Research and Documentation
in the Electronic Age

Fifth Edition

Research and Documentation
in the Electronic Age
Fifth Edition

Diana Hacker

Barbara Fister
Gustavus Adolphus College

Bedford / St. Martin's
Boston ◆ New York

For information, write: Bedford/St. Martin's, 75 Arlington Street,
Boston, MA 02116 (617-399-4000)

ISBN-10: 0-312-56672-7
ISBN-13: 978-0-312-56672-2

Acknowledgments

ACADEMIC ONEFILE screen shot. Copyright 2008 Salisbury State University. Reprinted with permission of Cengage Learning.

The Boston Globe Archives search results page screen shot. © Boston Globe/Landov. Reprinted by permission.

Columbia University Libraries. Library Home Page: Databases screen shot. © Columbia University Libraries. www.columbia.edu. Reprinted with permission of the Columbia University Libraries.

DILBERT: © Scott Adams/Dist. By United Features Syndicate, Inc. Reprinted by permission of United Media.

EBSCO Database Record screen shot. © 2009 EBSCO Information Services, a division of EBSCO Industries, Inc. All rights reserved. Reprinted by permission.

Thomas L. Friedman. Title and copyright pages from *Hot, Flat and Crowded.* Copyright © 2008 by Thomas L. Friedman. New York, NY: Farrar, Straus & Giroux. Reprinted by permission of International Creative Management.

Title page and page 151 from *Asian-American Literature: An Anthology* by Shirley Geok-lin Lim. © 2000 McGraw-Hill. Copyright page and brief excerpt of "Guilty on Both Counts" by Mitsuye Yamada. Copyright © 2000. Reprinted by permission of the McGraw-Hill Companies.

Google Search screen shots. Courtesy of Google, Inc.

Title page from *The Journal of Popular Culture,* Volume 41, Issue 3, 2008. Journal compilation © 2008, Blackwell Publishing, Inc. Reprinted with permission of Blackwell Publishing, Inc.

LINCC, Library Information Network for Community Colleges. Example of record with an abstract. Courtesy of SirsiDynix.

Minnesota Department of Health browser printout of Web site and on-screen view of document screen shots. www.health.state.mn. Reprinted with permission.

University of Minnesota Libraries. MNCAT Twin Cities screen shots. © Regents of the University of Minnesota. All rights reserved. Reprinted by permission.

New Bedford Whaling Museum. "Overview of American Whaling" screen shot. Copyright © 2008 Old Dartmouth Historical Society/New Bedford Whaling Museum. Courtesy of the New Bedford Whaling Museum.

(continued on page 288)

Contents

Introduction

This compact reference supplements Diana Hacker's handbooks and other titles published by Bedford / St. Martin's. It can be consulted for quick reference as you research and document sources in any college course. For advice about writing a research paper, consult *The Bedford Handbook*, Eighth Edition, by Diana Hacker and Nancy Sommers, or another Hacker handbook: *A Writer's Reference, Rules for Writers*, or *A Pocket Style Manual*.

Part I of this reference offers guidelines on posing an appropriate research question and mapping out a search strategy. Part II provides general strategies for finding, evaluating, and managing sources. Part III describes research practices in a variety of disciplines and lists specialized library and Web resources in thirty-one academic fields. Part IV includes guidelines for four documentation styles—MLA, APA, *Chicago*, and CSE—with documentation models for both print and electronic sources and a list of style manuals for several disciplines. Part V is a glossary of research terms.

An online version of this reference, *Research and Documentation Online*, is available at <http://hackerhandbooks.com/resdoc>.

Part I. Research Questions and Search Strategies

College research assignments ask you to pose a question worth exploring, to read widely in search of possible answers, to interpret what you read, to draw reasoned conclusions, and to support those conclusions with valid and well-documented evidence. Your search strategies—whether you search your library's databases or catalog, explore the Web, or gather information in the field—will vary depending on the research questions you have posed.

Posing a research question

Working within the guidelines of your assignment, pose a few questions that seem worth researching. Here, for example, are some preliminary questions jotted down by students enrolled in a variety of courses in different disciplines.

- Should the FCC broaden its definition of indecent programming to include violence?
- Which geological formations are the safest repositories for nuclear waste?
- What was Marcus Garvey's contribution to the fight for racial equality?
- How can governments and zoos help preserve Asia's endangered snow leopard?
- Why was amateur archaeologist Heinrich Schliemann such a controversial figure in his own time?

As you think about possible questions, make sure that they are appropriate lines of inquiry for a research paper. Choose questions that are narrow (not too broad), challenging (not too bland), and grounded (not too speculative).

Choosing a narrow question

If your initial question is too broad, given the length of the paper you plan to write, look for ways to restrict your focus. Here, for example, is how three students narrowed their initial questions.

TOO BROAD	NARROWER
What are the hazards of fad diets?	Why are low-carbohydrate diets hazardous?
What are the benefits of stricter auto emissions standards?	How will stricter auto emissions standards create new, more competitive auto industry jobs?
What causes depression?	How has the widespread use of antidepressant drugs affected teenage suicide rates?

Choosing a challenging question

Your research paper will be more interesting to both you and your audience if you base it on an intellectually challenging line of inquiry. Avoid bland questions that fail to provoke thought or engage readers in a debate.

TOO BLAND	CHALLENGING
What is obsessive-compulsive disorder?	Why is obsessive-compulsive disorder so difficult to treat?
Where is wind energy being used?	What makes wind farms economically viable?
How does DNA testing work?	How reliable is DNA testing?

You may need to address a bland question in the course of answering a more challenging one. For example, if you were writing about promising treatments for obsessive-compulsive disorder, you would no doubt answer the question "What is obsessive-compulsive disorder?" at some point in your paper. It would be a mistake, however, to use the bland question as the focus for the whole paper.

Choosing a grounded question

Finally, you will want to make sure that your research question is grounded, not too speculative. Although speculative questions—such as those that address philosophical, ethical, or religious issues—are worth asking and may receive some attention in a research paper, they are inappropriate central questions. The central argument of a research paper should be grounded in facts; it should not be based entirely on beliefs.

TOO SPECULATIVE	GROUNDED
Is it wrong to share music files on the Internet?	How has Internet file sharing affected the earning potential of musicians?
Do medical scientists have the right to experiment on animals?	How have technical breakthroughs made medical experiments on animals increasingly unnecessary?
Are youth sports too dangerous?	Why should school districts fund cardiac screening for all student athletes?

Mapping out a search strategy

A search strategy is a systematic plan for tracking down sources. To create a search strategy appropriate for your research question, consult a reference librarian and take a look at your library's Web site, which will give you an overview of available resources.

Getting started

Reference librarians are information specialists who can save you time by steering you toward relevant and reliable sources. With the help of an expert, you can make the best use of electronic databases, Web search engines, your library's catalog, and other reference tools.

Before you ask a reference librarian for help, be sure you have thought through the following questions:

- What is your assignment?
- In which academic discipline are you writing?
- What is your tentative research question?
- How long will the paper be?
- How much time can you spend on the project?

It's a good idea to bring a copy of the assignment with you.

In addition to speaking with a reference librarian, take some time to explore your library's Web site. You will typically find links to the library's catalog and to a variety of databases and electronic sources that you can access from any networked computer. You may also find resources listed by subject, research guides, information about interlibrary loans, and links to Web sites selected by librarians for their quality. Many libraries offer online reference assistance to help you locate information and refine your search strategy.

NOTE FOR DISTANCE LEARNERS: Even if you are unable to visit the library, as an enrolled student you can still use its resources. Most libraries offer chat reference services and access to online databases, though you may have to follow special procedures to use them. Check your library's Web site for information for distance learners.

Including the library in your plan

You may be tempted to ignore your library's resources, but using them can save you time and money in the end. Libraries weed out questionable sources and make a wide range of quality materials readily available.

While a general Internet search might seem quick and convenient, it is often more time-consuming and can be less reliable than a search in a library's databases. Initial Internet searches may generate thousands of results. Figuring out which of these are credible, relevant, and worth further investigation can require many additional steps:

- Refining search terms to generate fewer results (See the chart on refining keyword searches on p. 11.)
- Narrowing the domain to include only .org, .gov, or .edu sites
- Weeding out any advertisements associated with results
- Determining which sites might present useful arguments by scanning their titles and, in some cases, viewing their content
- Visiting sites that seem promising to determine their currency and relevance
- Combing through sites to determine the credibility of their authors

Starting with your library's collection of databases to run the same search can save you time and effort. Library database searches will turn up a manageable number of results, most of which are relevant, even if your initial search is broader than it should be. Because these searches are limited to only academic databases, you can count on finding reliable sources. Not all of the results will be worth examining in detail, but most library searches automatically sort them into subject categories that allow you to view narrowed results with just one click.

Using library databases can also save money. Most college assignments will require using at least some books and scholarly journal articles. Internet search engines can help you locate such sources, but the published texts are often not free online. *Google Scholar*, for example, provides scholarly results, but often you have to pay a fee or purchase a subscription to access the full texts. Most libraries subscribe to databases that will give you unlimited access to many of these materials as well as scholarly resources that might not turn up outside of a database. You will be able to do some of your work from any computer that can connect to the campus network.

LIBRARY DATABASES PAGE

Choosing an appropriate search strategy

No single search strategy works for every topic. For some topics, it may be appropriate to search for information in newspapers, magazines, and Web sites. For others, the best sources might be found in scholarly journals and books and specialized reference works. Still other topics might be enhanced by field research—interviews, surveys, or direct observation. When in doubt about the kinds of sources appropriate for your topic, check with your instructor or a reference librarian.

Part II. Finding and Evaluating Sources

Once you have discussed your topic with a reference librarian and sketched out your research strategy, you are ready to begin finding the sources you need. You will use a variety of research tools—such as databases, your library's catalog, and the Web—to find sources appropriate for the research question you have posed.

Finding Sources

Finding articles using a database or print index

Libraries subscribe to a variety of electronic databases (also called *periodical databases*) that give students access to articles and other materials without charge. Because many databases are limited to recent works, you may need to consult a print index as well.

What databases offer

Your library has access to databases that can lead you to articles in periodicals such as newspapers, magazines, and scholarly or technical journals. Some databases cover several subject areas; others cover one subject area in depth. Your library might subscribe to some of the following databases.

General databases College libraries typically subscribe to one or more general databases. The information in those databases is not restricted to a specific discipline or subject area. You may find searching a general database helpful in the early stages of your research process.

> *Academic Search Premier.* An interdisciplinary database that indexes thousands of popular and scholarly journals on all subjects, offering many articles in full text.

Expanded Academic ASAP. An interdisciplinary database that indexes the contents of magazines, newspapers, and scholarly journals in all subject areas. It also includes many full-text articles.

JSTOR. A full-text archive of scholarly journals from many disciplines; unlike most databases, it includes articles published decades ago but does not include articles from the most recent issues of publications.

LexisNexis. A database that is particularly strong in coverage of news, business, legal, and political topics. Nearly all of the material is available in full text.

ProQuest. A database of periodical articles, many in full text. Through *ProQuest*, your library may subscribe to databases in subjects such as nursing, biology, and psychology.

Subject-specific databases   Libraries have dozens of specialized databases covering many different subjects. Your library's Web site will guide you to what's available. The following are examples of subject-specific databases.

ERIC. A database offering education-related documents and abstracts of articles published in education journals.

MLA Bibliography. A database of literary criticism, with citations to help researchers find articles, books, and dissertations.

PsycINFO. A comprehensive database of psychology research, including abstracts of articles in journals and books.

Public Affairs Information Service (PAIS). A database that indexes books, journals, government documents, statistical directories, and research reports in the social sciences.

PubMed. A database offering millions of abstracts of medical research studies.

Many databases include the full text of at least some articles; others list only citations or citations with short summaries called *abstracts*. In the case of full-text articles, you may have the option to print an article, save it, or e-mail it to yourself.

When full text is not available, the citation will give you enough information to track down an article. Your library's Web site will help you determine which articles are available in your library, either in print or in electronic form. If the library does not own the item you want, you can usually request a copy through interlibrary loan; check with a librarian to find out how long it may take for the source to arrive.

How to search a database

To find articles on your topic in a database, start with a keyword search. If the first keyword you try results in too few or no matches, experiment with synonyms or ask a librarian for suggestions. For example, if you're searching for sources on a topic related to education, you might also try the terms *teaching*, *learning*, *pedagogy*, and *curriculum*. If your keyword search results in too many matches, narrow it by using one of the strategies in the chart on page 11.

When to use a print index

A print index to periodical articles is a useful tool when you are researching a historical topic, especially from the early to mid-twentieth century. The *Readers' Guide to Periodical Literature* or *Poole's Index to Periodical Literature* indexes magazine articles beginning around 1900, many of which are too old to appear in electronic databases. You can usually access the print articles themselves in your library's shelves, on microfilm or microfiche, or by interlibrary loan.

Finding books in the library's catalog

The books your library owns are listed in its catalog, along with other resources such as videos. You can search the catalog by author, title, or subject keywords. The screens on pages 12 and 13 illustrate a search of a library catalog.

Refining keyword searches in databases and search engines

Although command terms and characters vary among electronic databases and Web search engines, some of the most commonly used functions are listed here.

- Use quotation marks around words that are part of a phrase: "gateway drug".

- Use AND to connect words that must appear in a document: hyperactivity AND children. In some search engines—*Google*, for example—*and* is assumed, so typing it is unnecessary. Other search engines require a plus sign instead: hyperactivity +children.

- Use NOT in front of words that must not appear in a document: shepherd NOT dog. Some search engines require a minus sign (hyphen) instead: shepherd -dog.

- Use OR if only one of the terms must appear in a document: "mountain lion" OR cougar.

- Use an asterisk as a substitute for letters that might vary: "marine biolog*" (to find *marine biology* or *marine biologist*, for example).

- Use parentheses to group a search expression and combine it with another: (standard OR student OR test*) AND reform.

NOTE: Many search engines and databases offer an advanced search option that makes it easy to refine your search.

If your first search calls up too few results, try different keywords or search for books on broader topics. If your search gives you too many results, use the strategies in the chart at the top of this page or try an advanced search tool to combine concepts and limit your results. If those strategies don't work, ask a librarian for suggestions.

Sometimes catalogs don't use the words you would expect—for example, *motion pictures* is used as a subject heading instead of *movies* or *films*.

LIBRARY CATALOG SCREEN 1:
ADVANCED SEARCH

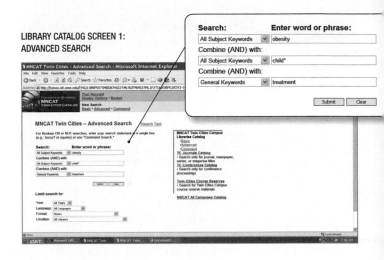

LIBRARY CATALOG SCREEN 2: SEARCH RESULTS

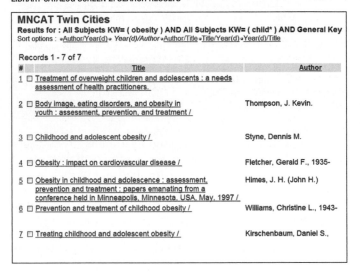

MNCAT Twin Cities
Results for : All Subjects KW= (obesity) AND All Subjects KW= (child*) AND General Key
Sort options : *Author/Year(d)* *Year(d)/Author* *Author/Title* *Title/Year(d)* *Year(d)/Title*

Records 1 - 7 of 7

#	Title	Author
1 ☐	Treatment of overweight children and adolescents : a needs assessment of health practitioners.	
2 ☐	Body image, eating disorders, and obesity in youth : assessment, prevention, and treatment /	Thompson, J. Kevin.
3 ☐	Childhood and adolescent obesity /	Styne, Dennis M.
4 ☐	Obesity : impact on cardiovascular disease /	Fletcher, Gerald F., 1935-
5 ☐	Obesity in childhood and adolescence : assessment, prevention and treatment : papers emanating from a conference held in Minneapolis, Minnesota, USA, May, 1997 /	Himes, J. H. (John H.)
6 ☐	Prevention and treatment of childhood obesity /	Williams, Christine L., 1943-
7 ☐	Treating childhood and adolescent obesity /	Kirschenbaum, Daniel S.,

LIBRARY CATALOG SCREEN 3: COMPLETE RECORD FOR A BOOK

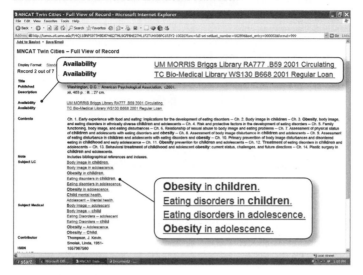

If a search gives you too many results, you will need to narrow your search. Many catalogs offer an advanced search option that will help you combine concepts and limit your results. For example, a search for the term *obesity* might turn up more than fifty hits, an unmanageable number. An advanced search could significantly limit your results, as shown in screens 1 and 2.

Once you have narrowed your search to a list of relevant sources, you can display or save the complete record for each source, which includes its bibliographic information (author, title, publication information) and a call number. Screen 3 shows the complete record for the second title on the list generated by the advanced search for *obesity* AND *child** AND *treatment*. The call number, listed beside *Availability*, is the book's address on the library shelf. When you're retrieving a book from the shelf, take the time to scan other books in the area since they are likely to be on the same topic.

LIBRARIAN'S TIP: The catalog record for a book lists related subject headings. These headings are a good way to locate other books on your subject. For example, the record in screen 3 lists the terms *obesity in children* and *obesity in adolescence* as related subject headings. By clicking on these new terms, you might find a few more books on this subject. Subject headings can be useful terms for a database search as well.

Finding a wide variety of sources online

You can find a variety of reliable sources using online tools beyond those offered by your library. For example, most government agencies post information on their Web sites, and federal and state governments use Web sites to communicate with citizens. The sites of many private organizations, such as Doctors without Borders and the Sierra Club, contain useful information about current issues. Museums and libraries often post digital versions of primary sources, such as photographs, political speeches, and classic literary texts.

Although the Internet at large can be a rich source of information, some of which can't be found anywhere else, it lacks quality control. The material on many sites has not necessarily been reviewed by experts. So when you're not working with your library's tools to locate online sources, carefully evaluate what you find (see p. 32).

This section describes the following general Web resources: search engines, directories, digital archives, government and news sites, blogs, and wikis.

Search engines

When using a search engine, such as *Google* or *Ask.com*, focus your search as narrowly as possible. You can refine your search by using many of the tips in the chart on page 11 or by using the search engine's advanced search form. For example, typing *Internet*, *surveillance*, *workplace*, and *privacy* into a search engine can yield tens of thousands of matches. To focus your search, you might try the phrases "*Internet surveillance*" and "*workplace privacy*" and *employee*. With an advanced search, you could further refine your search to include only organization-sponsored sites with URLs ending in *.org* that have been updated in the past three months. The resulting list will be even briefer and may include promising sources for your paper. (See the results screen on this page.)

Directories

If you want to find good resources on topics too broad for a search engine, try a directory. Unlike search engines, directories are put together by information specialists who choose

SEARCH ENGINE SCREEN: RESULTS OF AN ADVANCED SEARCH

Web Results 1 - 5 of about 9 over the past 3 months for "Internet surveillance" employee "workplace privacy"

Web Results 1 - 5 of about 9 over the past 3 months for "Internet surveillance" employee "workplace privacy" site:.org (0.44 seconds)

Tip: Try removing quotes from your search to get more results.

EPIC/PI - Privacy & Human Rights 2000
Now the supervision of **employee**'s performance, behavior and... [89]Information and Privacy Commissioner/Ontario, **Workplace Privacy**: The Need For a..
www.privacyinternational.org/survey/phr2000/threats.html - 131k Cached - Similar pages

   Privacy and Human Rights 2003: Threats to Privacy
   Other issues that raise **workplace privacy** concerns are employer requirements that **employees** complete medical tests, questionnaires, and polygraph tests..
   www.privacyinternational.org/survey/phr2003/threats.htm - 279k Cached - Similar pages
   [More results from www.privacyinternational.org]

[PDF] Monitoring **Employee** E-Mail And Internet Usage: Avoiding The..
File Format: PDF/Adobe Acrobat -View as HTML
Internet surveillance by employers in the American workplace. At present, US **employees** in the private workplace have no constitutional, common law or statu
lsr.nellco.org/cgi/viewcontent.cgi?article=1006&context=suffolk/ip - Similar pages

Previous EPIC Top News
The agencies plan to use RFID to track **employees**' movements and in ID cards... For more information on **workplace privacy**, see the EPIC **Workplace Privacy** ...
www.epic.org/news/2005.html - 163k Cached - Similar pages

reputable sites and arrange them by topic: education, health, politics, and so on.

Some directories are particularly useful for research. For example, links included in the *Internet Scout Project* are selected by an expert research team and include annotations that both describe and evaluate each site.

The following directories are especially useful for scholarly research:

Internet Scout Project <http://scout.wisc.edu/Archives>
Librarian's Internet Index <http://lii.org>
Open Directory Project <http://dmoz.org>
WWW Virtual Library <http://vlib.org>

Digital archives

Archives are a good place to find primary sources. They may contain the texts of poems, books, speeches, and historically significant documents; photographs; and political cartoons.

The materials in these sites are usually limited to official documents and older works because of copyright laws. The following online archives are impressive collections:

American Memory <http://memory.loc.gov>
Avalon Project <http://yale.edu/lawweb/avalon/avalon.htm>
Eurodocs <http://eudocs.lib.byu.edu>
Google Books <http:// books.google.com>
Google Scholar <http://scholar.google.com>
The Making of America <http://quod.lib.umich.edu/m/moagrp>
Online Books Page <http://onlinebooks.library.upenn.edu>

Government and news sites

For current topics, both government and news sites can prove useful. Many government agencies at every level provide online information. Government-maintained sites include resources such as legal texts, facts and statistics, government reports, and searchable reference databases. Here are just a few government sites:

Fedstats <http://www.fedstats.gov>

GPO Access <http://www.gpoaccess.gov>

United Nations <http://www.un.org>

University of Michigan Documents Center <http://www.lib .umich.edu/govdocs>

US Census Bureau <http://www.census.gov>

NOTE: You can access a state's Web site by putting the two-letter state abbreviation into a standard URL: <http://www .state.ga.us>. Substitute any state's two-letter abbreviation for the letters *ga*, which in this case stand for Georgia.

Many news organizations offer up-to-date information on the Web. Some require registration and may charge fees for some articles. Check with your library to see if it subscribes to online newspapers that you can access at no charge. The following are some free news sites:

BBC <http://www.bbc.co.uk>

Google News <http://news.google.com>

Kidon Media-Link <http://www.kidon.com/media-link>

New York Times <http://nytimes.com>

Blogs

A blog (short for *Weblog*) is a site that contains dated text or multimedia entries usually written and maintained by one person, with comments contributed by readers. Though some blogs are personal diaries and others are devoted to partisan politics, many journalists and academics maintain blogs that cover topics of interest to researchers. Some blogs feature short essays that provide useful insights or analysis; others point to new developments in an area of interest. Because blogs are frequently updated, you may want to subscribe to especially useful ones. The following Web sites can lead you to a wide range of blogs:

Academic Blog Portal <http://academicblogs.org>
Google Blog Search <http://www.google.com/blogsearch>
Science Blogs <http://scienceblogs.com>
Technorati <http://technorati.com>

Wikis

A wiki is a collaborative Web site with many contributors and with content that may change frequently. *Wikipedia*, the collaborative online encyclopedia, is one of the most frequently consulted wikis.

In general, *Wikipedia* may be helpful if you're checking for something that is common knowledge (facts available in multiple sources, such as dates and well-known historical events) or looking for very current information about a topic in contemporary culture that isn't covered elsewhere. However, many scholars do not consider *Wikipedia* and wikis in general to be appropriate sources for college research. Authorship is open to anyone, not limited to experts; articles may be written by enthusiastic amateurs who are not well informed. And because the articles can be changed by anyone, controversial texts are often altered to reflect a particular perspective and are especially susceptible to bias. When possible, locate and cite another, more reliable source for any useful information you find in a wiki. (Sometimes a wiki's own citations can lead you to such credible sources.) If you cannot find a second source, check with your instructor before integrating ideas from a wiki into your researched writing.

Considering other search tools

In addition to articles, books, and online sources, you may want to consult references such as encyclopedias and almanacs. Citations in scholarly works can also lead you to additional sources.

Reference works

The reference section of the library holds both general and specialized encyclopedias, dictionaries, almanacs, atlases, and biographical references, some available in electronic form through the library's Web site. Such works often provide a good overview of your subject and include references to the most significant works on a topic. Check with a reference librarian to see which works are most appropriate for your project.

NOTE: See Part III for descriptions of reference works and other resources likely to be useful in a variety of disciplines.

General reference works   General reference works are good places to check facts and get basic information. Here are a few frequently used general references:

> *American National Biography*
> *Chronology of World History*
> *National Geographic Atlas of the World*
> *The New Encyclopaedia Britannica*
> *The Oxford English Dictionary*
> *Statistical Abstract of the United States*

Although general encyclopedias are often a good place to find background about your topic, you should rarely use them in your final paper. Most instructors expect you to rely on more specialized sources.

Specialized reference works   Specialized reference works often explore a topic in depth, usually in the form of articles written by leading authorities. They offer a quick way to gain an expert's overview of a complex topic. Many specialized works are available, including these:

> *Contemporary Authors*
> *Encyclopedia of Bioethics*

Encyclopedia of Crime and Justice
Encyclopedia of Psychology
Encyclopedia of World Environmental History
International Encyclopedia of Communication
New Encyclopedia of Africa

See Part III for suggestions of specialized reference works by subject area.

Conducting field research

Your own field research can enhance or be the focus of a writing project. For a composition class, for example, you might want to interview a local politician about a current issue, such as the use of alternative energy sources. For a sociology class, you might decide to conduct a survey regarding campus trends in community service. At work, you might need to learn how food industry executives have responded to reports that their products are contributing to health problems.

NOTE: Colleges and universities often require researchers to submit projects to an institutional review board (IRB) if the research involves human subjects outside of a classroom setting. Before administering a survey or conducting other fieldwork, check with your instructor to see if IRB approval is required.

Interviewing

Interviews can often shed new light on a topic. Look for an expert who has firsthand knowledge of the subject or seek out someone whose personal experience provides a valuable perspective on your topic.

When asking for an interview, be clear about who you are, what the purpose of the interview is, and how you would prefer to conduct it: via e-mail, over the phone, or in person. Plan for the interview by writing down a series of questions. Try to avoid questions with yes or no answers or those that encourage vague rambling. Instead, ask questions that lead to facts, anecdotes, and opinions that will add a meaningful dimension to your paper.

INEFFECTIVE INTERVIEW QUESTIONS
How many years have you spent studying childhood obesity?
Is your work interesting?

EFFECTIVE INTERVIEW QUESTIONS
What are some current interpretations of the causes of childhood obesity?
What treatments have you found to be most effective? Why do you think they work?

When quoting your source in your paper, be as accurate and fair as possible. To ensure accuracy, you might want to ask permission to record the interview; if you cannot record it, take careful notes or conduct it by e-mail.

Surveying opinion

For some topics, you may find it useful to survey opinions through written questionnaires, telephone or e-mail polls, or questions posted on a Web forum. Many people are reluctant to fill out long questionnaires or answer long-winded telephone pollsters, so if you want a good response rate, you will need to limit your questions and frame them carefully.

When possible, ask yes/no questions or give multiple-choice options. Surveys with such queries can be completed quickly, and they are easy to tabulate.

SAMPLE YES/NO QUESTION
Do you favor the use of Internet surveillance in the workplace?

You may also want to ask a few open-ended questions to elicit more individual responses, some of which may be worth quoting in your paper.

What, if any, experiences have you had with Internet surveillance in the workplace?

Some online survey companies such as SurveyMonkey <http://www.surveymonkey.com> and Zoomerang <http://zoomerang.com> host Web-based surveys and provide for a limited number of questions and responses for free. They allow you to create easy-to-take online surveys and collate the results. See the note on page 20 if you intend to survey students on your campus.

Evaluating Sources

With electronic search tools, you can often locate dozens or even hundreds of potential sources for your topic—far more than you will have time to read. Your challenge will be to determine what kinds of sources you need and to zero in on a reasonable number of quality sources, those truly worth your time and attention.

Later, once you have decided on some sources worth consulting, your challenge will be to read them with an open mind and a critical eye.

Selecting sources worth your time and attention

The previous sections show how to refine searches in databases, in the library's book catalog, and in search engines. This section explains how to scan through the results for the most promising sources and how to preview them—without actually reading them—to see whether they are likely to live up to your expectations and meet your needs.

Scanning search results

As you scan through a list of search results, watch for clues indicating whether a source might be useful for your purposes or not worth pursuing. You will need to use somewhat differ-ent strategies when scanning search results from a database, a book catalog, and a Web search engine.

Databases   Most databases, such as *Expanded Academic ASAP*, list at least the following information, which can help you de-cide if a source is relevant, current, scholarly enough (see the chart on p. 25), and a suitable length for your purposes.

Title and brief description (How relevant?)

Date (How current?)

Name of periodical (How scholarly?)

Length (How extensive in coverage?)

Book catalogs   The library's book catalog usually lists basic information about books, enough for a first impression (see also p. 13). A book's title and date of publication will often be your first clues about whether the book is worth consult-ing. Be cautious about books that were published ten or more years ago; depending on the topic, they may be outdated. If a title looks interesting, you can click on it for information about the book's subject matter and its length. The table of contents may also be available, offering a glimpse of what's inside.

Web search engines   Because anyone can publish a Web site, legitimate sources and unreliable sources live side-by-side online. As you scan through search results, look for the fol-lowing clues about the probable relevance, currency, and reli-ability of a site—but be aware that the clues are by no means foolproof.

The title, keywords, and lead-in text (How relevant?)

A date (How current?)

An indication of the site's sponsor or purpose (How reliable?)

The URL, especially the domain name extension: for example, .com, .edu, .gov, or .org (How relevant? How reliable?)

Previewing sources

Once you have decided that a source looks promising, preview it quickly to see whether it lives up to its promise. If you can reject irrelevant or unreliable sources before actually reading them, you will save yourself time. Techniques for previewing an article from your library's subscription database or a book are relatively simple; strategies for investigating the likely worth of a Web site are more complicated.

Previewing an article The techniques for previewing an article are fairly straightforward, and a few minutes spent scanning an article can help you decide whether it is worth your time.

Here are a few strategies for previewing an article:

- Consider the publication in which the article is printed. Is it a scholarly journal (see the chart on p. 25)? A popular magazine? A newspaper with a national reputation?
- For a magazine or journal article, look for an abstract or a statement of purpose at the beginning; also look for a summary at the end.
- For a newspaper article, focus on the headline and the opening paragraphs, known as the *lead*.
- Skim any headings and look at any visuals—charts, graphs, diagrams, or illustrations—that might indicate the article's focus and scope.

Previewing a book As you preview a book, keep in mind that even if the entire book is not worth your time, parts of it may prove useful. Try any or all of the following techniques to preview a book:

- Glance through the table of contents, keeping your research question in mind.

- Skim the preface in search of a statement of the author's purposes.

- Use the index to look up a few words related to your topic.

- If a chapter looks useful, read its opening and closing paragraphs and skim any headings.

- Consider the author's style and approach. Does the style suggest enough intellectual depth, or is the book too specialized for your purposes? Does the author present ideas in an unbiased way?

Determining if a source is scholarly

For many college assignments, you will be asked to use scholarly sources. These are written by experts for a knowledgeable audience and usually go into more depth than books and articles written for a general audience. (Scholarly sources are sometimes called *refereed* or *peer-reviewed* because the work is evaluated by experts in the field before publication.) To determine if a source is scholarly, you should look for the following:

- Formal language and presentation

- Authors who are academics or scientists

- Footnotes or a bibliography documenting the works cited by the author in the source

- Original research and interpretation (rather than a summary of other people's work)

- Quotations from and analysis of primary sources (in humanities disciplines such as literature, history, and philosophy)

- A description of research methods or a review of related research (in the sciences and social sciences)

NOTE: In some databases, searches can be limited to refereed or peer-reviewed journals.

Previewing a Web site   It is a fairly quick and easy job to track down numerous potentially useful sources on the Web, but evaluating those sources can require some detective work. Web sites can be created by anyone, and their authors and purposes are not always apparent. In addition, there are no required standards for the design of Web sites, so you may need to do a fair amount of clicking and scrolling before you locate clues about a site's reliability.

As you preview a Web site, check for relevance, reliability, and currency:

- Browse the home page. Do its contents and links seem relevant to your research question?

- Ask yourself what the site is trying to do: Sell a product? Promote an idea? Inform the public? Is the site's purpose consistent with your research?

- Look for the name of an author or a Webmaster and, if possible, review his or her credentials. Often a site's author is named at the bottom of the home page. If you have landed on an internal page of a site and no author is evident, try navigating to the home page, either through a link or by truncating the URL (see the tip on p. 31).

- Check for a sponsor name, and consider possible motives the organization might have for sponsoring the site. Is the group likely to look at only one side of an issue?

- Find out when the site was created or last updated. Is it current enough for your purposes?

TIP: When conducting academic research, do not rely on sites that give very little information about authors or sponsors.

Distinguishing between primary and secondary sources

As you begin assessing evidence in a source, determine whether you are reading a primary or a secondary source. Primary sources are original documents such as letters, diaries, legislative bills, laboratory studies, field research reports, and eyewitness accounts. Secondary sources are commentaries on primary sources—another writer's opinions about or interpretation of a primary source.

Although a primary source is not necessarily more reliable than a secondary source, it has the advantage of being a first-hand account. Naturally, you can better evaluate what a secondary source says if you have first read any primary sources it discusses.

Selecting appropriate versions of electronic sources

An online source may appear as an abstract, an excerpt, or a full-text article or book. It is important to distinguish among these versions of sources and to use a complete version of a source, preferably one with page numbers, for your research.

Abstracts and excerpts are shortened versions of complete works. An abstract—a summary of a work's contents—might appear in a database record for a periodical article (see p. 28) and can give you clues about the usefulness of an article for your paper. Abstracts are brief (usually fewer than five hundred words) and usually do not contain enough information to function alone as sources in a research paper. Reading the complete article is the best way to understand the author's argument before referring to it in your own writing. When you determine that the full article is worth reading, scroll through the record to find a link to the complete text in your library's databases. If you cannot access the article from a database, see if the library has a print copy on the shelves. Ask a librarian for assistance if you are unsure whether your library keeps the periodical.

An excerpt is the first few sentences or paragraphs of a newspaper or magazine article and sometimes appears in a list of hits in an online search (see p. 29). From an excerpt, you can often determine whether the complete article would be useful for your paper. Sometimes, however, the thesis or topic sentence of the article is buried deeper in the article than the excerpt reveals. In these cases, the headline might be a clue to the relevance of the complete article. Be sure to retrieve and read the full text of any article you might want to cite. If you are working with an Internet search engine such as *Google*, you may find that your results lead to articles available only for a fee. Before paying a fee, see if you can get the article through your library system.

A full-text work may appear online as a PDF (portable document format) file or as an HTML file (sometimes called a *text file*). A PDF file is usually an exact copy of the pages of a periodical article as they appeared in print, including the page numbers. Some corporate and government reports are presented online as PDF files, and they are usually paginated. A full-text document that appears as an HTML or a text file is not paginated. If your source is available in both formats, choose the PDF file for your research because you will be able to cite specific page numbers.

DATABASE RECORD WITH AN ABSTRACT

LINCC, Library Information Network for Community Colleges
Expanded Academic ASAP

—— Article 1 of 2 —— ▶

☐   *Civil War History*, June 1996 v42 n2 p116(17)
Mark

"These devils are not fit to live on God's earth": war crimes and the Committee on the Conduct of the War, 1864-1865. *Bruce Tap*.

Abstract: The Committee on the Conduct of the War's report on the April 1864 Fort Pillow massacre of black Union soldiers by Confederate forces influenced public opinion against the atrocities of the Confederate troops and accelerated the reconstruction program. Hostility against blacks and abolition in the South prompted the Confederates to target black troops and deny them prisoner of war status. Investigation exposed the barbaric act and the Northern prisoners' suffering in Southern prisons. The report helped the inclusion of black troops in the prisoner exchange program.

Article A18749078

SEARCH RESULT WITH AN EXCERPT

▾ BOSTON GLOBE ARCHIVES

Your search for **((fort AND pillow AND massacre))** returned **1** article(s) matching your terms. To purchase the full-text of an article, follow the link that says "Click for complete article."

| Perform a new search |

Your search results:

TALES OF BLACKS IN THE CIVIL WAR, FOR ALL AGES
Published on March 23, 1998
Author(s):   Scott Alarik, Globe Correspondent

For African Americans, the Civil War was always two wars. It was, of course, the war to save the union and destroy slavery, but for the nearly 180,000 black soldiers who served in the Union Army, it was also a war to establish their rights as citizens and human beings in the United States. Their role in defeating the Confederacy is grandly chronicled in two new books, the massively complete "Like Men of War" and the superbly readable children's book "Black, Blue and

Click for complete article *(782 words)*

Reading with an open mind and a critical eye

As you begin reading the sources you have chosen, keep an open mind. Do not let your personal beliefs prevent you from listening to new ideas and opposing viewpoints. Your research question—not a snap judgment about the question—should guide your reading.

When you read critically, you are not necessarily judging an author's work harshly; you are simply examining its assumptions, assessing its evidence, and weighing its conclusions.

TIP: When you research on the Web, it is easy to ignore views different from your own. Web pages that appeal to you will often link to other pages that support the same viewpoint. If your sources all seem to agree with you—and with one another—try to find sources with opposing views and evaluate them with an open mind.

Being alert for signs of bias

Both in print and online, some sources are more objective than others. If you were exploring the conspiracy theories surrounding John F. Kennedy's assassination, for example, you wouldn't look to a supermarket tabloid for answers. Even publications that are considered reputable can be editorially biased. For example, *USA Today*, *National Review*, and *Ms.* are all credible sources that are likely to interpret events quite differently from one another. If you are uncertain about a periodical's special interests, consult *Magazines for Libraries*. To check for bias in a book, see what book reviewers have written about

Evaluating all sources

Checking for signs of bias

- Does the author or publisher endorse political or religious views that could affect objectivity?
- Is the author or publisher associated with a special-interest group, such as Greenpeace or the National Rifle Association, that might present only one side of an issue?
- Are alternative views presented and addressed? How fairly does the author treat opposing views?
- Does the author's language show signs of bias?

Assessing an argument

- What is the author's central claim or thesis?
- How does the author support this claim—with relevant and sufficient evidence or with just a few anecdotes or emotional examples?
- Are statistics consistent with those you encounter in other sources? Have they been used fairly? Does the author explain where the statistics come from? (It is possible to "lie" with statistics by using them selectively or by omitting mathematical details.)
- Are any of the author's assumptions questionable?
- Does the author consider opposing arguments and refute them persuasively?
- Does the author fall prey to any logical fallacies?

it. A reference librarian can help you locate reviews and assess the credibility of both the book and the reviewers.

Like publishers, some authors are more objective than others. If you have reason to believe that a writer is particularly biased, you will want to assess his or her arguments with special care. For a list of questions worth asking, see the chart on page 30.

Assessing the author's argument

In nearly all subjects worth writing about, there is some element of argument, so don't be surprised to encounter experts who disagree. When you find areas of disagreement, you will want to read each source's arguments with special care, testing them with your own critical intelligence. The questions in the chart on page 30 can help you weigh the strengths and weaknesses of each author's arguments.

Assessing Web sources with special care

Web sources can provide valuable information, but verifying their credibility may take time. Before using a Web source in your paper, make sure you know who created the material and for what purpose.

TIP: If both the sponsorship and the authorship of a site are unclear, think twice about using the site for your research. To discover a site's sponsor, you may have to shorten the full URL to its domain name.

> FULL URL: http://www.bankofamerica.com/environment/dex
> .cfm?template=env_reports_speeches&context=smartgrowth
>
> DOMAIN NAME: http://www.bankofamerica.com
>
> SPONSOR: Bank of America

Many sophisticated-looking sites contain questionable information. Even a well-designed hate site may at first appear unbiased and informative. Sites with reliable information, however, can stand up to careful scrutiny. For a checklist on evaluating Web sources, see the following chart.

Evaluating Web sources

Authorship

- Does the Web site or document have an author? You may need to do some clicking and scrolling to find the author's name. If you have landed directly on an internal page of a site, for example, you may need to navigate to the home page or find an "about this site" link to learn the name of the author.

- If there is an author, can you tell whether he or she is knowledgeable and credible? When the author's qualifications aren't listed on the site itself, look for links to the author's home page, which may provide evidence of his or her interests and expertise.

Sponsorship

- Who, if anyone, sponsors the site? The sponsor of a site is often named and described on the home page.

- What does the URL tell you? The domain name extension often indicates the type of group hosting the site: commercial (.com), educational (.edu), nonprofit (.org), governmental (.gov), military (.mil), or network (.net). URLs may also indicate a country of origin: .uk (United Kingdom) or .jp (Japan), for instance.

Purpose and audience

- Why was the site created: To argue a position? To sell a product? To inform readers?

- Who is the site's intended audience?

Currency

- How current is the site? Check for the date of publication or the latest update, often located at the bottom of the home page or at the beginning or end of an internal page.

- How current are the site's links? If many of the links no longer work, the site may be too dated for your purposes.

Part III. Specialized Library and Web Resources

Researching in the Humanities

Research in the humanities generally involves interpreting a text or a work of art within a historical and cultural context, making connections, exploring meaning, and uncovering contradictions. Scholars in the humanities typically use library resources in at least three ways:

- to obtain primary sources to be interpreted or analyzed
- to find secondary sources to put primary sources in a critical context
- to seek answers to specific questions that arise during research

Research in the humanities is often interdisciplinary, bridging literature and history, philosophy and art, or music and religion. Because the subject areas are harder to categorize, the terminology used in humanities research may be less solid and agreed upon than that in other fields. Researchers in the humanities are more likely to draw material from texts and artifacts than from original data gathering and experimentation. They must be prepared to be

- flexible, both in search terminology and in search strategy
- tolerant of multiple perspectives on the same object of study
- prepared to use citations in relevant texts to locate other material and clarify connections among works
- willing to return to the library as new questions arise

Fortunately, there are many fine research tools to help. Those listed here are not available in every library, but they give you some ideas for how to start. Always bear in mind, too, that librarians are particularly user-friendly resources. Ask a librarian for recommended research tools as you begin your research, and use the librarian's expertise as your research progresses and your questions grow more specific.

General resources in the humanities

Databases and indexes in the humanities

Arts and Humanities Citation Index. Philadelphia: Institute for Scientific Information, 1978–. An interdisciplinary index to articles in more than 1,100 journals, searchable by author, keyword, and cited work. A Related Records search also lets you find articles that cite the same sources. It may be available at your library as *AHSearch* (through the *FirstSearch* database collection) or as part of the *Web of Knowledge* database.

Humanities Index. New York: Wilson, 1974–. An interdisciplinary index to about 500 of the most prominent English-language journals in the humanities, including art, music, history, and literature. Searchable by author or subject, the index includes many cross-references and subheadings that break large topics into components. In some libraries, the database includes full texts of selected articles.

Web resources in the humanities

The Online Books Page <http://digital.library.upenn.edu/books>. Provides links to over 35,000 full-text books and journals in English and allows searching by author and title. The site includes special exhibits on women writers, banned books, and prize winners. It is edited by John Mark Ockerbloom at the University of Pennsylvania.

Voice of the Shuttle <http://vos.ucsb.edu>. A wide-ranging index to sites of interest to researchers in humanities disciplines—art, literature, philosophy, religion, and cultural studies—with links to higher education and publishing sites. The site is maintained by Allen Liu and others in the English Department at the University of California, Santa Barbara.

Reference books in the humanities

The Humanities: A Selective Guide to Information Sources. By Ron Blazek and Elizabeth Smith Aversa. 5th ed. Englewood: Libraries Unlimited, 2000. A guide to research tools in the humanities, including the arts, philosophy, religion, and language and literature. A critical annotation is provided for each source listed.

New Dictionary of the History of Ideas. 6 vols. New York: Scribner, 2005. Covers concepts in intellectual history, with long, scholarly discussions of important ideas. An update of the 1974 classic, this revised work includes global perspectives in over 750 articles.

Art and architecture

Databases and indexes in art and architecture

Art Index. New York: Wilson, 1930–. An author and subject index to more than 400 art periodicals, covering all periods and media, including film and photography. The work is particularly helpful for locating reproductions in periodicals, for research studies, and for news of sales and exhibitions.

ARTbibliographies Modern. Bethesda: Cambridge Scientific Abstracts, 1974–. An electronic index containing citations to and descriptive abstracts of articles, books, catalogs, and essays on modern art and photography from the late nineteenth century to the present.

ARTstor. New York: ARTstor, 2003–. A collection of about a million high-quality images of works of art, architecture, and cultural artifacts that can be searched and used for educational purposes.

Bibliography of the History of Art (BHA). Santa Monica: John Paul Getty Trust, 1991–. Comprehensive and up-to-date coverage of art in Europe and the Americas from antiquity to the present. This database provides citations and abstracts for books, articles, dissertations, and exhibit catalogs published since 1973.

Web resources in art and architecture

Artcyclopedia <http://www.artcyclopedia.com>. Provides links to art images on the Web. The site is searchable by artist, work, and museum and browsable by subject, medium, or nationality. It includes information about art movements with examples of relevant artworks and a section on women artists. The site was created and is maintained by John Maylon.

Art History Resources on the Web <http://witcombe.sbc.edu/ARTHLinks.html>. Provides links to hundreds of sites related to all periods of art history, from prehistoric to twenty-first century, arranged by period and region. Many links are to museums and galleries or to artists' pages that provide biographical information and images. The site is maintained by Christopher Whitcombe, professor of art history at Sweet Briar College.

Great Buildings Collection <http://www.greatbuildings.com>. Offers information on about 1,000 works of architecture and hundreds of architects from all periods and regions. Searchable by building, architect, and place, the site provides biographical information about architects, basic information on works, extensive images, and links to articles published in *Architecture Week*. The site also provides selected 3-D images and listings of buildings by chronology, building type, and architectural style.

Image Collections and Online Art <http://www.umich.edu/~hartspc/histart/mother/images.html>. Lists sources of art images by geographic region.

Timeline of Art History <http://www.metmuseum.org/toah/splash.htm>. A chronology of art from the Metropolitan Museum of Art in New York, with links to images primarily in the museum's collections. The site is organized both thematically and geographically and includes an alphabetical index and a search engine.

WorldImages <http://worldimages.sjsu.edu>. A source for over 70,000 art images, searchable or browsable in over 650 "portfolios," that may be used for educational purposes.

Absolute Arts <http://www.absolutearts.com>. A commercial site particularly strong in studio arts and the business side of the art professions, offering information about works by over 24,000 artists and news for the arts community.

Reference books in art and architecture

Contemporary Artists. Ed. Sarah Pendergast et al. 5th ed. Detroit: Gale Group, 2002. Provides biographies of more than 800 twentieth-century artists from around the world, including information on their work, lists of their exhibits, and bibliographies for further research.

The Dictionary of Art. Ed. Jane Turner. 34 vols. New York: Grove's Dictionaries, 1996. An exhaustive encyclopedia of world art containing scholarly articles on artists, movements, works, and subjects, with bibliographical references and an index.

Encyclopedia of Aesthetics. Ed. Michael Kelly. 4 vols. New York: Oxford University Press, 1998. Includes 600 substantial articles on philosophical concepts relating to art and aesthetics, including overviews of movements, major theorists, national and regional aesthetics, and subjects such as cyberspace, law and art, cultural property, and politics and aesthetics. Each article is followed by an up-to-date bibliography.

Encyclopedia of Twentieth-Century Architecture. Ed. R. Stephen Sennott. 3 vols. New York: Fitzroy Dearborn, 2003. Offers over 700 illustrated articles on architects and buildings as well as styles, building types, and movements worldwide. The work includes coverage of architecture's roles in communities and regions.

Encyclopedia of World Art. 16 vols. New York: McGraw-Hill, 1959–. Includes supplements. Offers thorough, scholarly articles on artists, movements, media, periods, national traditions, and so on. Each volume has text in the front and a section of plates in the back. The entire set is indexed, and supplementary volumes present newer information. Though dated, this set remains valuable for its erudite overview articles and well-indexed plates.

The Oxford Companion to Western Art. Ed. Hugh Brigstocke. Oxford: Oxford University Press, 2001. Provides basic information on artists, movements, forms, materials, and techniques, covering the Western world from classical times to the present.

Classics

Databases and indexes in classics

L'Année philologique: bibliographie critique et analytique de l'antiquité Gréco-Latine. Paris: Société Internationale de Bibliographie Classique (SIBC), 1924/26–. The most thorough database available for classics, covering books and articles on all aspects of Greek and Latin cultures, including archaeology, literature, and philosophy. The index is international in scope and includes works in all languages.

TLG: Thesaurus Linguae Graecae. Irvine: University of California, Irvine, 2000–. This online archive includes every Greek text in existence from the age of Homer (eighth century BCE) to 600 CE, as well as most Greek texts up to the fall of Byzantium.

TOCS-IN: Tables of Contents of Journals of Interest to Classicists <http://www.chass.utoronto.ca/amphoras/tocs.html>. A Web-based index of the contents of 185 classics journals and collections of essays compiled by a team of classics scholars. Though most of the references date only to the early 1990s, when the project was started, some older material is included. The entries provide basic bibliographic information, with a few including abstracts and/or links to full text.

Web resources in classics

Ancient World Mapping Center <http://www.unc.edu/awmc>. From the University of North Carolina, Chapel Hill, this site provides maps of the ancient world as well as sophisticated cartographic tools.

Classical Art Research Centre (The Beazley Archive, Oxford University). Offers a dictionary and a searchable database of thousands of images of artwork, pottery, sculpture, and gems and photographs of ancient sites.

Forum Romanum <http://www.forumromanum.org>. A vast collection of Latin texts, translations, and teaching materials for the study of the Roman world.

Metis <http://www.stoa.org/metis>. Though little textual information is provided, links lead to animated panoramas of Greek archaeological sites, with options to scan a site or zoom in on specific areas. The site, a project of the Stoa Consortium, includes links to related materials on the *Perseus Project* Web site (see next entry).

The Perseus Project <http://www.perseus.tufts.edu>. A digital library of resources for students researching the ancient world. Constructed and maintained by the Classics Department at Tufts University, the site focuses on ancient Greece and Rome and includes information on everything from lexicons to images, maps, art, and ancient texts and translations.

Reference books in classics

Ancient Writers: Greece and Rome. Ed. T. James Luce. 2 vols. New York: Macmillan Library Reference, 1982. Offers lengthy critiques and overviews of the works of classical writers. Each essay is written by an expert and is followed by a selected bibliography of editions, translations, commentaries, and criticism.

Brill's New Pauly: Encyclopedia of the Ancient World. Ed. Christine F. Salazar and David E. Orton. 20 vols. Leiden: Brill, 2002. The most complete encyclopedia of classics, including antiquity and the classical tradition.

The Cambridge Ancient History. Ed. I. E. S. Edwards et al. 3rd ed. 14 vols. Cambridge: Cambridge University Press, 1970–. Covers the ancient world chronologically and includes chapters written by experts in particular eras. Individual volumes are updated periodically; some volumes are still in their second edition. There is a separate volume of plates for the first two volumes.

Civilization of the Ancient Mediterranean. Ed. Michael Grant and Rachel Kitzinger. 3 vols. New York: Scribner, 1988. Provides lengthy articles on such topics as language and dialects, farming and animal husbandry, myths and cosmologies, women in the ancient world, and building techniques.

Oxford Classical Dictionary. Ed. Simon Hornblower and Anthony Spawforth. Rev. 3rd ed. New York: Oxford University Press, 2003. Provides concise and informative articles on people, places, events, works of art, and figures in mythology. It is a well-regarded classic in the field.

Oxford Companion to Classical Literature. Ed. M. C. Howatson. 2nd ed. New York: Oxford University Press, 1989. A handy guide to writers and works from classical times, with concise discussions of the social and cultural context of the literature.

Oxford Encyclopedia of Archaeology in the Near East. Ed. Eric M. Meyers. 5 vols. New York: Oxford University Press, 1997. Covers archaeological sites, regions, countries, and peoples in the Near East, from prehistoric times through the Crusades. The work also covers specific areas of archaeology, such as ethics, history, and underwater archaeology.

The Oxford Guide to Classical Mythology in the Arts, 1300–1990s. Ed. Jane Davidson Reid. 2 vols. New York: Oxford University Press, 1993. Lists examples of Western art from medieval to modern times that use figures and subjects from classical mythology as themes. Paintings, sculptures, musical compositions, ballets, and literary works are included.

Place-Names in Classical Mythology: Greece. By Robert E. Bell. Santa Barbara: ABC-CLIO, 1989. Provides descriptions of significant locations referred to in classical mythology and literature.

Literature

Databases and indexes in literature

Literature Resource Center. Detroit: Gale Group, 1998–. An online portal to a number of literature resources including the text of *Contemporary Authors, Contemporary Literary Criticism, Dictionary of Literary Biography,* Twayne's Authors Series, Scribner Writers Series, and the full text of other reference works. Many libraries have some of the contents of this database in print form (see Reference Books in Literature, p. 41, for descriptions).

MLA International Bibliography. New York: Modern Language Association, 1921–. The most important ongoing index of scholarship in literature and linguistics. Includes citations to books, book chapters, articles, and dissertations in all languages on literature, linguistics, folklore, and some film criticism. It covers literary criticism in depth; book reviews and articles appearing in popular magazines are not included.

Web resources in literature

Internet Public Library Online Literary Criticism Collection <http://ipl .org/div/litcrit>. A collection of links to literary criticism and biographical information available on the Web, organized by author, title, nationality, and period.

Internet Shakespeare Editions <http://internetshakespeare.uvic.ca>. A site that offers a search engine for Shakespeare's plays and poems as well as information about his life and times, critical studies, and performance history.

The Online Books Page <http://digital.library.upenn.edu/books>. See this entry in Web Resources in the Humanities, page 34.

Reference books in literature

American Writers. 4 vols. New York: Scribner, 1979–87. With supplements. Offers essays analyzing the life and work of major American writers, arranged chronologically with an alphabetical index. Scribner publishes a similar series for British, Latin American, and European writers. These works are also available in electronic format as part of the *Literature Resource Center* (see Databases and Indexes in Literature, p. 40).

Bloomsbury Guide to Women's Literature. By Claire Buck. Upper Saddle River: Prentice-Hall, 1992. A thorough compendium of information on women's literature from around the world, from early times to the present. This text provides concise and informative articles and includes lengthy regional surveys. Its coverage of non-Western women writers is particularly useful.

Concise Oxford Dictionary of Literary Terms. By Chris Baldick. 2nd ed. New York: Oxford University Press, 2001. Defines and briefly discusses terms used in current critical theory. Notable for its clear and succinct language, this dictionary is also available in electronic format.

Contemporary Authors. Detroit: Gale Group, 1962–. 275 vols. to date. A long-running series that offers profiles of modern authors, including some whose work is not strictly literary. To locate author profiles, consult the most recent index. This work is available online as a separate database or as part of the *Literature Resource Center* (see Databases and Indexes in Literature, p. 40).

Contemporary Literary Criticism. Detroit: Gale Group, 1973–. 264 vols. to date. A series that offers background on contemporary authors, with excerpts from critical essays and reviews. Citations for original sources are included. Consult the most recent cumulative index, which includes cross-references to other Gale biographical series. This series provides a quick sense of how a writer's work has been received. Available online as *Contemporary Literary Criticism Select* or as part of the *Literature Resource Center* (see Databases and Indexes in Literature, p. 40).

Dictionary of Literary Biography (*DLB*). Detroit: Gale Group, 1978–. 352 vols. to date. A series that offers lengthy biographies of authors with criticism of their works. Volumes are arranged thematically. To find an author, consult the index in the most recent volume. Though the *DLB* emphasizes American and British literary authors, it offers substantial coverage of writers from other countries and of journalists and historians. This work is available online as part of the *Literature Resource Center* (see Databases and Indexes in Literature, p. 40).

Encyclopedia of German Literature. Ed. Matthias Konzett. 2 vols. Chicago: Fitzroy Dearborn, 2000. Covers authors and topics such as literary movements.

Encyclopedia of World Literature in the 20th Century. Ed. Steven R. Serafin. 3rd ed. 4 vols. Farmington Hills: St. James, 1999. Covers twentieth-century authors and movements and provides lengthy surveys of the modern literature of different countries.

Guide to French Literature. Ed. Anthony Levi. 2 vols. Chicago: St. James, 1992. Includes biographical information as well as entries on movements and themes, covering Francophone Africa, the Caribbean, and France.

Literary Research Guide: A Guide to Reference Sources for the Study of Literatures in English and Related Topics. By James L. Harner. 5th ed.

New York: Modern Language Association, 2008. A guide to tools and methods of literary scholarship, emphasizing English literature; includes annotated lists of reference sources.

The Oxford Companion to English Literature. Ed. Margaret Drabble. 6th ed. New York: Oxford University Press, 2000. Brief descriptions of writers, literary works, schools and movements, and places of literary significance, arranged alphabetically. A number of *Oxford Companion*s cover other national literatures and genres.

The Oxford English Dictionary (OED). Ed. J. A. Simpson and E. S. C. Weiner. 2nd ed. 20 vols. Oxford: Clarendon, 1989. Includes supplements. An invaluable source for understanding the meanings of words and their changing definitions, the *OED* provides chronological examples showing how a word has been used throughout history. It is unequaled in its depth of coverage.

Music

Databases and indexes in music

Music Index. Detroit: Information Coordinators, 1949–. A subject and author index to more than 600 music periodicals. International in scope, its citations cover both musicology and performance journals.

RILM Abstracts of Music Literature. New York: RILM, 1967–. Offers abstracts of articles appearing in over 5,000 international journals, books, and dissertations and other materials in the music field. Its coverage is especially strong for music history and musicology.

Web resources in music

The Classical Composer Database <http://www.classical-composers .org>. Offers basic biographical information about composers, both well known and obscure, and links to information about them on the Web. Includes composers' chronologies, news, and calendars. The list is maintained by Jos Smeets, a classical composer.

The Classical Music Navigator <http://www.wku.edu/~smithch/ music>. Provides information on over 400 composers with a list of works arranged by musical genre, a geographical roster, an index of forms and styles, and a glossary of musical terms. Maintained by Charles H. Smith of Western Kentucky University.

Music History 102: A Guide to Western Composers and Their Music from the Middle Ages to the Present <http://www.ipl.org/div/mushist>. A nicely organized chronological survey of music with images, audio files, and links to composer profiles. The author of this site is Robert Sherane, a librarian at the Juilliard School of Music; the site is part of the *Internet Public Library*.

Reference books in music

Baker's Biographical Dictionary of Musicians. Ed. Nicolas Slonimsky. 9th ed. 6 vols. New York: Schirmer, 2001. Compact biographies of composers and performers with bibliographies of works by and about them. This reference is good for a quick overview of a musician and his or her impact.

Encyclopedia of Popular Music. Ed. Colin Larkin. 4th ed. 10 vols. London: Muze, 2006. Offers brief entries on musicians, bands, musicals, and record labels as well as a song title index.

Garland Encyclopedia of World Music. 10 vols. New York: Garland, 1998–2002. Covers the music of peoples of the world in regional volumes that offer area profiles, social contexts for music, and in-depth information on the musical traditions of specific nations and ethnic groups. The work includes musical examples on accompanying CDs.

New Grove Dictionary of Music and Musicians. Ed. Stanley Sadie. 2nd ed. 29 vols. New York: Grove, 2001. The definitive source on music and music history. The articles in these volumes are carefully researched and documented and provide information on national music traditions, musical forms, composers and musicians, instruments, and more.

New Oxford History of Music. 11 vols. New York: Oxford University Press, 1957–1990. An excellent chronological exploration of all aspects of music. Each volume covers a different musical period. Some have been published in newer editions. The final volume includes chronologies, bibliographies, and an index to the set.

Oxford Companion to Music. Ed. Alison Latham. Oxford: Oxford University Press, 2002. Covers primarily Western classical music, offering brief entries on musicians, works, musical terms, and movements, with surveys of musical traditions in various countries.

The Oxford Dictionary of Music. By Michael Kennedy and Joyce Bourne. 2nd ed. rev. Oxford: Oxford University Press, 1999. Offers brief identifications of musical terms and musicians; a handy place to find dates and other quick facts.

Philosophy

Databases and indexes in philosophy

Philosopher's Index. Bowling Green: Philosophy Documentation Center, 1967–. Provides abstracts of articles from over 400 philosophy journals as well as anthologies and books published from 1940 to the present.

Web resources in philosophy

BioethicsWeb <http://www.intute.ac.uk/healthandlifesciences/ bioethicsweb>. A UK-based guide to reputable Web resources on topics such as genetically modified food, medical ethics, cloning, stem cell research, and animal welfare.

Contemporary Philosophy, Critical Theory, and Postmodern Thought <http://carbon.cudenver.edu/~mryder/itc_data/postmodern.html>. A compilation of Web-based sources on postmodernism, including important philosophers, background information, and primary texts. The site was created by Martin Ryder of the University of Colorado at Denver.

Ethics Matters <http://ethics.sandiego.edu>. Provides bibliographic essays and links to content on ethics theory, teaching and learning, and applied ethics topics such as euthanasia, animal rights, bioethics, and world hunger. The site includes audio and video files as well as textual information. Edited by Lawrence W. Hinman at the Values Institute, University of San Diego.

Internet Encyclopedia of Philosophy <http://www.iep.utm.edu>. A site for peer-reviewed survey articles by philosophy scholars about topics in the field. The articles in the collection are extensive and thoroughly documented.

Stanford Encyclopedia of Philosophy <http://plato.stanford.edu>. Offers authoritative articles that are updated to reflect changes in the field. Entries are kept current by experts in philosophy and reviewed by an editorial board, based at the Metaphysics Research Lab of Stanford University. Because the project is a work in progress, some topics have not yet been covered.

Reference books in philosophy

Encyclopedia of Applied Ethics. Ed. Ruth Chadwick. 4 vols. San Diego: Academic Press, 1998. Provides lengthy, scholarly discussions of the ethical aspects of issues such as affirmative action, animal rights, and genetic screening as well as contemporary views on theories of humanism, hedonism, and utilitarianism.

Encyclopedia of Bioethics. Ed. Stephen G. Post. 3rd ed. 5 vols. New York: Macmillan, 2004. Covers issues and controversies in bioethics in lengthy, scholarly articles, each accompanied by a bibliography of key sources.

Encyclopedia of Philosophy. Ed. Donald M. Borchert. 2nd ed. 10 vols. New York: Macmillan, 2006. Offers articles on movements, concepts, and philosophers. A good starting place for research, offering clearly written and accessible overviews and bibliographies of key works.

Oxford Dictionary of Philosophy. By Simon Blackburn. New York: Oxford University Press, 1994. Offers succinct definitions of terms in philosophy, primarily Western, and biographical entries on individual philosophers.

Routledge Encyclopedia of Philosophy. 10 vols. London: Routledge, 1998. This specialized encyclopedia covers classical approaches to the field as well as approaches based on feminism, postcolonialism, poststructuralism, deconstruction, and postmodernism.

Religion

Databases and indexes in religion

ATLA. Evanston: American Theological Library Association, 1949–. The most thorough database for articles, books, selections in books, and reviews for the field of religion, including theology, biblical studies, church history, comparative religions, archaeology and antiquities, and pastoral work.

Web resources in religion

Christian Classics Ethereal Library <http://www.ccel.org>. A digital archive of key Christian historical texts and other material, such as the Early Church Fathers series; works of Boethius, Erasmus, and Luther; and modern works by G. K. Chesterton and Dorothy L. Sayers. Material can be searched or browsed by author, title, subject, or type of text.

The Five Gospel Parallels <http://www.utoronto.ca/religion/ synopsis>. A tool for comparing the text of the New Testament Gospels as well as several apocryphal texts, including the Gospel of Thomas, side-by-side. An interesting feature of this program is that users can locate the passages in different texts that deal with the same parables and events. The site is maintained by John W. Marshall of the Department for the Study of Religion, University of Toronto.

Internet Sacred Texts Archive <http://sacred-texts.com>. A varied collection of texts on religion, mythology, folklore, and esoteric topics such as alchemy and UFOs, which can be browsed by religion, subject, or world region.

Judaism and Jewish Resources <http://shamash.org/trb/judaism.html>. A directory of selected Internet resources related to almost any aspect of Judaism and its history. The site includes annotated links on a variety of academic and social topics, with links to museums, libraries, organizations, and the government and news media of modern Israel. Maintained by Andrew Tannenbaum.

Religious Worlds <http://www.religiousworlds.com/index.html>. Offers selective, annotated links to Web material on religious traditions, contemporary issues, religious experience, religious studies programs, and reference sources. Maintained by Gene R. Thursby of the University of Florida.

Religion Newswriters: Religion Online Library <http://www.rna.org/library.php>. Offers a collection of sites useful to journalists covering religion as well as to anyone interested in how religion is reflected in contemporary culture and current affairs.

Internet Guide to Religion <http://www.wabashcenter.wabash.edu/resources/guide_headings.aspx>. A selective annotated directory of Web sites arranged by subject and type of material. Sites of particular note are highlighted, and the directory covers topics such as the history of Christianity, world religions, social issues, theology, and archaeology. Maintained by Charles K. Bellinger at Wabash College.

Pew Forum on Religion and Public Life <http://pewforum.org>. A project that provides information about issues at the intersection of religion and public affairs based on news tracking and independent research. Sections cover religion and law, politics, social welfare, public schools, bioethics, international affairs, and timely topics such as evolution, stem cell research, same-sex marriage, and the death penalty. This site is funded by the Pew Charitable Trusts.

Reference books in religion

Anchor Bible Dictionary. Ed. David Noel Freedman et al. 6 vols. New York: Doubleday, 1992. A definitive encyclopedia covering names, places, and events of the Bible as well as cultural history, social institutions, archaeological sites, and other topics of interest to biblical scholars.

Contemporary American Religion. Ed. Wade Clark Roof. 2 vols. New York: Macmillan Reference, 2000. Five hundred articles that address the religious pluralism of the United States and provide contemporary analyses of practices, traditions, and trends.

Encyclopedia of Buddhism. Ed. Robert E. Buswell. 2 vols. Detroit: Gale, 2004. Covers basic concepts and practices of Buddhism around the world, including art, architecture, rites, and festivals.

Encyclopedia of Hinduism. Ed. Denise Cush, Catherine Robinson, and Michael York. New York: Routledge, 2008. Offers over 900 articles of varying depth on terms and concepts related to Hinduism as a religious tradition as well as its social and cultural aspects.

Encyclopaedia Judaica. 2nd ed. 22 vols. Detroit: Macmillan Reference, 2007. An excellent source of information on Jewish culture and religion, offering in-depth scholarly articles and ample illustrations.

Encyclopedia of Islam and the Muslim World. Ed. Richard C. Martin. 2 vols. New York: Macmillan Reference, 2004. Identifies and discusses important events, concepts, historical movements, and key figures in the Islamic world.

Encyclopedia of Protestantism. Ed. Hans H. Hillerbrand. 4 vols. New York: Routledge, 2004. Offers articles on traditions and faith groups; creeds and professions; historical events, movements, and figures; and cultural and social issues as they relate to Protestantism.

Encyclopedia of Religion. Ed. Lindsay Jones. 2nd ed. 16 vols. New York: Macmillan, 2005. Covers religions from around the world, including information about their ideas, histories, and cultures. The articles are written by experts in their fields and include excellent bibliographies.

Mythologies. Ed. Yves Bonnefoy. 2 vols. Chicago: University of Chicago Press, 1991. An encyclopedia surveying mythologies of the world, with articles on cosmology, cults, and myth traditions arranged in geographical sections. The articles are long and scholarly, and they are accompanied by illustrations and thorough bibliographies.

New Catholic Encyclopedia. Ed. Bernard L. Marthaler. 2nd ed. 15 vols. Detroit: Gale Group, 2002. An authoritative source for Catholic theology, canon law, liturgical matters, and the church's position on social issues such as euthanasia and biomedical research. This encyclopedia also has articles on the history of the church, biographical sketches, and institutions.

Oxford Dictionary of the Christian Church. Ed. F. L. Cross. 3rd ed. New York: Oxford University Press, 1997. A compact compendium that contains vast amounts of information, with short, descriptive entries that run from *Aaron* to *Zwingli*. The entries provide concise starting points for understanding and identifying people, concepts, events, places, and biblical references that are important in Christian church history.

Oxford Encyclopedia of the Modern Islamic World. Ed. John L. Esposito. 4 vols. New York: Oxford University Press, 1995. Covers countries of the Islamic world and topics related to Islamic religion, history, and culture. The articles are long and scholarly as well as up-to-date.

Theater, dance, and film

Databases and indexes in theater, dance, and film

Film and Television Literature Index. Albany: Film and Television Documentation Center, SUNY Albany, 1975–. The most complete index to international, trade, popular, and scholarly publications about film and television. Very thorough in its coverage of reviews, interviews, criticism, and production information. A retrospective version of this database, covering only publications from 1975 through 2001, is available online for free at <http://webapp1.dlib.indiana.edu/fli>.

MLA International Bibliography. New York: Modern Language Association, 1921–. Useful for scholarly criticism of dramatic works, this database lists citations to books, book chapters, articles, and dissertations. It offers in-depth coverage of literary analysis of plays, but performance reviews and information about stagecraft and acting technique are not typically included.

Web resources in theater, dance, and film

Artslynx International Arts Resources <http://www.artslynx.org>. An index of links to performing arts, including theater, dance, music, and film, as well as sources for arts management and the arts in personal and community enrichment. The editor is Richard Finkelstein of James Madison University.

The Internet Movie Database <http://imdb.com>. The oldest and most comprehensive Internet film Web site. The database includes information on hundreds of thousands of movies from early silent films to the latest releases, offering information on the release, script, cast, reviews, and additional information. Users can search by movie title, cast or crew member, year, genre, country, production company, or combinations thereof. Industry news and information about upcoming releases are available through articles and message boards. Now affiliated with *Amazon.com,* this site retains the flavor of its fan-based origins. Some features designed specifically for industry professionals are available only by subscription.

Theatre History on the Web <http://www.videoccasions-nw.com/ history/jack.html>. Includes links of interest to the student, the researcher, and the dramaturge, organized by period and topic. The site is maintained by Jack Wolcott, a retired professor of drama at the University of Washington.

Reference books in theater, dance, and film

American Playwrights, 1880–1945: A Research and Production Sourcebook. Ed. William W. Demastes. Westport: Greenwood, 1995. Covers the lives, works, critical reception, and impact of 40 American playwrights, some prominent and others lesser known, including many women and minority writers who have not received much critical attention. Each entry is followed by a detailed bibliography of the playwright's works, criticism, and reviews. Greenwood publishes similar sourcebooks for contemporary British and American dramatists as well as volumes devoted to specific playwrights.

Drama Criticism. Detroit: Gale, 1991–. 36 vols. to date. Provides biocritical information about playwrights and plays. Much of this series is available through the *Literature Resource Center* database (see Databases and Indexes in Literature, p. 40).

Cambridge Guide to Theatre. Ed. Martin Banham. 2nd ed. Cambridge: Cambridge University Press, 1995. Offers international coverage of major playwrights, actors, directors, works, traditions, theories, companies, venues, and events as well as information on theater history, design, and architecture.

Encyclopedia of Documentary Film. Ed. Ian Aitken. 3 vols. New York: Routledge, 2006. Covers the documentary genre with more than 700 entries from international scholars on films, filmmakers, themes, and techniques.

Encyclopedia of the Musical Theatre. By Kurt Ganzl. 2nd ed. 3 vols. New York: Schirmer, 2001. Surveys musical theater, providing detailed background on musicals and profiles of those involved with them.

Film Encyclopedia. By Ephraim Katz and Ronald Dean Nolen. 6th ed. New York: HarperCollins, 2008. Offers brief entries on terms, topics, styles, genres, industry jargon, and individuals related to the history of film. Though it fits into a single volume, this work contains a wealth of handy information.

International Encyclopedia of Dance. 6 vols. New York: Oxford University Press, 1998. The most exhaustive reference work on dance, covering the historical evolution of dance throughout the world, analysis of dance techniques, theories of aesthetics, influential individuals, important companies, and significant works.

McGraw-Hill Encyclopedia of World Drama. 2nd ed. 5 vols. New York: McGraw-Hill, 1984. Contains articles on playwrights, periods of theater history, and notable figures in theater. Brief critical comments on plays are given under author entries. Though dated, this work is particularly useful for its coverage of past productions and includes many illustrations.

World Encyclopedia of Contemporary Theatre. Ed. Don Rubin. 6 vols. London: Routledge, 2000. An authoritative, up-to-date guide to current theater with a global perspective and thorough coverage organized by country.

World languages and linguistics

Databases and indexes in world languages and linguistics

MLA International Bibliography. New York: Modern Language Association, 1921–. See this entry in Databases and Indexes in Literature, page 40.

Web resources in world languages and linguistics

Ethnologue <http://www.ethnologue.com>. A database of information on world languages, including information about geographic distribution, dialects, numbers of speakers, and linguistic affiliation.

The site includes a bibliography. Maintained by SIL International, an organization that promotes language study for international faith-based work, this database is particularly strong for basic information about lesser-known and endangered languages.

iLoveLanguages <http://www.ilovelanguages.com>. Formerly known as *The Human-Languages Page,* this site offers links to language-related Internet resources. Of particular interest is the Languages section, which contains categories such as languages, dictionaries, lessons, and so on.

Reference books in world languages and linguistics

Encyclopedia of Language and Education. Ed. Nancy H. Hornberger. 2nd ed. 10 vols. New York: Springer, 2008. Covers a wide range of topics, from bilingual education and language policy to language testing and research methods.

International Encyclopedia of Linguistics. Ed. William J. Frawley. 2nd ed. 4 vols. New York: Oxford University Press, 2003. Includes scholarly articles on all aspects of linguistics along with helpful bibliographies for further research.

Researching in History

Research in history involves developing an understanding of the past through the examination and interpretation of evidence. Evidence may exist in the form of texts, physical remains of historic sites, recorded data, pictures, maps, artifacts, and so on. The historian's job is to find evidence, analyze its content and biases, corroborate it with further evidence, and use that evidence to develop an interpretation of past events that holds some significance for the present.

Historians use libraries to

- locate primary sources (firsthand information such as diaries, letters, and original documents) for evidence

- find secondary sources (historians' interpretations and analyses of historical evidence)

- verify factual material as inconsistencies arise

Doing historical research is a little like excavating an archaeological site. It requires patience, insight, and imagination as well as diligence and the proper tools. As you find and examine primary sources, you need to imagine them in their original context and understand how your present-day point of view may distort your interpretation of them. You need to recognize not only your own biases but also the biases that shaped primary materials in their own period. You need to brush away the layers of interpretation that time has imposed on these materials and imaginatively re-create the complexities of the environment in which they originated. Students doing historical research should be prepared to

- survey historians' interpretations of the past while recognizing how their purposes or backgrounds might influence those interpretations

- understand the context in which primary sources were generated

- identify conflicting evidence and locate factual and interpretive information that can help resolve or illuminate inconsistencies

Many bibliographies can help you identify primary and secondary sources related to a topic or historical period. Be sure to examine bibliographies and footnotes in secondary sources as you find them, since they will often lead you to primary sources. Finally, innumerable encyclopedias, dictionaries, handbooks, and chronologies can provide information to round out your interpretations and ground them in fact. Consult a librarian to find out what the reference shelves offer for your topic and whether the library has any special collections of microfilm, archives, manuscripts, or other primary sources especially suited to your research.

General resources in history

Databases and indexes in history

Humanities Index. New York: Wilson, 1974–. An interdisciplinary index to about 400 prominent English-language journals in the humanities, including art, music, history, and literature. Searchable by author or subject, the index includes many cross-references and subheadings that break large topics into components.

JSTOR. New York: JSTOR, 1995–. A multidisciplinary historical archive of scholarly journals. The complete contents of core journals have been digitized from the first issues. The most current issues (typically from the past three to five years) are not included. This archive is particularly useful to historians because many prominent history journals are included (such as the *American Historical Review*) and, since the contents go back to the nineteenth century, full-text searches can reveal the historical development of concepts, words, and phrases in scholarly publications.

Social Sciences Citation Index. Philadelphia: Institute for Scientific Information, 1956–. Part of the *Web of Knowledge,* this multidisciplinary database of social science journals includes history, women's studies, and urban studies. Searchable by author or keyword, the index allows searches by cited source, which is an efficient way to trace the influence of a particular work. The Related Search feature also identifies works that cite one or more of the same sources.

Web resources in history

Make History <http://bcs.bedfordstmartins.com/makehistory>. A database of digital content relevant to United States, ancient, and Western history. Searchable by topic or chronological period.

Best of History Websites <http://www.besthistorysites.net>. Though the audience for this site is K–12 history teachers, it is a useful and up-to-date guide to reputable Web sites, arranged by region and period, with links to art history, maps, news, and teaching materials. The site was created by Tom Daccord of the Center for Teaching History with Technology.

WWW Virtual Library: History Central Catalogue <http://vlib.iue.it/history/index.html>. The premier meta-site for history, organized by research methods and materials, historical topics, countries and regions, and eras and epochs.

Reference books in history

American Historical Association Guide to Historical Literature. Ed. Mary Beth Norton and Pamela Gerardi. 3rd ed. 2 vols. New York: Oxford University Press, 1995. Offers citations of important historical publications, arranged in 48 sections covering theory, international history, and regional history. Though it does not include recent publications, it remains an indispensable guide to the best work in the field.

Dictionary of Historical Terms. By Chris Cook. 2nd ed. New York: Peter Bedrick, 1990. Covers a wide variety of terms related to historical events, places, and institutions in a remarkably small package. This is a good place for quick identification of terms used by historians.

Encyclopedia of Historians and Historical Writing. Ed. Kelly Boyd. 2 vols. London: Fitzroy Dearborn, 1999. Provides information on historians, regions, periods, and topics in the field such as history of religion, women's and gender history, and art history.

World history

Databases and indexes in world history

Historical Abstracts. Santa Barbara: ABC-CLIO, 1955–. Provides citations and abstracts of articles, book reviews, books, and dissertations from over 2,000 journals in world history from 1450 to the present. North American history is covered in the companion index *America: History and Life.*

Web resources in world history

ABZU: A Guide to Information Related to the Study of the Ancient Near East on the Web <http://www.etana.org/abzu>. Links to thousands of Web-accessible texts—articles, books, papers, and scholarly editions of the world's earliest texts—searchable or browsable by author or title. A collaborative project undertaken by several organizations, including the Oriental Institute at the University of Chicago, this resource is valuable for archaeologists and historians.

Finding World History <http://chnm.gmu.edu/worldhistorysources/ whmfinding.php>. A selection of reputable sites with brief reviews organized by region and time period. Also includes guides to analyzing evidence and documents. A project of the Center for History and New Media at George Mason University.

Reference books in world history

Cambridge History of Africa. 8 vols. Cambridge: Cambridge University Press, 1986. Covers African history chronologically and in depth. Use the table of contents and indexes for access. Other Cambridge History works cover many countries and regions such as China, Japan, Latin America, and Southeast Asia.

Civilization of the Ancient Mediterranean. Ed. Michael Grant. 3 vols. New York: Scribner, 1988. Provides lengthy articles that introduce many facets of the classical world. Each article is followed by a helpful bibliography.

Civilizations of the Ancient Near East. Ed. Jack M. Sasson. 4 vols. New York: Scribner, 1995. A collection of essays on the culture and history of Egypt, Syro-Palestine, Mesopotamia, and Anatolia. The work includes some coverage of Arabian, northeast African, and Aegean cultures as well as extensive bibliographies.

Companion Encyclopedia of the History of Medicine. Ed. W. F. Bynum and Ray Porter. 2 vols. New York: Routledge, 1994. Includes essays on body systems and how they have been perceived through time, theories of illness (including the history of specific diseases and their treatments), clinical history, and medicine in society and culture.

Dictionary of the Middle Ages. Ed. Joseph R. Strayer. 13 vols. New York: Scribner, 1982–89. With supplements. An encyclopedia covering people, events, ideas, movements, texts, and cultural features of the medieval world. Articles are often illustrated with period artwork and are followed by bibliographies of primary and secondary sources.

Encyclopedia of Asian History. Ed. Robin Lewis and Ainslie Embree. 4 vols. New York: Macmillan Library Reference, 1988. Discusses people, places, events, and topics in detailed and well-documented essays covering central Asia, southern Asia, and the Far East.

Encyclopedia of European Social History from 1350 to 2000. Ed. Peter N. Stearns. 6 vols. New York: Scribner, 2001. Offers substantial, well-documented survey essays on topics such as social change, urban and rural life, gender, popular culture, religion, and everyday life.

Encyclopedia of Latin American History and Culture. Ed. Jay Kinsbruner and Eric D. Langer. 2nd ed. 6 vols. Detroit: Gale, 2008. Presents a wide variety of topics in more than 5,000 articles that together constitute an overview of current knowledge about the region. Entries cover countries, topics (such as slavery, art, Asians in Latin America), and biographical sketches.

Encyclopedia of the Enlightenment. Ed. Alan Charles Kors. 4 vols. Oxford: Oxford University Press, 2002. Covers ideas, figures, historical events, and culture in Europe from the 1670s to the early nineteenth century.

Encyclopedia of the Holocaust. Ed. Israel Gutman. 4 vols. New York: Macmillan Library Reference, 1996. Offers lengthy articles on people, places, events, and concepts related to the Holocaust, each followed by a selective bibliography.

Encyclopedia of the Renaissance. Ed. Paul F. Grendler. 6 vols. New York: Scribner, 1999. Offers nearly 1,200 substantial articles on topics related to the culture and history of the period.

Encyclopedia of the Vietnam War: A Political, Social, and Military History. Ed. Spencer C. Tucker. 3 vols. Santa Barbara: ABC-CLIO, 1998. Includes 900 entries covering prominent figures, military events, and war protests. The third volume offers a wealth of primary source documents in English and English translation.

New Cambridge Modern History. 14 vols. Cambridge: Cambridge University Press, 1957–79. Covers world history from 1493 to 1945, chronologically and by topic, providing detailed and lengthy narrative surveys of the times. New editions of individual volumes are occasionally published. Similar works published by Cambridge University Press cover ancient and medieval history.

The Oxford Encyclopedia of the Reformation. Ed. Hans J. Hillerbrand. 4 vols. New York: Oxford University Press, 1996. Lengthy, scholarly articles treat people, places, events, documents, and ideas related to the Reformation. Each article reflects current research and interpretation and is followed by a selective bibliography.

Times Atlas of World History. Ed. Geoffrey Barraclough and J. R. Overy. 4th ed. London: Times Books, 1993. Offers more than 600 maps showing historical periods and movements such as the spread of world religions, the industrial revolution, and European expansion. The maps are supplemented by explanations and discussions of each period. For more specialized maps of particular places or periods, search your library catalog for *historical atlas.*

Chronology of World History. Ed. H. E. L. Mellersh. 4 vols. Santa Barbara: ABC-CLIO, 1999. Provides year-by-year coverage of global events, including developments in the arts, politics, science, and society.

American history

Databases and indexes in American history

America: History and Life. Santa Barbara: ABC-CLIO, 1964–. This companion to *Historical Abstracts* provides citations and abstracts of articles, books, dissertations, and book reviews on U.S. and Canadian history and culture. Searchable by keyword, author, subject, and source, the index offers in-depth coverage of scholarly publications in North American history and allows for interdisciplinary examinations of American culture.

Web resources in American history

American Women's History: A Research Guide <http://frank.mtsu.edu/~kmiddlet/history/women.html>. Offers clearly organized information on more than 2,000 print and online resources. Includes a subject guide, a state index, and an introduction to research tools for primary and secondary sources. The site is maintained by Ken Middleton, a reference librarian at Middle Tennessee State University.

WWW Virtual Library: History: United States <http://vlib.iue.it/history/USA>. Organized by period and topic, with links to research tools and associations, this selective directory focuses on history sites of interest to scholars.

Reference books in American history

American National Biography. Ed. John Arthur Garraty and Mark C. Carnes. 24 vols. New York: Oxford University Press, 1999. Compiled under the auspices of the American Council of Learned Societies, this is the most important and comprehensive biographical reference work on American historical figures. Each sketch is a detailed scholarly profile followed by a critical bibliography.

Dictionary of American History. Ed. Stanley I. Kutler. 3rd ed. 10 vols. New York: Scribner, 2003. An encyclopedia of terms, places, and concepts in U.S. history, with maps and illustrations as well as references for further research.

Encyclopedia of African-American Culture and History.   Ed. Colin A. Palmer. 2nd ed. 6 vols. Detroit: Gale, 2006. A wide-ranging encyclopedia covering people, places, events, concepts, and topics of all sorts. Articles are written by specialists and feature bibliographies.

Encyclopedia of American Cultural and Intellectual History. Ed. Mary Kupiec Cayton and Peter W. Williams. 3 vols. New York: Scribner, 2001. Provides in-depth articles on American thought and culture. Topics include historical approaches, cultural groups, major cultural regions, and political thought.

Encyclopedia of American Social History. Ed. Mary Kupiec Cayton et al. 3 vols. New York: Scribner, 1993. Fills in the gaps left by conventional political-biographical history sources. The work presents lengthy and well-documented articles covering topics such as religion, class, gender, race, popular culture, regionalism, and everyday life in the United States from pre-Columbian to modern times. Organized thematically rather than alphabetically.

Encyclopedia of the American Civil War. 5 vols. Santa Barbara: ABC-CLIO, 2000. Subtitled *A Political, Social, and Military History,* this source offers over 1,600 articles on topics related to the Civil War and its contexts, including events leading up to the war and its consequences. A special section is devoted to primary sources; photographs, drawings, and maps are included.

Encyclopedia of the Confederacy. Ed. Richard N. Current. 4 vols. New York: Simon and Schuster, 1993. Covers Confederate society, culture, and politics as well as events and people in the Civil War–era South. Articles are arranged alphabetically.

Encyclopedia of the North American Colonies. Ed. Jacob Ernest Cook. 3 vols. New York: Scribner, 1993. A collection of lengthy essays covering government and law, economic life, labor, social issues, families, the arts, education, and religion, arranged thematically. The third volume contains a thorough index.

Encyclopedia of the United States in the Nineteenth Century. Ed. Paul Finkelman. 3 vols. New York: Scribner, 2001. Covers major ideas and issues in American social, political, and military history.

Encyclopedia of the United States in the Twentieth Century. Ed. Stanley I. Kutler. 4 vols. New York: Scribner, 1996. An ambitious survey of U.S.

cultural, social, and intellectual history in broad articles arranged topically. Each essay is followed by a thorough bibliography.

United States History: A Multicultural, Interdisciplinary Guide to Information Sources. By Ron Blazek and Anna Perrault. 2nd ed. Westport: Libraries Unlimited, 2003. A selective and descriptive guide to research materials in U.S. history.

Primary sources

Primary sources are original documents such as letters, diaries, legislative bills, laboratory studies, field research reports, and eyewitness accounts published during the era you are researching. There is no simple, foolproof way to find primary sources for historical research; rather, locating such sources tends to be an intuitive and creative process involving guesswork and blind alleys. To get started, try searching the library catalog with the search term *sources* or *documents* added to your keyword, or use the names of prominent figures as authors. Additionally, check with a reference librarian to find out if your library subscribes to any primary source databases. Primary documents may also be available in your library or on the Web through the following sources.

Databases and indexes: The popular press

American Periodicals Series, 1741–1900. Ann Arbor: University Microfilms International, 1946–79. 2,770 microfilm reels. A large collection of articles from journals published from colonial times through the nineteenth century. This database identifies journals focused on specific topics and offers full-text articles. Available on microfilm or in electronic format.

The Civil War: A Newspaper Perspective. Wilmington: Accessible Archives, 1995–. Offers selected full-text articles in plain-text format from more than 2,500 issues of newspapers representing both southern and northern perspectives for the years 1860–1865. The database includes eyewitness accounts, hundreds of maps, official reports of battles, and advertisements from the period.

HarpWeek. Norfolk: HarpWeek, 1990–. An electronic edition of the contents of *Harper's Weekly*, a popular illustrated publication, for the years 1857–1916. Images of the pages have been digitally scanned to retain the original appearance and include both illustrations and full text. Some libraries may have only segments of this database covering the Civil War and/or Reconstruction.

Historical Newspapers Online. Ann Arbor: ProQuest, 1999–. Offers the searchable full text of the *New York Times*, the *Wall Street Journal*, and other newspapers from their first issue on. Users can view both the article in its original format and the entire page on which the article appeared.

New York Times Index. New York: New York Times, 1851–. A valuable print source for finding newspaper coverage on a particular historical topic. Topics are grouped under broad subjects with individual stories listed chronologically. Each index citation provides the date, section, page, and column of a story. Even without reading the stories themselves, users can get a detailed sequence of events from the index. Though the keyword search capability of *Historical Newspapers Online* offers some advantages, this print index provides a unique chronological record of events.

The Official Index to the Times. London: Times Publishing, 1966–. An excellent source for news on British life and world affairs from 1790 on. Offers citations for articles from the *London Times*. Sections of this index are published as *Palmer's Index to the Times*.

Poole's Index to Periodical Literature, 1802–1881. 6 vols. Boston: Houghton Mifflin, 1892. With supplement covering 1882–1906. Provides citations to American and English periodicals, books, newspapers, and government documents of the nineteenth century. An electronic edition is also available, with 3.8 million citations and enhanced indexing.

Readers' Guide to Periodical Literature. New York: Wilson, 1900–. Indexes popular magazines by subject. This index is a good source for popular reactions to events, literary topics, and popular culture of the twentieth century. Available in print or electronic format. A companion index covers 1890–1900.

Web resources: Primary documents

American Memory <http://memory.loc.gov>. A rich source of electronic reproductions of texts, images, sound, and film from the collections of the Library of Congress and collaborating libraries and museums. Materials include motion pictures from as early as 1897, sound recordings from World War I, and more than 300 pamphlets written by African Americans between Reconstruction and World War I. Browse collections by topic, period, document type, and region.

The Avalon Project at the Yale Law School: Documents in Law, History, and Diplomacy <http://avalon.law.yale.edu>. A well-edited, high-quality collection of full-text primary source documents particularly rich in legal and diplomatic history and human rights. Organized by period and topic and searchable by keyword, documents include internal links to materials referenced in the text.

EuroDocs: Primary Historical Documents from Western Europe <http://eudocs.lib.byu.edu>. A wealth of primary source material from 22 countries (plus Vatican City). Sites are sorted by country and listed chronologically. Available sources include letters, facsimiles of paintings and photographs, journals, and official documents. The links are compiled by Richard Hacken at Brigham Young University Library.

Internet History Sourcebooks Project <http://www.fordham.edu/halsall/index.html>. A large collection of online texts and primary documents for the study of history. Three major sourcebooks, edited by Paul Halsall of Fordham University, cover ancient, medieval, and modern history; other collections focus on the history of science, African history, Islamic history, women's history, and more.

Making of America <http://quod.lib.umich.edu/m/moagrp>. A digital archive of books and journals from the antebellum period through Reconstruction. It is extremely useful for the study of American social history, with strengths in education, science and technology, psychology, and sociology. A work in progress, it already includes the full text of over 10,000 books and 50,000 journal articles published in the nineteenth century.

Web resources: Government documents

Foreign Relations of the United States: Diplomatic Papers <http://www
.state.gov/www/about_state/history/frusonline.html>. Provides collected correspondence, memoranda, treaties, presidential messages,
and other documents related to U.S. foreign policy, arranged chronologically and by region. Online volumes cover the years spanning
the Truman and Johnson administrations. For earlier documents,
see the print collection *Foreign Relations of the United States: Diplomatic Papers* (Washington: Government Printing Office, 1861–).

Public Papers of the Presidents of the United States <http://www
.gpoaccess.gov/pubpapers/index.html>. A repository of proclama-
tions, speeches, statements, photographs, and other presidential
papers. Documents from the George H. W. Bush administration
and later are currently available online. Papers from Hoover on will
eventually be added; until then, see the print version of *Public Papers of the Presidents of the United States* (Washington: Office of the
Federal Register, 1957–).

Reprint series

American Culture Series. Ann Arbor: University Microfilms International, 1941–74. 643 microfilm reels. Reproduces over 6,000
American books and pamphlets published between 1493 and 1875.
The materials are organized by 12 disciplines. Series I spans 1493–
1806; the larger Series II expands the pre-1806 material and extends
to 1875.

American Women's Diaries. New Canaan: Readex, 1980–. 90 microfilm
reels. Reproduces the diaries of women who lived and traveled in
the western, southern, and eastern United States. Available on microfilm only.

Early English Books, 1475–1640. Ann Arbor: University Microfilms
International, 1938–67. 2,034 microfilm reels. *Early English Books,
1641–1700.* Ann Arbor: University Microfilms International, 1961–.
2,396 microfilm reels. A vast collection of books from the first texts
printed in England to the Restoration. Also available as a database
titled *Early English Books Online* (*EEBO*).

Early English Text Society Series. 287 vols. London: Early English Text Society and IDC Publisher, 1864–. A long-running scholarly series that republishes Old English and Middle English texts in scholarly editions, bringing unpublished manuscripts, medieval dramas, and historical documents into print. New volumes of the series are being published by the Oxford University Press.

March of America Facsimile Series. 103 vols. Ann Arbor: University Microfilms International, 1966. A reprint series of original editions of early English accounts of travel to the New World. Available in print only.

Oral and local history collections

You may want to undertake an oral history project or track down oral histories that others have compiled by consulting the *Oral History Index* (Westport: Meckler, 1990), by seeing if your library subscribes to the *Oral History Online* database, or by browsing *Oral History Projects (by Subject)* <http://www.h-net.org/~oralhist/projects .html>. Alternatively, you can simply search your library's catalog with the term *oral history* or combine *oral history* with a keyword. Also consider getting primary sources from a county or state historical society's collections or even from the archives of your own college or university. You may find yourself working with material that no one else has yet analyzed.

Researching in the Social Sciences

Social scientists interpret and analyze human behavior, generally using empirical methods of research. Though original data gathering and analysis are central to social sciences research, researchers also use library and Internet resources to

- obtain raw data for model building or analysis
- locate information about a particular model, theory, or methodology to be used in a research project
- review the literature to place new research in context

Subjects of study in the social sciences sometimes cross disciplines and may be difficult to locate through typical subject headings in indexes and abstracts. In addition, new theories may take some time to circulate in the literature, especially in print sources. Consequently, the researcher should be prepared to

- identify potential search terms by scanning indexes and abstracts in relevant works
- use the references in published articles and books to trace connections among theories and ideas
- work from the most recent to older sources

A review of the literature for a social sciences research project not only should identify what research has been done but should also compare and contrast the available information and evaluate its significance.

Each of the social sciences has a well-developed set of research tools to help you find relevant material. The tools listed here will give you ideas for beginning your research. Consult a librarian for help in refining your search.

General resources in the social sciences

Databases and indexes in the social sciences

American Statistics Index. Washington: Congressional Information Service, 1974–. A useful index to statistics that are buried within government publications. The online version, called *Statistical Masterfile* or *LexisNexis Statistical*, contains some links to full texts. It is searchable by keyword, subject, author, title, agency, or year and can be limited by demographic, geographic, or other variables.

Social Sciences Citation Index. Philadelphia: Institute for Scientific Information, 1956–. An interdisciplinary database covering more than 1,700 journals in the social sciences. Search by author, keyword, or cited source, a good way to trace the influence of a particular work. Part of the *Web of Knowledge,* this database also offers a powerful Related Records search, which identifies articles that cite one or more of the same sources.

Social Sciences Index. New York: Wilson, 1974–. An interdisciplinary index to over 600 key journals in the social sciences, including anthropology, psychology, sociology, economics, and political science. In some libraries, the database includes the full texts of selected articles.

Web resources in the social sciences

FedStats <http://www.fedstats.gov>. A well-organized portal for statistical information available from more than 100 U.S. government agency sites. Statistics can be searched by keyword or browsed by topic or agency. Links to downloadable data sets are included.

Internet Crossroads in Social Science Data <http://www.disc.wisc.edu/newcrossroads/index.asp>. Offers more than 800 annotated links to online data sources. Searchable by keyword or browsable by category, the site includes links to government and nongovernment sites concerned with domestic and international economics and labor, health, education, geography, history, politics, sociology, and demography. The site is maintained by the Data and Program Library Service at the University of Wisconsin, Madison.

Intute Social Sciences <http://www.intute.ac.uk/socialsciences>. A selective catalog of thousands of Web sites in the social sciences, hosted in the United Kingdom. Users can browse by topic and region or search by keyword. Each entry has been reviewed and is annotated. The focus is on high-quality sites that provide information directly rather than just link to other sites. It is an excellent resource for international social sciences data.

U.S. Census Bureau <http://www.census.gov>. Offers access to an astounding amount of demographic, social, and economic data. The search engine can pinpoint relevant statistical tables and reports. The site is updated almost daily with newly released reports.

Reference books in the social sciences

The Gallup Poll. Wilmington: Scholarly Resources, 1972–. An annual print compilation of opinion poll statistics gathered by the Gallup organization from 1935 to the present.

Historical Statistics of the United States: Earliest Times to the Present. Ed. Susan B. Carter. Rev. ed. 5 vols. New York: Cambridge University Press, 2006. Offers vital statistics, economic figures, and social data for the United States over time; it includes a subject index. For more recent figures, consult the latest volume of the *Statistical Abstract of the United States*.

International Encyclopedia of the Social and Behavioral Sciences. Ed. Neil J. Smelser and Paul B. Baltes. 26 vols. Amsterdam: Elsevier, 2001. A vast compendium of scholarly articles on topics in the social sciences. International and interdisciplinary in perspective, this work is particularly useful for its cross-references among related topics.

International Historical Statistics, 1750–2000: Europe. By B. R. Mitchell. 5th ed. New York: Palgrave, 2003. Offers time-series data for European countries, including figures on population, agriculture, the economy, transportation, communications, and education. Other volumes by the same author cover different regions of the world.

The Social Sciences: A Cross-Disciplinary Guide to Selected Sources. Ed. Nancy L. Herron. 3rd ed. Englewood: Libraries Unlimited, 2003. Provides information about the most important tools for social sciences research, with essays describing the structure of each discipline's literature.

Statistical Abstract of the United States. Washington: Government Printing Office, 1879–. Perhaps the single most useful collection of statistical information available in a small package. It includes hundreds of tables with figures on areas such as population, economics, and social factors as well as references to the original sources. An index provides easy access. Statistical abstracts from 1995 to the present are available on the Web at <http://www.census.gov/compendia/statab>.

Anthropology

Databases and indexes in anthropology

AnthroSource. Arlington: American Anthropological Association, 2005–. This database is the most important online resource for the field and contains the full text of publications of the association from the first issues.

Anthropology Plus. Mountain View: OCLC, 2002–. An online index to anthropology publications from the eighteenth century to the present. This work combines indexes maintained by the British Museum Anthropology Library and Harvard's Tozzer Library.

Human Relations Area Files (HRAF). Ann Arbor: University Microfilms International, 1968–. A huge collection of anthropological data, including books, articles, and field reports, sorted into cultural classifications. The electronic version of this resource has two parts: *eHRAF World Cultures* and *eHRAF Archaeology*.

Web resources in anthropology

Anthropology Resources on the Internet <http://www.aaanet.org/resources>. A selective guide to sites on anthropology, archaeology, and ethnology as well as organizations, institutions, and online discussion groups. The list is part of the Web site of the American Anthropological Association.

Anthropology Resources on the Internet: WWW Virtual Library: History: Archaeology / Prehistory <http://www.anthropologie.net>. Founded in 1995, a directory of sites primarily devoted to anthropology. Includes journals, organizations, institutions, research and data arranged by region and links to topics such as law, cultural heritage and paleoanthropology. The site is edited by Bernard Olivier Clist.

Reference books in anthropology

Atlas of World Cultures: A Geographic Guide to Ethnographic Literature. By David H. Price. Newbury Park: Sage, 1989. Provides geographic context for bibliographic information about cultures. Forty maps are used to locate 3,500 cultural groups, for which bibliographies are provided.

Cambridge Encyclopedia of Human Evolution. Ed. Steve Jones et al. Cambridge: Cambridge University Press, 1992. A handy source for overviews of the field. The work surveys human evolution in thematic chapters.

Countries and Their Cultures. Ed. Melvin Ember and Carol Ember. 4 vols. New York: Macmillan Reference, 2001. Covers world cultures, including both the national culture held in common by citizens of a country and variations within the country. The work includes demographic, historical, economic, political, and religious information about each culture.

Dictionary of Anthropology. Ed. Thomas Barfield. Oxford: Blackwell, 1997. Defines and explores terms and concepts in social and cultural anthropology. The work includes some biographical sketches and longer articles on theoretical topics.

Encyclopedia of Cultural Anthropology. Ed. David Levinson and Melvin Ember. 4 vols. New York: Holt, 1996. Offers 340 lengthy articles written by specialists on approaches, methods, concepts, and topics related to cultural anthropology. Articles are followed by bibliographies of key research.

Encyclopedia of Prehistory. Ed. Peter N. Peregrine and Melvin Ember. 9 vols. New York: Kluwer, 2001. Provides information on all cultures known through archaeology, arranged by region. Major traditions are surveyed along with specific information about archaeological sites. The work is published in conjunction with the *Human Relations Area Files.*

Encyclopedia of World Cultures. Ed. David Levinson. 10 vols. Boston: G. K. Hall, 1991–. With supplements. Covers more than 1,500 cultural groups, arranged alphabetically within regions. Entries summarize information on the distribution, belief systems, kinship structures, and history of the groups and provide selective bibliographies. The encyclopedia is based on information in the *Human Relations Area Files.*

Business and economics

Databases and indexes in business and economics

ABI/Inform. Ann Arbor: ProQuest, 1971–. Covers industries, management techniques, business trends, and profiles of corporations and corporate leaders. Includes full text of financial news sources, journals, working papers, country reports, and more.

Accounting and Tax Index. Ann Arbor: ProQuest, 1992–. A detailed index of over 2,000 publications covering taxation and accounting, standards, conference papers, reports, journals, and books.

Business and Company Resource Center. Detroit: Gale Group, 2001–. An online database of business magazine articles, trade publications, company histories, rankings, and industry information. Many of the materials are available in full text.

Business Source Premier. Ipswich: EBSCO, 1990–. A database of journals and magazines in business and economics, with some full-text coverage (including a few titles going as far back as the 1920s). Coverage includes management, finance, accounting, and international business.

EconLit. Nashville: American Economic Association, 1969–. Provides citations (most with abstracts) to articles in scholarly journals in the field, covering all aspects of economics worldwide.

LexisNexis: Business. New York: LexisNexis, 1998–. A collection of full-text databases of continuously updated business news sources, industry news, and company and financial data as well as other news and legal sources. Includes company dossiers, profiles, SEC filings, accounting news, and business information from global sources. This resource can also be found as a tab in the *LexisNexis Academic* database.

Web resources in business and economics

Bureau of Labor Statistics <http://www.bls.gov>. A mine of current statistical data and reports covering consumer spending, employment, wages, productivity, occupations, international trade, and industries as well as "The U.S. Economy at a Glance." The bureau is a unit of the U.S. Department of Labor.

Economic Census, 2007 <http://www.census.gov/econ/census07>. Undertaken every five years, the economic census gathers data on retail, wholesale, manufacturing, and other business by state and local subdivision. Results from the 2007 census are being released in parts from 2009 to 2011 and will be integrated into the *American FactFinder* system at <http://factfinder.census.gov>; data are also available online from the 2002 and 1997 economic censuses.

Economic Report of the President <http://www.gpoaccess.gov/eop/index.html>. Prepared annually by the chair of the Council of Economic Advisers, this publication explains the rationale for the president's budget submitted to Congress. Of particular interest are the tables that cover income, production, and employment in time series.

globalEDGE <http://globaledge.msu.edu>. Offers worldwide business information, including methods of comparing country data, country background information, an annual compilation of market potential indicators, breaking news of interest to the business community, and a glossary of international business terms. The site was created by the Center for Business Education and Research at Michigan State University.

OSU Virtual Finance Library <http://fisher.osu.edu/fin/overview.htm>. Well-organized links on banks, exchanges, and market news, with pages for various audiences: students, researchers, executives, investors, and educators. The site is provided by the Department of Finance, Ohio State University.

SEC Filings and Forms (EDGAR) <http://www.sec.gov/edgar.shtml>. Provides information about publicly held corporations, which are required by federal law to file reports on their activities with the U.S. Securities and Exchange Commission. Most reports from 1994 to the present are publicly available through the *EDGAR (Electronic Data Gathering, Analysis, and Retrieval System)* database at this site. Information in company reports includes financial status, chief officers, stock information, company history, pending litigation that might have an economic impact on the company, and more. The site provides a brief tutorial for searching *EDGAR*.

U.S. Congressional Budget Office <http://www.cbo.gov>. Offers material compiled by a nonpartisan office for congressional decision making. The site includes federal budget analysis; the economic outlook; analysis of specific topics on housing, health, education, national security, and telecommunications; and more.

VIBES: Virtual International Business and Economics Resources <http://libweb.uncc.edu/ref-bus/vibehome.htm>. Provides nearly 3,000 links to sites related to international business and economics. Links include free full-text files of recent articles, reports, and statistical tables, which are organized by topics such as international trade law, patents, emerging markets, and regional and national sites. Compiled by Jeanie M. Welch of the J. Murrey Atkins Library, University of North Carolina at Charlotte.

Reference books in business and economics

Blackwell Encyclopedia of Management: Business Ethics. Ed. Patricia Werhane and R. Edward Freeman. 2nd ed. Cambridge: Blackwell, 2005. Offers substantial entries written by experts in business ethics on such topics as equal opportunity, corporate crime, participatory management, environmental risk, business ethics in different cultures, and electronic surveillance. This work is part of the 12-volume *The Blackwell Encyclopedia of Management.*

Encyclopedia of Business and Finance. Ed. Burton S. Kaliski. 2nd ed. 2 vols. Detroit: Macmillan Reference, 2007. Offers over 300 articles on accounting, economics, finance, information systems, ethics, management, and marketing, with a U.S. focus.

Encyclopedia of Political Economy. Ed. Philip Anthony O'Hara. 2 vols. London: Routledge, 1999. Provides analyses of topics related to money and finance, labor, family and gender, political ideologies, development, theoretical schools, and methodology.

New Palgrave Dictionary of Economics. Ed. Steven N. Durlauf and Lawrence E. Blume. Rev. ed. 8 vols. New York: Palgrave Macmillan, 2008. A revision of the classic *Palgrave's Dictionary of Political Economy,* offering scholarly analyses of economic theories and theorists.

International Encyclopedia of Public Policy and Administration. Ed. Jay M. Shafritz. 4 vols. Boulder: Westview, 1998. A scholarly compendium of over 850 articles on management, public institutions, theories, legal concepts, and definitions of terms, with an interdisciplinary and global perspective.

Oxford Encyclopedia of Economic History. Ed. Joel Mokyr. 5 vols. New York: Oxford University Press, 2003. Covers concepts and theories, economic development, background on countries and regions, and the history of specific products such as oil and coffee.

Communication studies

Databases and indexes in communication studies

Communication Abstracts. Beverly Hills: Sage, 1978–. Provides abstracts from more than 150 scholarly journals, books, and research reports in the field.

Communication and Mass Media Complete. Ipswich: EBSCO, 2004–. An online database that covers both scholarly articles on communication studies and trade and popular coverage of the media. A substantial portion of the contents is linked to full text, with especially rich historical material on communication theory.

The Year's Work in Cultural and Critical Theory. Oxford: Blackwell, 1994–. An annual roundup of recent research on feminist theory, postcolonial studies, popular culture, virtual culture, film theory, cultural policy, and visual culture, presented as evaluative review essays written by leading scholars. This work is published in conjunction with the English Association (UK).

Web resources in communication studies

American Rhetoric Online Speech Bank <http://www.americanrhetoric .com/speechbank.htm>. Offers over 5,000 speeches, many of them as audio or visual files as well as written texts.

Communication   Studies   Resources   <http://www.uiowa.edu/ ~commstud/resources>. A well-organized directory of Web resources useful for research. The directory covers advertising, culture studies, digital media, film studies, interpersonal and small-group commu- nication, journalism and mass media, media studies, and rhetoric as well as online tools for communication studies researchers. It is maintained by Karla Tonella of the University of Iowa Department of Communication Studies.

First Amendment Handbook <http://www.rcfp.org/handbook/index .html>. Provides detailed analyses of constitutional law issues as they relate to the practice of journalism. Sections cover access to courts, places and people, the Freedom of Information Act, confi- dentiality, surreptitious recording, libel, invasion of privacy, prior restraint, and copyright. From the Reporters Committee for Free- dom of the Press, compiled by Gregg P. Leslie.

Journalism.org: Research, Resources, and Ideas to Improve Journalism <http://www.journalism.org>. News about the news industry, infor- mation for working journalists, background on issues of concern to journalists, and a detailed survey of the state of the news media, including print, broadcast, cable news, magazines, local TV, alterna- tive media, and online news sources. The site is jointly maintained by the Project for Excellence in Journalism and the Committee of Concerned Journalists.

MCS: The Media and Communications Studies Site <http://www.aber.ac .uk/media>. A well-organized, searchable collection of links to Web content on a wide variety of topics: gender and ethnicity, news media, advertising, film studies, visual images, textual analysis, media influence, and more. The site is based at the University of Wales, Aberystwyth.

Reference books in communication studies

American Voices: Significant Speeches from American History, 1640–1945. Ed. James Andrews and David Zarefsky. New York: Longman, 1991. A chronologically arranged anthology of major speeches of historical and oratorical significance. A companion volume covers speeches from 1945 to the end of the 1980s.

Encyclopedia of American Journalism. Ed. Steven L. Vaughn. New York: Routledge, 2008. Offers articles on news organizations, journalists, significant publications, legal and political terms, and topics such as ethics, cameras in the courtroom, and blogs.

Encyclopedia of Rhetoric. Ed. Thomas O. Sloane. Oxford: Oxford University Press, 2001. Offers substantial, scholarly overviews of research on such topics as invention, ethos, fallacies, rhetoric, and social movements.

History of the Mass Media in the United States: An Encyclopedia. Ed. Margaret A. Blanchard. Chicago: Fitzroy Dearborn, 2000. Covers all forms of mass media from 1690 to 1990, offering short articles on technological, legal, economic, and political developments as well as major organizations and institutions.

International Encyclopedia of Communication. Ed. Wolfgang Donsbach. 12 vols. Malden: Blackwell, 2008. A definitive and global source for information about every aspect of communication, including interpersonal and group communication as well as mass media and visual communication.

Museum of Broadcast Communications Encyclopedia of Television. Ed. Horace Newcomb et al. 3 vols. Chicago: Fitzroy Dearborn, 2000. Covers genres, programs, people, organizations, and topics related to television history. Information on television programs includes casts, producers, programming history, and bibliographies. The same publisher also offers *Encyclopedia of Radio* (2004).

Criminal justice

Databases and indexes in criminal justice

Criminal Justice Abstracts. Thousand Oaks: Sage, 1968–. Provides abstracts of articles, books, reports, and government documents that deal with crime trends, crime prevention and deterrence, juvenile justice, police, courts, punishment, and sentencing. Published in conjunction with the Criminal Justice Collection of Rutgers University Libraries.

Web resources in criminal justice

Bureau of Justice Statistics <http://www.ojp.usdoj.gov/bjs>. Provides information about crime and victimization, law enforcement, corrections, prosecutions, courts and sentencing, drugs, firearms, and more. This authoritative source for data and analysis of crime in the United States is a unit of the U.S. Department of Justice.

Criminal Justice Links <http://www.criminology.fsu.edu/cjlinks>. A long-running directory of international resources on crime, the courts, forensic sciences, crime in the news and popular culture, and other aspects of the field. The site is maintained by Cecil Greek of the Florida State University School of Criminology.

Internet Resources <http://www.lib.jjay.cuny.edu/links>. Prepared by librarians at one of the premier criminal justice libraries in the world, the Lloyd Jay Sealy Library of the John Jay College of Criminal Justice. This directory has a wealth of material on a variety of criminal justice topics, including history, domestic and international issues, and statistics, with special emphasis on New York City. All links are annotated; the site is updated frequently.

National Criminal Justice Reference Service <http://www.ncjrs.org>. A federal information resource offering a huge amount of information on corrections, juvenile justice, the courts, law enforcement, drug interdiction, victimization, and more. It includes a database of criminal justice articles, some with full text. Provided by the U.S. Department of Justice.

Zeno's Forensic Site <http://forensic.to/links/pages>. Provides annotated links to information on arson investigation, firearms identification, DNA analysis, fingerprints, toxicology, forensic entomology, forensic psychology, and more. Based in the Netherlands and maintained by Zeno Geradts.

Reference books in criminal justice

Encyclopedia of Crime and Justice. Ed. Josua Dressler. 2nd ed. 4 vols. New York: Macmillan Reference, 2002. One of the best sources for overall coverage of the field. Includes issues in law, criminology, and sociology and references to classic studies and recent research. Though the focus is on criminal justice in the United States, international perspectives are included.

Encyclopedia of Crime and Punishment. Ed. David Levinson. 4 vols. Thousand Oaks: Sage, 2002. Covers a huge range of topics in an accessible manner, from crimes to enforcement to corrections.

Encyclopedia of Criminology and Deviant Behavior. Ed. Clifton D. Bryant. 4 vols. Philadelphia: Brunner-Routledge, 2001. Provides substantial, scholarly articles on theory and research on crime, sexual deviance, and self-destructive behaviors. This work is particularly useful for understanding the psychological and sociological context of crime.

Encyclopedia of Forensic Sciences. Ed. Jay A. Siegel. 3 vols. San Diego: Academic Press, 2000. The most comprehensive reference work of its type, this encyclopedia provides information on processing crime scenes, handling evidence and witnesses, understanding forensic medicine, identifying firearms, analyzing DNA, and more, in detailed, technical articles.

Education

Databases and indexes in education

Education Index. New York: Wilson, 1929–. An author-subject database of articles in education journals, books, and yearbooks, including both research-based studies and material on classroom practice. Online versions of this index may include abstracts and full text of selected journals.

ERIC: Education Resources Information Center. Washington: Institute of Education Sciences, 1966–. Provides descriptive abstracts of over a million journal articles and ERIC documents—research reports, conference papers, curriculum guides, and other materials—that are not formally published otherwise. This database service is sponsored by the U.S. Department of Education and is available free online at <http://www.eric.ed.gov>.

Web resources in education

Educator's Reference Desk <http://www.eduref.org>. A directory of resource guides and lesson plans, searchable by grade level, as well as a collection of questions and answers about a variety of education topics. The site is a project of the Information Institute of Syracuse.

GEM: The Gateway to Educational Materials <http://thegateway.org>. A directory of online classroom materials. This site, sponsored by the U.S. Department of Education, offers a sophisticated search engine as well as options to browse by keyword, subject, grade level, or type of resource. Search results lead to lesson plans, curriculum units, and other Web materials for educators.

National Center for Education Statistics <http://nces.ed.gov>. Provides a wealth of statistical data on schools and libraries in the United States, including academic achievement; the condition of schools; comparative information on school districts, colleges, and libraries; dropout rates; enrollment trends; school safety; and more. The center is a unit of the U.S. Department of Education.

SMETE <http://www.smete.org>. A digital library of materials for teaching science, mathematics, engineering, and technology for K–12 and higher. The site offers an advanced search of materials by type of learning resource, grade level, and keyword.

Reference books in education

Encyclopedia of Early Childhood Education. Ed. Leslie R. Williams and Doris P. Fromberg. New York: Garland, 1992. Offers articles on historical, political, economic, sociocultural, intellectual, and educational influences on early childhood education.

Encyclopedia of Education. Ed. James W. Guthrie. 2nd ed. 8 vols. New York: Macmillan Reference, 2003. More than 850 articles cover education theory, history of education, education and social forces, and education reform efforts. Emphasis is on the U.S. experience but the work provides some international perspectives. Volume 8 includes primary sources and a thematic outline.

Encyclopedia of Educational Psychology. Ed. Neil J. Salkind. 2 vols. Los Angeles: Sage, 2008. Provides accessible overviews of research in the field, including cognitive development, gender, peers and peer influence, testing, and classroom management.

Philosophy of Education: An Encyclopedia. Ed. J. J. Chambliss. New York: Garland, 1996. Offers substantial analyses covering various philosophers and their contributions to the field of education; philosophical topics such as behaviorism, critical thinking, and epistemology; and concepts such as school and truth from a philosophical angle.

World Education Encyclopedia: A Survey of Educational Systems World-wide. Ed. Rebecca Marlow-Ferguson. 2nd ed. 3 vols. Detroit: Gale Group, 2002. Provides overviews of education at all levels throughout the world and some discussion of administration and finance, research, and the state of the profession. The appendix includes comparative statistical tables and maps.

Ethnic and area studies

Databases and indexes in ethnic and area studies

Bibliography of Asian Studies. Ann Arbor: Association for Asian Studies, 1956–. An index to European-language scholarly publications in Asian studies. Organized by country with subdivisions by topic, the index provides more than 410,000 bibliographic citations.

Ethnic NewsWatch. Ann Arbor: ProQuest, 1985–. A full-text database specializing in publications by ethnic communities in the United States, which are often left out of general news and magazine databases. Providing valuable alternative insights, this work includes many publications in Spanish and can be searched in a Spanish-language interface.

Handbook of Latin American Studies. Austin: University of Texas Press, 1935–. A selective, annotated bibliography of scholarly works on Latin America. This is an excellent source of citations for any topic in Latin American studies, including Hispanic populations in the United States. Now prepared by the Hispanic Division of the Library of Congress, an electronic version of this work, *HLAS Online,* is available at <http://lcweb2.loc.gov/hlas>. The site can be searched by keyword or subject heading in English, Spanish, or Portuguese.

HAPI: Hispanic American Periodical Index. Los Angeles: UCLA Latin American Center, 1970–. An index to articles in over 400 scholarly journals published in Latin America or covering topics relevant to Latin America and Latin Americans living in North America.

Web resources in ethnic and area studies

African American Digital Initiatives <http://www.howard.edu/library/ Assist/Guides/Afro-Am_Digital.htm>. A directory of links to high-quality archival material online from libraries and museums around the country. The list is maintained by the Howard University Libraries.

Africa South of the Sahara <http://www-sul.stanford.edu/depts/ssrg/ africa/guide.html>. Annotated links to selected sites arranged by country and topic, with sources for current news from Africa. The site is maintained by Karen Fung for the African Studies Association.

Asian Studies WWW Virtual Library <http://coombs.anu.edu.au/ WWWVL-AsianStudies.html>. Covers information on all regions of Asia and the Middle East. The site is comprehensive, frequently updated, and organized by an alphabetical index and a hierarchical topical index. It is edited by T. Matthew Ciolek of the Australian National University.

Center for World Indigenous Studies <http://www.cwis.org>. Offers information on various indigenous peoples and issues of political and cultural identity and nationhood. Of particular note is the Fourth World Docu-Program, which provides full-text documents related to communities around the world as well as relevant international and multilateral documents.

LANIC: Latin American Network Information Center <http://lanic .utexas.edu>. Provides over 12,000 links to Web resources for Latin America, arranged by country or by topic, such as economy, education, and government. The site is affiliated with the Lozano Long Institute of Latin American Studies, University of Texas at Austin, one of the premier Latin American Studies programs in the world.

NativeWeb: Resources for Indigenous Cultures around the World <http:// www.nativeweb.org>. A rich site for information on native peoples, particularly on Native North Americans, but global in scope. The site includes cultural, historical, educational, and current affairs information.

Pew Hispanic Center <http://www.pewhispanic.org/index.jsp>. Includes the text of several reports as well as information on demographics, economics, labor, immigration, education, health, and Latinos in the military. The Pew Hispanic Center, a research organization, is a project of the Pew Research Center.

Reference books in ethnic and area studies

Africana: The Encyclopedia of the African and African American Experience. Ed. Kwame Anthony Appiah and Henry Louis Gates Jr. 2nd ed. 5 vols. New York: Oxford University Press, 2005. Offers over 4,000 articles on Africa and the African diaspora, with extensive coverage of African American history and culture.

American Immigrant Cultures: Builders of a Nation. Ed. David Levinson and Melvin Ember. 2 vols. New York: Macmillan Library Reference, 1997. Offers in-depth profiles of immigrant communities in the United States, including their defining features, patterns of cultural variation, immigration history, demographics, and cultural characteristics.

Atlas of the North American Indian. By Carl Waldman. Rev. ed. New York: Facts on File, 2000. Offers maps on tribal locations, reservations, sites of cultural and archaeological importance, and other significant places. Includes related text and bibliographies.

Dictionary of Native American Mythology. By Sam D. Gill and Irene F. Sullivan. Santa Barbara: ABC-CLIO, 1992. Provides quick access to information about individuals, events, and topics in Native American mythology, from all tribes and periods. Includes a bibliography.

Encyclopedia Latina: History, Culture, and Society in the United States. Ed. Ilan Stavans and Harold Augenbraum. 4 vols. Danbury: Grolier, 2005. Covers Latino/a culture in the United States, including influential people and topics in the areas of history, family life, education, the arts, popular culture, immigration, historical periods, and places of origin.

Encyclopedia of African American Civil Rights: From Emancipation to the Twenty-First Century. Ed. Charles D. Lowery and John F. Marszalek. Rev. ed. 2 vols. New York: Greenwood, 2003. A dictionary of terms, events, and prominent people related to the civil rights movement. The work includes selected primary sources.

Encyclopedia of African-American Culture and History. Ed. Colin A. Palmer. 2nd ed. 6 vols. Detroit: Macmillan Reference, 2006. Offers extensive articles on people, institutions, events, issues, and themes related to African Americans. Includes many illustrations and bibliographies.

Encyclopedia of American Immigration. Ed. James Climent. 4 vols. Armonk: Sharpe, 2001. Covers immigration history, demographics, and political, economic, and cultural issues as well as background on specific immigrant groups. Includes the text of several essential primary documents.

Encyclopedia of Contemporary French Culture. Ed. Alex Hughes and Keith Reader. London: Routledge, 1998. Short articles on a wealth of topics related to French and Francophone culture from 1945 to the present. Other volumes cover contemporary German, Spanish, Italian, Japanese, and other cultures.

Encyclopedia of Latin American History and Culture. Ed. Jay Kinsbruner and Erick Detlef Langer. 2nd ed. 6 vols. Detroit: Gale, 2008. Covers a wide variety of topics in over 5,000 articles that together constitute an overview of current knowledge about Latin America. Entries are organized by country and by topic (such as slavery, art, and Asians in Latin America); biographical entries are included.

Encyclopedia of Modern Asia. Ed. David Levinson and Karen Christensen. 6 vols. New York: Scribner, 2002. Covers twentieth-century culture in East, Southeast, and central Asia, from Japan to Turkey and from Kazakhstan to Indonesia.

Encyclopedia of the Modern Middle East and North Africa. Ed. Philip Mattar. 2nd ed. 4 vols. Detroit: Macmillan Reference, 2004. Covers political, historical, social, economic, and cultural topics in substantial, well-documented articles.

Gale Encyclopedia of Multicultural America. Ed. Julie Galens et al. 2nd ed. 3 vols. Detroit: Gale Group, 2000. Offers more than 100 extensive essays on ethnic groups in the United States, covering origins, circumstances of arrival, family, community, culture, economy, politics, and significant contributions. Each essay ends with a bibliography and contacts for further research.

Gale Encyclopedia of Native American Tribes. 4 vols. Detroit: Gale Group, 1998. Offers information on the history and current status of nearly 400 tribes, with historical background, past and current location, religious beliefs, language, means of subsistence, healing practices, customs, oral literature, and current issues.

Handbook of North American Indians. 15 vols. to date. Washington: Smithsonian Institution, 1978–. Offers scholarly essays on the history, social situation, politics, religion, economics, and tribal traditions of Native American groups. The work covers aboriginal cultures in North America by region and topics such as relations between settlers and indigenous tribes and Native American art and language.

Oxford Encyclopedia of the Modern Islamic World. 4 vols. New York: Oxford University Press, 1995. Covers Islamic peoples, movements, and issues throughout the world.

Geography

Databases and indexes in geography

GEOBASE. New York: Elsevier, 1989–. An index to books and articles relevant to human and physical geography, including some coverage of geology and ecology. Also known as *Geographical Abstracts.*

The Online Geographical Bibliography. Milwaukee: American Geographical Society, 1985–. An index to journal articles, books, and maps from the American Geographical Society collection available at <http://geobib.lib.uwm.edu>. This work provides citations to research on topics such as biogeography, climatology, human geography, hydrology, and physical geography as well as regional geography. Additions to this database are given in *Current Geographical Publications,* a list of the tables of contents of current journals that is available at the same site.

Web resources in geography

American FactFinder <http://factfinder.census.gov>. Provides a wealth of information about populations and places in the United

States. The powerful search facility can be used to pinpoint tables of data and to create maps based on the variables that users supply, with tools that enable creation of thematic maps from national to street level. The site is sponsored by the U.S. Census Bureau.

Geosource <http://www.library.uu.nl/geosource>. A directory of Web sources for human geography, physical geography, planning, geoscience, and environmental science. The information is organized by topic, region, and country and by type, such as organizations, journals, and institutions. The site is maintained by Jeroen Bosman of the Central Library, Utrecht University.

Google Maps <http://maps.google.com>. Offers global street maps and satellite views as well as a street-level view for selected cities. *Google* also provides a downloadable program, *Google Earth* <http://earth.google.com>, that offers 3-D views of terrain from cities to the sea floor.

National Atlas <http://nationalatlas.gov>. An online atlas that offers dynamic maps of agriculture, biology, climate, history, transportation, water, and demographics as well as a mapping tool for creating customized maps. Offered by the U.S. Department of the Interior.

Perry Castañeda Library Map Collection <http://www.lib.utexas.edu/maps/index.html>. An excellent and frequently updated list of links to over 2,400 online maps in digital form. Organized primarily by region and country, the site also includes maps of current interest, linked to world events. The site is a service of the General Libraries, University of Texas at Austin.

Places Online <http://www.placesonline.org>. A map-based set of links to "the world's best" sites for visual information about places around the world. The site is a service of the Association of American Geographers.

Worldmapper <http://www.sasi.group.shef.ac.uk/worldmapper>. A source of intriguing cartograms: maps that resize countries to reflect data. Over 300 maps illustrate social dynamics such as education, religion, poverty, pollution, health, religion, and more. The project is supported by an international collaboration that includes the University of Michigan, the University of Sheffield, and the Geographical Association.

Reference books in geography

Columbia Gazetteer of the World. Ed. Saul B. Cohen. 2nd ed. 3 vols. New York: Columbia University Press, 2008. Provides the exact location of places and geographical features around the world and gives a very brief definition or description. This is the most complete gazetteer available.

Dictionary of Human Geography. Ed. Ron Johnson et al. 5th ed. New York: Blackwell, 2009. Defines and discusses terms, topics, and concepts in human geography. Includes a bibliography and a detailed index.

Encyclopedic Dictionary of Physical Geography. Ed. Andrew Goudie et al. 2nd ed. New York: Blackwell, 1999. Defines and discusses terms and concepts in physical geography and includes brief, selective bibliographies.

Special resources in geography

Maps and atlases are basic tools for the geographer. Because of their sometimes unusual size and shape, they are often housed in special collections. Coverage in atlases can extend far beyond the reach of familiar reference works, such as the *Atlas of the World,* 16th ed. (New York: Oxford University Press, 2009), to provide information on population, trade, history, water resources, and so on. Additionally, GIS (Geographic Information Systems) software may be available for creating your own maps.

Law

Databases and indexes in law

Index to Legal Periodicals and Books. New York: Wilson, 1994–. Index to legal journals, law reviews and books, government publications, institutions, and bar associations. Some libraries have an accompanying archive that covers publications from 1908 to the present in addition to full texts of over 300 law journals.

LexisNexis: Legal. Bethesda: LexisNexis, 1998–. The *LexisNexis* databases include cases, codes, and research under the Legal tab. Of particular note is the ability to search for the full text of state and federal court decisions (also known as *case law*) by keyword, party name, or citation, and the Law Reviews section, which offers the full text of scholarly articles that analyze legal issues in depth.

WestLaw Campus Research. Eagan: West, 2002–. A database of legal research materials, including laws, cases, legal articles, and reference material as well as analysis of legal issues provided by West and an integrated system that indicates which cases remain precedent setting.

Web resources in law

Code of Federal Regulations <http://www.gpoaccess.gov/cfr>. Provides access to federal "administrative law"—regulations set by federal government agencies to spell out how a law passed by Congress will be carried out. The *CFR* is searchable by keyword, title, or citation information or can be browsed by topic or title.

EISIL: Electronic Information System for International Law <http://www.eisil.org>. A directory of information on international legal issues, including international human rights, criminal law, use of force, environmental law, and economic law. Each section includes the text of important international agreements and links to significant organizations. *EISIL* is a service of the American Society of International Law.

FindLaw U.S. Supreme Court Decisions <http://www.findlaw.com/casecode/supreme.html>. Provides the full text of Supreme Court decisions from 1893 to the present, with handy links to cited decisions. Searchable by citation, party name, or keyword, the database is part of *FindLaw,* a commercial portal to legal information.

Guide to Law Online: Nations of the World <http://www.loc.gov/law/guide/nations.html>. A country-by-country directory of legal information, including constitutional, executive, legislative, and judicial law, as well as related information such as human rights reports. The links are compiled by the Law Library of Congress.

LII: Legal Information Institute <http://www.law.cornell.edu>. A directory to legal information on the Web, including texts of case law and statutes for state, federal, and international jurisdictions. The site, organized alphabetically by topic, also provides links to court opinions and directories to law organizations and journals. The institute is a project of the Cornell University Law School.

Oyez: Supreme Court Multimedia <http://www.oyez.org/oyez>. Offers information about the U.S. Supreme Court, most notably audio files of all oral arguments held before the Court since 1995, with selected landmark cases as far back as 1955. Oral arguments offer a fascinating glimpse into the background of decisions. The site also provides current Supreme Court news and a link to *On the Docket,* a news feed on Supreme Court matters. The site is supported by grants from the National Science Foundation, Northwestern University, and other donors.

U.S. Code <http://uscode.house.gov>. From the Office of the Law Revision Council, U.S. House of Representatives, this site provides the text of federal laws of the United States currently in force, arranged by title and section. The site offers an option to search or browse the code and provides a link to *Thomas,* a site maintained by the Library of Congress that provides the text of bills introduced in Congress. For state laws, consult official state Web sites or the *LII* directory in this section.

Reference books in law

Black's Law Dictionary. Ed. Bryan A. Garner and Henry Campbell Black. 8th ed. St. Paul: West, 2004. Offers brief technical definitions of legal terms, with an emphasis on the U.S. legal system.

Encyclopedia of the American Constitution. Ed. Leonard Williams Levy et al. 2nd ed. 6 vols. New York: Macmillan Library Reference, 2000. Covers essential topics and landmark cases related to constitutional law.

Encyclopedia of the American Judicial System. Ed. Robert J. Janosik. 3 vols. New York: Macmillan Library Reference, 1987. Offers substantial articles covering the workings of the court system and its effects on society.

Historic U.S. Court Cases: An Encyclopedia. Ed. John W. Johnson. 2nd ed. 2 vols. New York: Routledge, 2001. Essays on major cases that have had an impact on American law and society, with sections on civil liberties, minority rights, women, and economics.

West's Encyclopedia of American Law. Ed. Jeffrey Lehman, Shirelle Phelps. 2nd ed. 13 vols. Detroit: Gale, 2005. Presents legal issues clearly in articles written for a general audience. This work is supplemented by *The American Law Yearbook.*

Political science

Databases and indexes in political science

CIAO: Columbia International Affairs Online. New York: Columbia University Press, 1997–. A digital library of working papers, journals, books, course materials, and case studies on world affairs.

LexisNexis: Congressional. Bethesda: LexisNexis, 1970–. The most comprehensive database of information on the U.S. Congress. This database provides bibliographic citations, descriptive abstracts, and the full texts of many documents including bills, laws (with legislative histories), committee reports, the *Congressional Record,* and more.

Monthly Catalog of United States Government Publications. Washington: Government Printing Office, 1895–. An index to publications from federal agencies and Congress, arranged by issuing body and indexed by author, title, subject, and series or report number. Current years are available online, with free access to the index from 1995 to the present, at <http://catalog.gpo.gov>.

PAIS International. New York: Public Affairs Information Service, 1972–. An index to books, articles, and government documents on public affairs, including politics, social issues, and economics. International in scope, this work combines the *Public Affairs Information Service* (1915–90), a long-running publication that is a good resource for historical analysis of politics, and *PAIS Foreign Language Index* (1972–90).

Web resources in political science

Country Studies <http://lcweb2.loc.gov/frd/cs/cshome.html>. Online editions of book-length country profiles produced for U.S. diplomats by the Federal Research Division of the Library of Congress. The site includes substantial information on each nation's culture, history, economy, and political system and is searchable by topic and country. Be sure to note publication dates; some country studies are more than ten years old and may include outdated information. Some libraries may have print versions.

LSU Libraries Federal Agencies Directory <http://www.lib.lsu.edu/gov/index.html>. Offers links to searchable federal agency Web sites, arranged hierarchically and alphabetically.

National Security Archive <http://www.gwu.edu/~nsarchiv>. The Web site of a project based at George Washington University that has collected the world's largest nongovernmental archive of declassified documents that were obtained through the Freedom of Information Act, many of them covering controversial issues. Though some of the documents are not accessible through the Web site, large collections of papers called *briefing books* are available on a variety of foreign affairs topics. This site offers a rich set of primary source documents on key international issues.

THOMAS: Legislative Information on the Internet <http://thomas.loc.gov>. Provides the text of bills introduced in Congress along with committee action from the 104th Congress (1995) to the present. Users can search the site by bill number or keyword to learn about the legislative process, find a state's members of Congress, or access a comprehensive database on current and past legislation. A service of the Library of Congress, the site also provides a full-text search of the *Congressional Record,* a daily record of activity in Congress, and committee information. Most official state Web sites provide similar bill-tracking information for state legislatures.

United Nations <http://www.un.org>. Offers news releases, virtual tours, documents, and basic information about the United Nations and its bodies. Three different search engines explore a large database and list of links. The site includes a wealth of reports, statistical data, and other information on human rights, international law, peacekeeping missions, and other topics.

University of Michigan Documents Center <http://www.lib.umich.edu/govdocs>. Offers a well-organized and current list of links to local, state, federal, foreign, and international Web sites, with official information as well as links to statistical information sources and a guide to political science material on the Web.

Reference books in political science

Almanac of American Politics. Ed. Michael Barone and Richard E. Cohen. Washington: National Journal, 1972–. Provides an overview of American politics at both national and state levels, giving voting results on key issues and state-by-state analyses of political concerns. Updated every two years.

America Votes. Ed. Richard M. Scammon. Washington: Congressional Quarterly, 1956–. A biennial summary of state and national election returns; useful for historical as well as current information.

Congressional Quarterly's Guide to Congress. 6th ed. 2 vols. Washington: Congressional Quarterly, 2007. Provides detailed histories and discussions of congressional processes and issues. Similar guides put out by the same publisher cover the presidency, the Supreme Court, and U.S. elections.

CQ Almanac Plus. Washington: Congressional Quarterly, 2001–. An annual summation of U.S. politics that analyzes key issues, important legislation, voting records of congressional representatives, and major Supreme Court decisions. Continues *Congressional Quarterly Almanac* (1945–2000). Some libraries may provide access to this series through *CQ Almanac Online*.

CQ Weekly Report. Washington: Congressional Quarterly, 1967–. A weekly publication covering events in Washington. Includes a detailed index every six months. Another weekly that provides similar coverage is the *National Journal*.

Encyclopedia of American Foreign Policy. 2nd ed. 3 vols. New York: Scribner, 2002. Offers essays on topics related to foreign-policy issues and doctrines, such as terrorism, environmental diplomacy, and refugee policies. This work is more theoretical than the *Encyclopedia of U.S. Foreign Relations* (see next entry).

Encyclopedia of U.S. Foreign Relations. Ed. Bruce W. Jentleson and Thomas G. Paterson. 4 vols. New York: Oxford University Press, 1997. Includes more than 1,000 articles covering historical events, relations with other countries, biographical sketches of leaders associated with foreign policy, treaties, doctrines, and key concepts. Published under the auspices of the Council on Foreign Relations, the work also provides chronologies and comparative country data.

International Encyclopedia of Public Policy and Administration. Ed. Jay M. Shafrirz. 4 vols. Boulder: Westview, 1998. Covers topics in public administration such as regional development, emergency management, budget reform, cost of living adjustments, and more. This work includes coverage of principles, theories, legal concepts, and management topics as well as definitions of terms used in the field of public policy.

Political Handbook of the World. Ed. Arthur S. Banks and Thomas C. Muller. Binghamton: CSA Publications, 1927–. Covers countries of the world, giving basic background information, discussions of political parties and structures, and analyses of current political trends. Updated annually.

United States Government Manual. Washington: Government Printing Office, 1973–. Outlines the organization of federal government agencies, providing organizational charts, contact names and addresses, and descriptions of agencies' missions. Also available online at <http://www.gpoaccess.gov/gmanual>.

Psychology

Databases and indexes in psychology

PsycINFO. Washington: American Psychological Association, 1927–. Formerly called *Psychological Abstracts.* This database provides more than 2.5 million references to journal articles, books, book chapters, and dissertations in psychology and related fields published from 1840 to the present. Most sources include abstracts; some also provide a complete list of cited works and links to publications that cite the source.

Web resources in psychology

American Psychological Association <http://www.apa.org>. The site for the discipline's premier organization, providing news from the field; a roundup of selected research on topics such as anger, trauma, addictions, and depression; and information about the organization, such as the APA's Code of Ethics. Some of the information on this site is available to members only, though some of it, such as the

PsycINFO database and APA journals, is likely available through your library.

National Institute of Mental Health <http://www.nimh.nih.gov>. From the federal agency charged with research into mental health and illness, this site offers useful information about health topics and statistics, with links to current research findings and clinical trials.

Psychology World Wide Web Virtual Library <http://www.vl-site.org/psychology/index.html>. A directory of selected links with brief descriptions. Areas covered include psychology of religion, transpersonal psychology, school psychology, mental health, and the history of psychology. Maintained by Gene R. Thursby of the University of Florida.

Social Psychology Network <http://www.socialpsychology.org>. A deep directory of resources on topics such as gender and psychology, social cognition, and interpersonal psychology as well as information on programs and organizations, research reports online, and social research groups. The site is maintained by Scott Plous at Wesleyan University.

Reference books in psychology

Corsini Encyclopedia of Psychology and Behavioral Science. Ed. W. Edward Craighead and Charles B. Nemeroff. 3rd ed. 4 vols. New York: Wiley, 2001. Defines and discusses terms, theories, methodology, and issues in psychological practice and offers brief biographies of important psychologists.

Diagnostic and Statistical Manual of Mental Disorders (DSM-IV). 4th ed. rev. Washington: American Psychiatric Association, 2000. Classifies and describes mental disorders and includes diagrams to aid diagnosis as well as a glossary of technical terms. A fifth edition is in development, with publication projected for 2012.

Encyclopedia of Human Behavior. Ed. V. S. Ramachandran. 4 vols. San Diego: Academic Press, 1994. Offers articles on a wide range of topics, such as left- or right-handedness, blushing, interpersonal communications, and intelligence. Each article provides an overview of the current state of knowledge about a topic and provides references to research.

Encyclopedia of Mental Health. Ed. Howard S. Friedman et al. 3 vols. San Diego: Academic Press, 1998. Includes substantial articles on major disciplines in the field, research areas, and topics of public interest. Designed for both students and health professionals, this work provides current and thorough coverage of mental disorders, treatments, personality traits, and psychological aspects of such topics as television viewing, parenting, and homelessness.

Encyclopedia of Psychology. Ed. Alan E. Kazdin. 8 vols. Washington: American Psychological Association, 2000. The most thorough and scholarly treatment of psychology topics, including methodology, findings, advances in research, and applications.

Handbook of Psychology. Ed. Irving B. Weiner. 12 vols. New York: Wiley, 2003. A thematically arranged overview of research in the field, with volumes devoted to history; research methods; experimental psychology; and developmental, clinical, educational, organizational, and forensic psychology.

Mental Measurements Yearbook. Lincoln: Buros Institute of Mental Measurements, 1938–. An essential reference work for those interested in psychological tests available to researchers. This work surveys and reviews tests of aptitude, education, achievement, and personality and includes bibliographies of related research.

Sociology

Databases and indexes in sociology

Sociological Abstracts. San Diego: Sociological Abstracts, 1952–. The most detailed index for the field, covering journal articles, book chapters, dissertations, and conference presentations on cultural and social structure, demography, family and social welfare, social development, studies of violence and power, and more. Recently added material includes the sources cited in an article and links to works that have cited a given article.

Web resources in sociology

SocioSite <http://www.sociosite.net>. A collection of links arranged in 18 categories and, within those categories, by country. Of particular note are the sections on sociologists, subjects in sociology, and data archives. The site is maintained by Albert Benschop of the University of Amsterdam.

Urban Institute <http://www.urban.org>. The Web site of a nonpartisan organization devoted to research on economic and social policy. The site includes a wealth of reports by topic as well as analysis of issues.

Social Work and Social Services Web Sites <http://gwbweb.wustl.edu/ Resources/Pages/socialservicesresourcesintro.aspx>. A topical list of recommended sites on topics such as abuse and violence, evidence-based social work, family issues, poverty, and welfare. A service of the George Warren Brown School of Social Work at Washington University in St. Louis.

Reference books in sociology

Blackwell Encyclopedia of Sociology. Ed. George Ritzer. 11 vols. Malden: Blackwell, 2007. Offers thorough coverage of sociological theory and topics such as alcohol and crime, community, consumption, prejudice, the public sphere, and hundreds more.

Encyclopedia of American Social Movements. Ed. Immanuel Ness. 4 vols. Armonk: Sharpe, 2004. Covers a range of social movements including civil rights; antiwar protests; the labor movement; religious movements; the gay, lesbian, bisexual, and transgender movements; nativist and conservative movements; and women's rights.

Encyclopedia of Social Theory. Ed. George Ritzer. 2 vols. Thousand Oaks: Sage, 2005. A handy place to find overviews of theories and theorists, both classical and cutting-edge. A good starting place for tracking down key ideas and core sources.

International Encyclopedia of Marriage and Family. Ed. James J. Ponzetti. 2nd ed. 4 vols. New York: Macmillan Reference, 2003. Covers aspects of family life including adolescent parenthood, family violence, fatherhood, and gender in a cross-cultural context.

Encyclopedia of Sociology. Ed. Edgar G. Montgomery et al. 2nd ed. 5 vols. New York: Macmillan Library Reference, 2000. Provides scholarly discussions of such topics as class and race, ethnicity, economic sociology, and social structure. The articles are written by specialists and include excellent bibliographies.

Violence in America: An Encyclopedia. Ed. Ronald Gottsman and Richard Maxwell Brown. 3 vols. New York: Scribner, 1999. A wide-ranging exploration of political, social, and psychological aspects of violence, including violence in sports and popular culture as well as violence against the environment, economic aspects of violence, and violence against specific populations. Experts from many disciplines contributed over 600 essays; the third volume includes an index to the set.

Gender and Women's Studies

Databases and indexes in gender and women's studies

Contemporary Women's Issues. Farmington Hills: Gale Group, 1992–. A full-text database of journal articles, newsletters, alternative press publications, and reports produced by nongovernmental organizations on women's issues. It includes material from 190 countries.

GenderWatch. Ann Arbor: ProQuest, 1998–. A database of full-text articles from 175 publications, some dating to the 1970s, on women's issues, including scholarly journals, magazines, and newsletters as well as conference proceedings and reports.

Women's Studies: Core Books <http://digicoll.library.wisc.edu/ACRLWSS>. A searchable database of the most important books in print on issues ranging from girlhood to aging, covering women's studies approaches to religion, sports, the arts, law, media, politics, and more. Books are chosen for inclusion by specialists in the Women's Studies Section of the Association of College and Research Libraries.

Women's Studies International. Baltimore: NISC, 1972–. Indexes scholarly materials including books and journals, with some popular magazines as well. Some libraries may offer *Gender Studies,* an expanded version of this database.

Web resources in gender and women's studies

Institute for Women's Policy Research <http://www.iwpr.org>. Links to information on violence, employment and economic change, democracy and society, poverty and welfare, the family and work, and health care policy. The Institute for Women's Policy Research is a nonprofit organization that conducts scientific research for use by women's organizations.

Women's Studies/Women's Issues Resource Sites <http://userpages .umbc.edu/~korenman/wmst/links.html>. A substantial, selective directory of hundreds of sites on topics such as women and activism, cyberculture, health, higher education, sports and recreation, and women of color. All entries are annotated. The site also offers an international directory of women's studies programs and research centers. Maintained by Joan Korenman of the Center for Women and Information Technology, University of Maryland, Baltimore County.

WSSLinks: Women and Gender Studies <http://libr.org/wss/WSSLinks/ index.html>. Annotated links for women's studies covering art, education, film, health, history, sexuality, music, philosophy, politics, science and technology, and theology. Links are chosen by an editorial team from the Women's Studies Section of the Association of College and Research Libraries.

WWW Virtual Library: Women's History <http://www.iisg.nl/ w3vlwomenshistory>. A directory of annotated links to women's history resources, arranged by period, location, and topic, with additional links to discussion lists, conferences, associations, and more. Maintained by Jenneke Quast for the International Institute of Social History.

Reference books in gender and women's studies

The Dictionary of Feminist Theory. By Maggie Humm. 2nd ed. Columbus: Ohio State University Press, 1995. Covers theoretical issues in feminism and is particularly useful for placing these issues in historical context. The work is also helpful for pinpointing primary documents related to feminist theory.

Encyclopedia of Lesbian, Gay, Bisexual, and Transgender History in America. Ed. Marc Stein. 3 vols. New York: Scribner, 2004. Offers over 500 articles on individuals, professions, legal issues, events, and communities that are significant in GLBT history.

Encyclopedia of Women and Gender: Sex Similarities and Differences and the Impact of Society on Gender. Ed. Judith Worell. 2 vols. San Diego: Academic Press, 2001. Provides lengthy technical articles on the psychology of women and gender, covering such topics as gender and achievement, aging, child care, and body image concerns.

Routledge International Encyclopedia of Women: Global Women's Issues and Knowledge. Ed. Cheris Kramarae and Dale Spender. 4 vols. New York: Routledge, 2000. A record of women's knowledge and experience, offering essays on international approaches to the arts, economic development, education, health and reproduction, sexuality, households, families, politics, and peace and violence.

Women in the Third World: An Encyclopedia of Contemporary Issues. Ed. Edith H. Altbach and Nelly P. Stromquist. New York: Garland, 1998. Offers substantial overviews of topics related to women in the developing world, including theoretical issues, political and legal contexts, sex-role ideologies, demographics, economics, and the environment. It also provides regional surveys.

Women in World History: A Biographical Encyclopedia. Ed. Anne Commire and Deborah Klezmer. 17 vols. Waterford: Yorkin, 1999–2002. The largest compilation of biographical material on the world's women. This work contains biographies of historically significant women from all walks of life and from all countries.

The Women's Movement Today: An Encyclopedia of Third-Wave Feminism. Ed. Leslie L. Heywood. 2 vols. Westport: Greenwood, 2006. Covers developments since the early 1990s. The first volume surveys important figures and issues ranging from riot grrrls to zines, and the second contains 77 documents showcasing third-wave feminist articles and essays.

Researching in the Sciences

Research in the sciences generally involves recognizing a scientific problem to be solved, setting up an experiment designed to yield useful data, and interpreting the data in the context of other scientific knowledge. Researchers use library resources to

- keep up with current thinking in the field so they can identify questions worth asking
- review what is known about a given phenomenon so they can place new knowledge in context
- locate specific information they need to successfully carry out an experiment or a project

The massive volume of scientific literature being produced can be daunting at first. However, a number of resources are available to help you find what is relevant to your research. Students planning to search for scientific materials should be prepared to

- choose search terms carefully so that they match those used by the sources
- work from the most recent publications to earlier ones, sorting out schools of thought and lines of inquiry
- know when to stop, when they have uncovered a selection of the most important and relevant research for their topic

The resources listed here will give you an idea of where to start. Consult a librarian to determine which resources are best for your research.

General resources in the sciences

Databases and indexes in the sciences

General Science Index. New York: Wilson, 1978–. An index designed for the nonspecialist, covering about 190 major research publications and popular science magazines. Some libraries subscribe to an electronic version that includes abstracts and full text of selected articles.

Science Citation Index. Philadelphia: Institute for Scientific Information, 1961–. An interdisciplinary index to nearly 6,000 science journals. It can be searched by author or keyword and allows searches by cited source, an efficient way to trace the influence of a piece of research. The electronic version, part of the *Web of Knowledge,* has a powerful Related Records search, which identifies articles that cite one or more of the same sources.

Web resources in the sciences

EurekAlert <http://www.eurekalert.org>. A regularly updated source for information about research advances in science, medicine, health, and technology. The site includes links to other science sites, access to databases, and a searchable archive of news releases. Content for the site is screened by an advisory committee of journalists and public-information specialists. The site was founded by the American Association for the Advancement of Science.

National Science Digital Library <http://nsdl.org>. Offers hundreds of collections of digitized material about math and science, intended to enhance science education at all levels. Users can search or browse collections or submit a question to a panel of experts. Sponsored by the National Science Foundation.

Science.gov <http://www.science.gov>. A portal for science information from the U.S. government. The site includes cross-searching of 30 databases as well as links to science pages contributed by 12 federal agencies. It offers an advanced search as well as a browsable directory of resources by topic.

Science Blogs <http://scienceblogs.com>. A portal for over 60 entertaining and informative blogs on the life sciences, physical sciences, medicine and health, brain and behavior, and the interaction of science with politics and society. Interested readers can follow a particular blog or scan new content from all blogs at the main site. Sponsored by the Seed Media Group.

Scirus <http://www.scirus.com>. A search engine that focuses on science materials only. It searches both free Web content and several databases that include abstracts to published research, including *Medline, Science Direct,* and *NASA Technical Reports.* The site is sponsored by Elsevier, a major science publisher.

Reference books in the sciences

Dictionary of Scientific Biography. Ed. Charles Coulston Gillispie, 14 vols. New York: Macmillan Library Reference, 1970–2000. With supplements. Profiles scientists from early to modern times, considering both their lives and technical aspects of their work. Each biography is followed by a bibliography of primary and secondary sources. For basic biographical information on living scientists, consult *American Men and Women of Science,* published by Thomson Gale.

McGraw-Hill Dictionary of Scientific and Technical Terms. 6th ed. New York: McGraw-Hill, 2003. Offers concise, up-to-date definitions of technical terms beyond those found in a standard dictionary.

McGraw-Hill Encyclopedia of Science and Technology. 10th ed. 20 vols. New York: McGraw-Hill, 2007. A specialized encyclopedia covering scientific topics in detail. Technical discussions are fully illustrated with charts, diagrams, and photographs.

Biology

Databases and indexes in biology

Agricola. Beltsville: National Agricultural Library, 1970–. A database of books, articles, and documents on agriculture, including veterinary science, entomology, plant sciences, forestry, aquaculture and fisheries, farming and farming systems, agricultural economics, and nutrition. Searches can be limited to books in the National Agricultural Library, to articles, or both. The database is available at <http://agricola.nal.usda.gov>.

BIOSIS. Philadelphia: Biosis, 1926–. The most thorough index to biological literature, with more than 30 million records of biology research dating back to 1926 and including the latest findings. In some libraries, this database is part of the *Web of Knowledge.*

CSA Biological Sciences. Bethesda: Cambridge Scientific Abstracts, 1994–. Provides citations and abstracts to the contents of over 6,000 biology journals as well as selected conference proceedings and books, covering publications from 1982 to the present.

Web resources in biology

Animal Diversity Web <http://animaldiversity.ummz.umich.edu/site/index.html>. Provides information on animals: mammals, birds, amphibians, reptiles, sharks, bony fish, mollusks, arthropods, and echinoderms. Each animal is classified by phylum, order, class, and family; pictures, sounds, and background information are provided for many of them. The site is a service of the University of Michigan Museum of Zoology.

National Center for Biotechnology Information <http://www.ncbi.nlm.nih.gov>. Provides highly technical molecular biology information and tools. The site includes molecular databases, nucleotide and protein sequences, and genome databases as well as links to the *PubMed* database of medical research and *PubMed Central,* an archive of free and fully accessible full-text life sciences journals. The center is part of the U.S. National Library of Medicine.

Plants Database <http://plants.usda.gov>. Covers individual plants, invasive species, threatened and endangered plants, checklists by state, fact sheets, and over 40,000 photographs. From the U.S. Department of Agriculture.

Tree of Life Web Project <http://tolweb.org/tree/phylogeny.html>. A collaborative project compiled by biologists around the world. The site offers more than 1,300 schematic trees that map biological relationships and provide information about organisms. Detailed bibliographies are included.

Reference books in biology

Encyclopedia of Human Biology. Ed. Renato Dulbecco. 2nd ed. 9 vols. San Diego: Academic Press, 1997. Offers substantial articles on topics in human biology, including behavior, biochemistry, genetics, psychology, and medical research. The final volume includes an index to the set.

Encyclopedia of Microbiology. Ed. Joshua Lederberg. 2nd ed. 4 vols. San Diego: Academic Press, 2000. Covers topics in microbiology, reviewing research in such areas as bacteriophages, anaerobic respiration, and AIDS. The articles, written for the informed nonspecialist, are substantial and include bibliographies.

Fieldbook of Natural History. Ed. E. L. Palmer and G. A. Parker. 2nd ed. New York: McGraw-Hill, 1975. A handy compilation of information on the natural world, devoted chiefly to the description of plants and animals with some information on their environment and behavior. The work is arranged by topic with an alphabetical index.

Grzimek's Animal Life Encyclopedia. Ed. Bernhard Grzimek. 2nd ed. 17 vols. Detroit: Gale Group, 2003–04. A survey of animals, organized by taxonomic class. Entries discuss species' distribution, behavior, and appearance; the work includes numerous color plates.

Walker's Mammals of the World. By Ronald M. Nowak. 6th ed. 2 vols. Baltimore: Johns Hopkins University Press, 1999. Describes the appearance, habitat, behavior, and biology of every genus of living mammal. The work is arranged taxonomically.

Chemistry

Databases and indexes in chemistry

Beilstein. Frankfurt: Beilstein Information, 1997–. The world's largest database of references to publications about organic compounds, based on *Beilstein's Handbook for Organic Chemistry.* The work covers organic chemistry research back to 1771, updated with the contents of current journals. Inorganic compounds are covered in *Gmelin's Handbuch der Anorganischen Chemie.* Both of these may be available through the *CrossFire* platform or, with the addition of a patents database, *Reaxys*.

Chemical Abstracts. Columbus: American Chemical Society, 1907–. A comprehensive index to chemistry publications. Searches can be conducted by author, subject, chemical structure, formula, and more. Online access is provided through the services *STN* and *Sci-Finder Scholar.*

Web resources in chemistry

Molecule of the Month <http://www.chm.bris.ac.uk/motm/motm .htm>. Provides detailed graphic and textual information on molecules, from mustard gas to aspirin. Pages are contributed by chemists in universities and research labs around the world. Emphasis is on molecules of popular interest. The site is maintained by Paul May at the School of Chemistry, University of Bristol.

NIST Chemistry WebBook <http://wcbbook.nist.gov/chemistry>. Provides chemical structure and thermochemical data for over 6,500 organic and small inorganic compounds and over 9,800 reactions as well as a variety of spectra data. A service of the National Institute of Standards and Technology, the site is searchable by physical property, name, formula, and more.

WebElements Periodic Table <http://www.webelements.com>. Offers information about elements based on the periodic table. The site includes data about physical, electronic, and nuclear properties as well as information about abundance, use, and more. The site is maintained by Mark Winter at the University of Sheffield.

Reference books in chemistry

Chemistry: Foundations and Applications. Ed. J. J. Lagowski. 4 vols. New York: Macmillan Reference, 2004. Covers basic information on elements, biochemistry, applied chemistry, biographies of important chemists, and chemistry-related topics in other areas such as medicine, environmental chemistry, and energy.

Encyclopedia of Reagents for Organic Synthesis. Ed. Leo A. Paquette. 2nd ed. 14 vols. Chichester: Wiley, 2009. Comprehensively covers over 4,000 reagents in alphabetical order. The work is indexed by formula, reagent structural class, and reagent function. Each article includes ring diagrams and a bibliography of research sources. The online version is called *e-EROS*.

Kirk-Othmer Encyclopedia of Chemical Technology. 5th ed. 27 vols. New York: Wiley, 2007. Provides in-depth articles on chemical properties, manufacturing, and technology. A two-volume concise edition is also available.

Merck Index: An Encyclopedia of Chemicals, Drugs, and Biologicals. Ed. Maryadele J. O'Neil. 14th ed. Whitehouse Station: Merck, 2006. Contains about 10,000 entries on chemicals, including many pharmaceuticals, as well as chemical formulas, properties, uses, and references to literature.

World of Chemistry. Ed. Robin V. Young. Detroit: Gale Group, 2000. A collection of articles on theories, discoveries, concepts, and key scientists in chemistry.

Computer science

Databases and indexes in computer science

ACM Digital Library. New York: Association for Computing Machinery, 1947–. Contains full-text articles from journals, newsletters, and conference proceedings published by the Association for Computing Machinery. Though full text is limited to libraries that subscribe to the database, anyone can access the basic search and browse features for free at <http://portal.acm.org>.

Web resources in computer science

Collection of Computer Science Bibliographies <http://liinwww.ira.uka .de/bibliography/index.html>. Contains references to computing publications in broad categories including database research, distributed systems, object-oriented programming, and artificial intelligence. Compiled by Alf-Christian Achilles, of the University of Karlsruhe in Germany.

FOLDOC: Free Online Dictionary of Computing <http://foldoc.org>. A searchable dictionary of computer terms, including acronyms, jargon, computer languages, operating systems, companies, and theory. The site is maintained by the Department of Computing at the Imperial College, London.

WWW Virtual Library: Computing and Computer Science <http://vlib .org/Computing>. An index page for a wide variety of computer-related Web directories in the *WWW Virtual Library,* including cryptography, logic programming, and Web design.

Reference books in computer science

Encyclopedia of Computers and Computer History. Ed. Raúl Rojas. 2 vols. Chicago: Fitzroy Dearborn, 2001. An accessible work that provides entries on people, organizations, and developments in the history of computing "from the abacus to eBay."

Encyclopedia of Computer Science. Ed. Anthony Ralston, Edwin D. Reilly, and David Hemmendinger. 4th ed. Hoboken: Wiley, 2003. A technical compendium that covers hardware, computer systems, information and data, software, the mathematics of computing, theory of computation, methodologies, applications, and computing in general. An authoritative reference work for the field.

Engineering

Databases and indexes in engineering

Applied Science and Technology Index. New York: Wilson, 1983–. Covers over 400 core scientific and technical journals and important trade and industrial publications in engineering, mathematics, computer technology, the environment, and natural science. Some libraries also have access to abstracts and selected full-text articles.

CE Database <http://cedb.asce.org>. A database of journal articles, conference proceedings, books, manuals, and other publications produced by the American Society of Civil Engineers from 1970 to the present concerning all aspects of civil engineering.

EI Engineering Village. Hoboken: Elsevier Engineering Information, 2000–. The most comprehensive resource covering all engineering disciplines with over 10 million abstracts of journal articles, technical reports, selected Web sites, conference papers, and proceedings. Includes the contents of several long-running databases, among them *Compendex* and *Inspec*, and other industry-related resources.

TRIS Online <http://trisonline.bts.gov/sundev/search.cfm>. A comprehensive database of publications on transportation issues. In some cases, links to full text are provided. This work is a joint project of the National Transportation Library, the Transportation Research Board, and the Bureau of Transportation Statistics.

Web resources in engineering

Intute Engineering <http://www.intute.ac.uk/sciences/engineering>. Provides reviews of and access to thousands of reputable sites on engineering topics such as bioengineering, manufacturing, and nanotechnology. Those marked *editor's choice* are considered especially noteworthy.

MatWeb: The Online Materials Information Resource <http://www.matweb.com>. Links to over 40,000 material data sheets from manufacturers and professional societies covering plastics, metals, ceramics, and composites. Searchable by physical properties, material type, manufacturer, or trade name. Though access to the data sheets is free, some search features are available only by subscription.

Reference books in engineering

The Electronics Handbook. Ed. Jerry C. Whitaker. 2nd ed. Boca Raton: CRC, 2005. Covers theory and principles governing electronic devices and systems.

McGraw-Hill Dictionary of Engineering. 2nd ed. New York: McGraw-Hill, 2003. Covers all fields of engineering, including building construction. This work is based on the *McGraw-Hill Dictionary of Scientific and Technical Terms*.

Mechanical Engineers' Handbook. Ed. Myer Kutz. 3rd ed. 4 vols. New York: Wiley, 2006. Covers fundamental topics and emerging issues in mechanical engineering.

Perry's Chemical Engineers' Handbook. 8th ed. New York: McGraw-Hill, 2007. Covers all aspects of chemical engineering, including chemical and physical property data and the fundamentals of chemical engineering.

Standard Handbook of Engineering Calculations. Ed. Tyler G. Hicks et al. 4th ed. New York: McGraw-Hill, 2005. A classic compendium of step-by-step calculations for solving the most frequently encountered engineering problems in many engineering disciplines.

Structural Engineering Handbook. Ed. Wai-Fah Chen and Eric M. Lui. 2nd ed. Boca Raton: CRC, 2005. Covers a variety of engineering structures, theories, and topics such as seismic loading and fatigue and fracture.

Environmental sciences

Databases and indexes in environmental sciences

Environmental Sciences and Pollution Management. Bethesda: Cambridge Scientific Abstracts, 1994–. Provides abstracts of research from nearly 6,000 journals as well as reports, conference proceedings, and books published since 1967 on ecology, energy, pollution, waste management, toxicology, risk assessment, environmental biotechnology, and water resources.

Web resources in environmental sciences

National Library for the Environment <http://www.ncseonline.org/NLE>. A digital archive of material, including reports on "hot topics," Congressional Research Service reports, and abstracts and links to over 14,000 reports on population and the environment. This site is a project of the National Council for Science and the Environment.

U.S. Environmental Protection Agency <http://www.epa.gov>. Offers information on topics such as acid rain, lead, ozone, and wetlands as well as technical publications, legal and regulatory information, and a database of enforcement and compliance actions taken by the EPA. There is a browsable index to background information on topics ranging from ecosystems to environmental technology to human health as well as a searchable database of research publications at <http://www.epa.gov/nscep/>.

World Resources Institute <http://www.wri.org>. Offers many digital publications on environmental issues, including country profiles and *EarthTrends* (<http://earthtrends.wri.org>), a portal for a wealth of data on environmental topics including population, energy, water resources, biodiversity, and economic issues affecting the environment.

Reference books in environmental sciences

Encyclopedia of Biodiversity. Ed. Simon Asher Levin. 5 vols. San Diego: Academic Press, 2001. Provides in-depth, scholarly articles on topics ranging from agriculture, conservation, economic aspects of biodiversity, microbial biodiversity, public policy, and systematics.

Encyclopedia of Endangered Species. 2 vols. Detroit: Gale Group, 1994. Describes over 700 animals and plants currently threatened with extinction. Arranged taxonomically; an index provides access by common and scientific names. The status, description and biology, habitat and current distribution, and history and conservation measures for each species are described. Includes indexes by geographic location and a list of wildlife and conservation organizations.

Encyclopedia of Global Warming and Climate Change. Ed. S. George Philander. Los Angeles: Sage, 2008. Covers concepts, historical background, policies, and perspectives from chemists, development experts, political scientists, climatologists, and engineers. Also included are data tables and country profiles.

Encyclopedia of the Biosphere. Ed. Ramon Folch. 11 vols. Detroit: Gale Group, 2000. Covers world habitats such as tropical rain forests, savannahs, prairies, and lakes, in lavishly illustrated volumes. The work is based on a 1998 Catalan publication compiled under the sponsorship of UNESCO.

Encyclopedia of World Environmental History. Ed. Shepard Krech, J. R. McNeill, and Carolyn Merchant. 3 vols. New York: Routledge, 2004. Covers topics, events, people, natural resources, and aspects of human interaction with the environment worldwide. This work provides historical surveys of environmental issues such as deforestation and extinction; it also offers regional and national overviews as well as essays on subfields such as environmental philosophy.

Vital Signs: The Environmental Trends That Are Shaping Our Future. Ed. Lester R. Brown. New York: Norton, 1992–. A compilation of statistics and analyses of major trends in food production, energy, the atmosphere, the economy, and social factors such as population growth, epidemics, and refugeeism. This work was produced under the auspices of the Worldwatch Institute.

Geology

Databases and indexes in geology

GeoRef. Alexandria: American Geological Institute, 1966–. A comprehensive database of more than 2.3 million bibliographic citations to articles, books, maps, papers, reports, and theses covering the geosciences internationally.

Web resources in geology

Minerals Information <http://minerals.usgs.gov/minerals>. Includes an online version of *The Minerals Yearbook* with profiles of over 90 minerals, lists of mineral resources in over 175 countries, and current and historical international industry surveys and statistics. From the U.S. Geological Survey.

National Map: The Nation's Topographic Map for the 21st Century <http://nationalmap.gov>. This amazing tool from the U.S. Geological Survey allows users to zoom in on any part of the United States and choose map layers such as elevation, roads, water, land use, and even detailed aerial satellite images. Whether you're examining a region, a state, or a few city blocks, this tool offers access to a wealth of topographic information.

U.S. Geological Survey <http://www.usgs.gov>. Since 1879, this federal project has provided the nation with geologic information and mapping services. Its Web site catalogs information about earthquakes, environmental and biological material, geospatial data and mapping projects, and other geologic resources.

Reference books in geology

Encyclopedia of Earth Sciences Series. Ed. Rhodes W. Fairbridge et al. 20 vols. to date. Boston: Kluwer Academic Publishers, 1966–. Offers lengthy, scholarly articles on oceanography, atmospheric sciences and astrogeology, geochemistry, world regional geography, climatology, and structural geology. Each volume covers a different aspect of earth sciences.

Encyclopedia of Paleontology. Ed. Ronald Singer. 2 vols. Chicago: Fitzroy Dearborn, 1999. Includes information on principles and methods of the field as well as on paleontologists and their findings throughout the world. Entries cover dinosaurs and other animals and plants found in the fossil record.

Lexicon of Geologic Names of the United States (including Alaska). 2 vols. Washington: Government Printing Office, 1936. With supplements. Provides information from records kept since the 1880s by the Geological Names Committee of the U.S. Geological Survey. This work identifies the names of geological features by time period and location and provides reviews of the literature referring to the names. Supplements provide information on more recently named features. Most of the names from the print volumes are also provided online in the *Geolex* database at <http://ngmdb.usgs.gov/Geolex>.

Macmillan Encyclopedia of Earth Sciences. Ed. Julius E. Dasch. 2 vols. New York: Macmillan, 1996. Offers nearly 400 accessible articles on all aspects of earth science, including solid earth, oceanographic, and atmospheric sciences, as well as discussions of Earth's place in the solar system.

Mathematics

Databases and indexes in mathematics

MathSciNet. Lancaster: American Mathematical Society, 1940–. The most comprehensive database for mathematics research, covering all types of publications with annotations written by reviewers.

Web resources in mathematics

Biographies of Women Mathematicians <http://www.agnesscott.edu/ lriddle/women/women.htm>. An extensive collection of biographical information about the contributions of women to mathematics. The site can be searched or browsed alphabetically or chronologically. Profiles are compiled by students and faculty at Agnes Scott College.

MacTutorHistoryofMathematicsArchive<http://www-groups.dcs.st-and .ac.uk/~history>. Provides biographies, historical overviews of topics, the history of mathematics in different cultures, and a "famous curves" page with illustrations, formulas, and other information. Maintained by staff at the St. Andrews University (Scotland) School of Mathematics and Statistics.

Math Forum @ Drexel <http://mathforum.org>. An online resource for math teachers, offering problems and puzzles as well as a directory of quality Web sites. From Drexel University School of Education.

Math on the Web <http://www.ams.org/mathweb>. A directory of mathematics resources from the American Mathematical Society. The selection of sites by topic is particularly useful.

WISE: Web Interface for Statistics Education <http://wise.cgu.edu>. Offers a selection of teaching resources, including tutorials on statistics topics as well as applets that demonstrate statistics principles. From the School of Behavioral and Organizational Sciences at the Claremont Graduate University.

Reference books in mathematics

Companion Encyclopedia of the History and Philosophy of Mathematical Sciences. Ed. I. Grattan-Guinness. 2 vols. London: Routledge, 1994.

Offers lengthy, well-documented articles on the historical basis of mathematics and the cultural production of mathematical understanding.

CRC Concise Encyclopedia of Mathematics. Ed. Eric W. Weisstein. 2nd ed. Boca Raton: CRC, 2003. Offers over 3,000 pages of accessible information about mathematics and its applications in physics, biochemistry, chemistry, biophysics, and engineering.

Encyclopedia of Statistical Sciences. Ed. Samuel Kotz. 2nd ed. 16 vols. New York: Wiley, 2006. An in-depth exploration of all fields of inquiry in which statistical methods are used. The work includes articles on statistical terminology.

The World of Mathematics: A Small Library of the Literature of Mathematics from A'h-mose the Scribe to Albert Einstein. 4 vols. New York: Simon and Schuster, 1956. This gem can sometimes provide answers to the most arcane questions, while conducting a tour through the history and traditions of mathematics. The work is dated and therefore does not cover recent developments, but it has excellent background material that is easily accessed using the thorough index.

Nursing and health sciences

Databases and indexes in nursing and health sciences

CINAHL: Cumulative Index to Nursing and Allied Health Literature. Glendale: Cinahl Information Systems, 1977–. Covers publications related to nursing research and practice, providing references to articles, books and book chapters, pamphlets and other documents, and standards of professional practice and research.

PubMed.   Bethesda: National Library of Medicine, 1948–. The most comprehensive coverage of medical research. Based on the *Medline* medical database but including current in-process citations, this tool provides over 15 million abstracts of publications in medicine, nursing, dentistry, veterinary medicine, health care, and the preclinical sciences published from the 1950s to the present. *PubMed* is available at <http://www.pubmed.gov>, a public resource provided by the National Library of Medicine.

Web resources in nursing and health sciences

Centers for Disease Control and Prevention <http://www.cdc.gov>. The CDC is the federal government's lead agency for preventing disease and promoting health. The agency's Web site provides information on health and safety topics, an index of health information, technical publications such as *The Mortality and Morbidity Weekly Report,* and current news about health risks.

National Center for Health Statistics <http://www.cdc.gov/nchs>. Provides a wealth of statistical data on health in the United States, including analysis of trends, health reports on specific populations, and leading causes of death. The center is part of the Centers for Disease Control.

National Institute of Nursing Research <http://ninr.nih.gov/ninr>. A U.S. government program devoted to clinical and basic research efforts in patient care. Included on the site are many publications and an online course for nurses who wish to conduct research.

National Institutes of Health <http://www.nih.gov>. Offers information on current medical research funded by the U.S. government in the areas of cancer, mental health, human genomes, drug and alcohol abuse, and a wide variety of other illnesses and medical specialties. Though much of the information available from the NIH is technical, every subject area contains information written for a nonspecialist audience. The NIH is part of the U.S. Department of Health and Human Services.

Virtual Hospital: A Digital Library of Health Information <http://www.vh.org>. Offers a tremendous amount of information for health care providers and their patients. A service of the University of Iowa Health Care Program, the site includes the full text of scores of medical textbooks as well as easily accessible patient and provider information arranged by topic.

Reference books in nursing and health sciences

Cambridge World History of Human Disease. Ed. Kenneth F. Kiple. Cambridge: Cambridge University Press, 1993. A scholarly guide to the history of specific diseases across time and in all parts of the world.

Cecil Textbook of Medicine. Ed. Lee Goldman and Dennis Ausiello. 23rd ed. Philadelphia: Saunders, 2008. A classic general textbook of medicine.

Conn's Current Therapy. Ed. Robert E. Rackel and Edward T. Bope. Philadelphia: Saunders, annual. A basic guide to current diagnosis and treatment of diseases and injuries.

Encyclopedia of Public Health. Ed. Wilhelm Kirch. 2 vols. New York: Springer, 2008. Offers over 2,500 entries on topics such as disease prevention and health promotion from the perspectives of sociology, demographics, economics, and social work as well as from clinical medicine.

Gale Encyclopedia of Medicine. Ed. Jacqueline Longe. 3rd ed. 5 vols. Detroit: Gale Group, 2006. Written in accessible, nontechnical language, this reference covers basic consumer information on hundreds of medical disorders, tests, and treatments.

Handbook of Clinical Nursing Research. Ed. Ada Sue Hinshaw et al. Newbury Park: Sage, 1999. Provides a comprehensive review and critique of nursing research.

Stedman's Medical Dictionary for Nursing and Health Professionals. 6th ed. Philadelphia: Lippincott Williams and Wilkins, 2007. Contains brief, illustrated definitions of medical terms. This is an adaptation of *Stedman's Medical Dictionary*, the longer classic work for practitioners.

Physics and astronomy

Databases and indexes in physics and astronomy

Physical Review Online Archive (PROLA). College Park: American Physical Society, 1997–. Indexes and provides full-text access to articles published in the most prominent series of physics research journals from 1893 to the most recent five years. The database includes abstracts of current articles; full text is available only with a library subscription.

INSPEC. London: Institute of Electrical Engineers, 1903–. Provides abstracts of publications in physics, electrical engineering, electronics, communications, control engineering, computers and computing, and information technology.

Web resources in physics and astronomy

AstroWeb: Astronomy/Astrophysics on the Internet <http://www.cv.nrao.edu/fits/www/astronomy.html>. Offers links to publications and organizations in the field; to data from observations; and to information on topics such as radio, planetary, and solar astronomy.

Energy Citations Database <http://www.osti.gov/energycitations>. Provides abstracts and, in some cases, links to full-text research publications in fields such as chemistry, physics, materials science, environmental science, geology, engineering, mathematics, and related disciplines. This database covers publications from 1948 to the present and is made available by the Office of Scientific and Technical Information at the U.S. Department of Energy.

Information Bridge <http://www.osti.gov/bridge>. A searchable database of full-text reports of research projects sponsored by the Department of Energy. Projects cover physics, chemistry, materials science, biology, environmental science, energy technologies, engineering, and renewable energy from 1995 to the present. The database is made available by the Office of Scientific and Technical Information at the U.S. Department of Energy.

NASA Astrophysics Data System <http://adswww.harvard.edu>. A database of nearly 4 million abstracts of publications from journals, colloquia, symposia, proceedings, and internal NASA reports from 1993 to the present. The database covers astronomy and astrophysics, instrumentation, physics, and geophysics and includes preprints in astronomy. It is made available by the Harvard-Smithsonian Center for Astrophysics.

National Aeronautics and Space Administration (NASA) <http://www.nasa.gov>. Offers information for scientists and the public, including many visual resources and information about space missions.

Physics Reference Data <http://physics.nist.gov/PhysRefData/contents.html>. Includes physical constants, atomic and molecular spectroscopy data, X-ray and gamma-ray data, and nuclear physics data. From the National Institute of Standards and Technology.

PhysicsWeb <http://physicsweb.org>. News from the world of physics. Sponsored by the Institute of Physics, this site includes a Best of *PhysicsWeb* section with a selection of articles organized by subfield as well as a collection of resources for physicists and physics students.

PhysLink <http://www.physlink.com>. A commercial site rich in news and general information. It contains links to reference sites and materials for physics teachers and students.

Reference books in physics and astronomy

AIP Physics Desk Reference. Ed. E. Richard Cohen, David R. Lide, and George L. Trigg. 3rd ed. New York: American Institute of Physics, 2003. A concise source of tables, formulas, and bibliographies in 22 subdisciplines related to physics, including acoustics, astronomy, biological physics, quantum physics, optics, fluid mechanics, and molecular spectroscopy. This work includes sections on "mathematical basics" and practical laboratory data.

Dictionary of Physics. 4 vols. London: Macmillan, 2004. An updated translation of *Lexikon der Physik,* this work provides brief, technical articles on a wide variety of topics in the field.

Dictionary of Pure and Applied Physics. Ed. Dipak Basu. Boca Raton: CRC, 2001. Defines over 3,000 terms in acoustics, biophysics, medical physics, communication, electricity, electronics, geometrical optics, low-temperature physics, magnetism, and physical optics.

Encyclopedia of Astronomy and Astrophysics. Ed. Paul Murdin. 4 vols. Bristol: Institute of Physics, 2001. Includes 700 long articles on topics and themes in the field as well as hundreds of shorter articles that define terms and provide profiles of people and institutions.

Macmillan Encyclopedia of Physics. Ed. John S. Rigden. 4 vols. With supplements. New York: Macmillan Library Reference, 1996. Accessibly covers laws, concepts, fundamental theories, and the lives and work of important physicists throughout history.

The World of Physics: A Small Library of the Literature of Physics from Antiquity to the Present. 3 vols. New York: Simon and Schuster, 1987. An anthology of key historical texts in physics, presented with informative introductory essays. This work is a useful collection of primary sources in the history of physics.

Part IV. Documentation Styles

In academic research papers and any other writing that borrows information from sources, the borrowed information—quotations, summaries, paraphrases, and any facts or ideas that are not common knowledge—must be clearly documented.

Each academic discipline uses a particular editorial style for citing sources and listing the works that have been cited in a paper. The following sections give details for four documentation styles: MLA (Modern Language Association), used in English and other humanities; APA (American Psychological Association), used in psychology and other social sciences; *Chicago*, used in history and some humanities; and CSE (Council of Science Editors), used in biology and other sciences.

MLA Style: English and Other Humanities

In English and other humanities classes, you may be asked to use the MLA (Modern Language Association) system for documenting sources, which is set forth in the *MLA Handbook for Writers of Research Papers*, 7th ed. (New York: MLA, 2009).

MLA recommends in-text citations that refer readers to a list of works cited. An in-text citation names the author of the source, often in a signal phrase, and gives a page number in parentheses. At the end of the paper, a list of works cited provides publication information about the source; the list is alphabetized by authors' last names (or by titles for works without authors).

IN-TEXT CITATION

Jay Kesan notes that even though many companies now routinely monitor employees through electronic means, "there may exist less intrusive safeguards for employers" (293).

ENTRY IN THE LIST OF WORKS CITED

Kesan, Jay P. "Cyber-Working or Cyber-Shirking? A First Principles
    Examination of Electronic Privacy in the Workplace." *Florida Law
    Review* 54.2 (2002): 289-332. Print.

For a list of works cited that includes this entry, see page 181.

MLA in-text citations

MLA in-text citations are made with a combination of signal
phrases and parenthetical references. A signal phrase introduces information taken from a source (a quotation, summary, paraphrase, or fact); usually the signal phrase includes
the author's name. The parenthetical reference comes after
the cited material, often at the end of the sentence. It includes
at least a page number (except for unpaginated sources, such
as those found online).

IN-TEXT CITATION

Kwon points out that the Fourth Amendment does not give employees any
protections from employers' "unreasonable searches and seizures" (6).

Readers can look up the author's last name in the alphabetized
list of works cited, where they will learn the work's title and
other publication information. If readers decide to consult the
source, the page number will take them straight to the passage
that has been cited.

Basic rules for print and online sources

The MLA system of in-text citations, which depends heavily
on authors' names and page numbers, was created with print
sources in mind. Although many online sources have unclear
authorship and lack page numbers, the basic rules are the
same for both print and online sources.

The models in this section (items 1–5) show how the MLA
system usually works and explain what to do if your source
has no author or page numbers.

1. Author named in a signal phrase Ordinarily, introduce the material being cited with a signal phrase that includes the author's name. In addition to preparing readers for the source, the signal phrase allows you to keep the parenthetical citation brief.

Frederick Lane reports that employers do not necessarily have to use software to monitor how their employees use the Web: employers can "use a hidden video camera pointed at an employee's monitor" and even position a camera "so that a number of monitors [can] be viewed at the same time" (147).

The signal phrase—*Frederick Lane reports*—names the author; the parenthetical citation gives the page number of the book in which the quoted words may be found.

Notice that the period follows the parenthetical citation. When a quotation ends with a question mark or an exclamation point, leave the end punctuation inside the quotation mark and add a period at the end of your sentence: ". . . ?" (8).

2. Author named in parentheses   If a signal phrase does not name the author, put the author's last name in parentheses along with the page number. Use no punctuation between the name and the page number.

> Companies can monitor employees' every keystroke without legal penalty, but they may have to combat low morale as a result (Lane 129).

3. Author unknown   Either use the complete title in a signal phrase or use a short form of the title in parentheses. Titles of books are italicized; titles of articles are put in quotation marks.

> A popular keystroke logging program operates invisibly on workers' computers yet provides supervisors with details of the workers' online activities ("Automatically").

TIP: Before assuming that a Web source has no author, do some detective work. Often the author's name is available but is not easy to find. For example, it may appear at the end of the page, in tiny print. Or it may appear on another page of the site, such as the home page.

NOTE: If a source has no author and is sponsored by a corporation or government agency, name the corporation or agency as the author (see items 8 and 17 on pp. 124 and 128, respectively).

4. Page number unknown   Do not include the page number if a work lacks page numbers, as is the case with many Web sources. Even if a printout from a Web site shows page numbers, treat the source as unpaginated in the in-text citation because not all printouts give the same page numbers. (When the pages of a Web source are stable, as in PDF files, supply a page number in your in-text citation.)

> As a 2005 study by *Salary.com* and *America Online* indicates, the Internet ranked as the top choice among employees for ways of wasting time on the job; it beat talking with co-workers—the second most popular method—by a margin of nearly two to one (Frauenheim).

If a source has numbered paragraphs or sections, use "par." (or "pars.") or "sec." (or "secs.") in the parentheses: (Smith, par. 4). Notice that a comma follows the author's name in this case.

5. One-page source   If the source is one page long, MLA allows (but does not require) you to omit the page number. Many instructors will want you to supply the page number because without it readers may not know where your citation ends or, worse, may not realize that you have provided a citation at all.

NO PAGE NUMBER IN CITATION

> Anush Yegyazarian reports that in 2000 the National Labor Relations Board's Office of the General Counsel helped win restitution for two workers who had been dismissed because their employers were displeased by the employees' e-mails about work-related issues. The case points to the ongoing struggle to define what constitutes protected speech in the workplace.

PAGE NUMBER IN CITATION

> Anush Yegyazarian reports that in 2000 the National Labor Relations Board's Office of the General Counsel helped win restitution for two workers who had been dismissed because their employers were displeased by the employees' e-mails about work-related issues (62). The case points to the ongoing struggle to define what constitutes protected speech in the workplace.

Variations on the basic rules

This section describes the MLA guidelines for handling a variety of situations not covered by the basic rules in items 1–5. These rules for in-text citations are the same for both print and online sources.

6. Two or three authors   Name the authors in a signal phrase, as in the following example, or include their last names in the parenthetical reference: (Kizza and Ssanyu 2).

> Kizza and Ssanyu note that "employee monitoring is a dependable, capable, and very affordable process of electronically or otherwise recording all employee activities at work" and elsewhere (2).

When three authors are named in the parentheses, separate the names with commas: (Alton, Davies, and Rice 56).

7. Four or more authors   Name all of the authors or include only the first author's name followed by "et al." (Latin for "and others"). The format you use should match the format in your works cited entry (see item 3 on p. 135).

> The study was extended for two years, and only after results were reviewed by an independent panel did the researchers publish their findings (Blaine et al. 35).

8. Organization as author   When the author is a corporation or an organization, name that author either in the signal phrase or in the parentheses. (For a government agency as author, see item 17 on p. 128.)

> According to a 2001 survey of human resources managers by the American Management Association, more than three-quarters of the responding companies reported disciplining employees for "misuse or personal use of office telecommunications equipment" (2).

In the list of works cited, the American Management Association is treated as the author and alphabetized under *A*. When you give the organization name in parentheses, abbreviate common words in the name: "Assn.," "Dept.," "Natl.," "Soc.," and so on.

> In a 2001 survey of human resources managers, more than three-quarters of the responding companies reported disciplining employees for "misuse or personal use of office telecommunications equipment" (Amer. Management Assn. 2).

9. Authors with the same last name   If your list of works cited includes works by two or more authors with the same last name, include the author's first name in the signal phrase or first initial in the parentheses.

> Estimates of the frequency with which employers monitor employees' use of the Internet each day vary widely (A. Jones 15).

10. Two or more works by the same author   Mention the title of the work in the signal phrase or include a short version of the title in the parentheses.

> The American Management Association and ePolicy Institute have tracked employers' practices in monitoring employees' e-mail use. The groups' 2003 survey found that one-third of companies had a policy of keeping and reviewing employees' e-mail messages ("2003 E-mail" 2); in 2005, more than 55% of companies engaged in e-mail monitoring ("2005 Electronic" 1).

Titles of articles and other short works are placed in quotation marks; titles of books are italicized.

In the rare case when both the author's name and a short title must be given in parentheses, separate them with a comma.

> A 2004 survey found that 20% of employers responding had employees' e-mail "subpoenaed in the course of a lawsuit or regulatory investigation," up 7% from the previous year (Amer. Management Assn. and ePolicy Inst., "2004 Workplace" 1).

11. Two or more works in one citation   To cite more than one source in the parentheses, give the citations in alphabetical order and separate them with a semicolon.

> The effects of sleep deprivation among college students have been well documented (Cahill 42; Leduc 114; Vasquez 73).

Multiple citations can be distracting, so you should not overuse the technique. If you want to alert readers to several sources that discuss a particular topic, consider using an information note instead (see p. 170).

12. Repeated citations from the same source   When you are writing about a single work of fiction, you do not need to include the author's name each time you quote from or paraphrase the work. After you mention the author's name at the beginning of your paper, you may include just the page number in your parenthetical citations.

> In Susan Glaspell's short story "A Jury of Her Peers," two women accompany their husbands and a county attorney to an isolated house where a farmer named John Wright has been choked to death in his bed with a rope. The chief suspect is Wright's wife, Minnie, who is in jail awaiting trial. The sheriff's wife, Mrs. Peters, has come along to gather some personal items for Minnie, and Mrs. Hale has joined her. Early in the story, Mrs. Hale sympathizes with Minnie and objects to the way the male investigators are "snoopin' round and criticizin'" her kitchen (200). In contrast, Mrs. Peters shows respect for the law, saying that the men are doing "no more than their duty" (201).

In a second citation from the same nonfiction source in one paragraph, you may omit the author's name in the signal phrase as long as it is clear that you are still referring to the same source.

13. Encyclopedia or dictionary entry   Unless an encyclopedia or a dictionary has an author, it will be alphabetized in the list of works cited under the word or entry that you consulted (see item 18 on p. 144). Either in your text or in your parenthetical citation, mention the word or entry. No page number is required, since readers can easily look up the word or entry.

> The word *crocodile* has a surprisingly complex etymology ("Crocodile").

14. Multivolume work   If your paper cites more than one volume of a multivolume work, indicate in the parentheses the volume you are referring to, followed by a colon and the page number.

> In his studies of gifted children, Terman describes a pattern of
> accelerated language acquisition (2: 279).

If you cite only one volume of a multivolume work, you will include the volume number in the list of works cited and will not need to include it in the parentheses. (See the second example in item 17, p. 144.)

15. Entire work   Use the author's name in a signal phrase or a parenthetical citation. There is no need to use a page number.

> Lane explores the evolution of surveillance in the workplace.

16. Selection in an anthology   Put the name of the author of the selection (not the editor of the anthology) in the signal phrase or the parentheses.

> In "Love Is a Fallacy," the narrator's logical teachings disintegrate
> when Polly declares that she should date Petey because "[h]e's got a
> raccoon coat" (Shulman 379).

In the list of works cited, the work is alphabetized under *Shulman*, not under the name of the editor of the anthology.

> Shulman, Max. "Love Is a Fallacy." *Current Issues and Enduring
>   Questions*. Ed. Sylvan Barnet and Hugo Bedau. 8th ed.
>   Boston: Bedford, 2008. 371-79. Print.

17. Government document   When a government agency is the author, you will alphabetize it in the list of works cited under the name of the government, such as *United States* or *Great Britain* (see item 73 on p. 166). For this reason, you must name the government as well as the agency in your in-text citation.

> Online monitoring by the United States Department of the Interior over a one-week period found that employees' use of "sexually explicit and gambling websites . . . accounted for over 24 hours of Internet use" and that "computer users spent over 2,004 hours accessing game and auction sites" during the same period (3).

18. Historical document   For a historical document, such as the United States Constitution or the Canadian Charter of Rights and Freedoms, provide the document title, neither italicized nor in quotation marks, along with relevant article and section numbers. In parenthetical citations, use common abbreviations such as "art." and "sec." and abbreviations of well-known titles (US Const., art. 1, sec. 2).

> While the United States Constitution provides for the formation of new states (art. 4, sec. 3), it does not explicitly allow or prohibit the secession of states.

For other historical documents, cite as you would any other work, by the first element in the works cited entry (see item 74 on p. 167).

19. Legal source   For legislative acts (laws) and court cases, name the act or case either in a signal phrase or in parentheses. Italicize the names of cases but not the names of acts.

> The Jones Act of 1917 granted US citizenship to Puerto Ricans.

> In 1857, Chief Justice Roger B. Taney declared in *Dred Scott v. Sandford* that blacks, whether enslaved or free, could not be citizens of the United States.

20. Visual such as a photograph, map, or chart   To cite a visual that has a figure number in the source, use the abbreviation "fig." and the number in place of a page number in your parenthetical citation: (Manning, fig. 4). Spell out the word "figure" if you refer to it in your text.

To cite a visual that does not have a figure number in a print source, use the visual's title or a general description in your text and cite the author and page number as for any other source.

For a visual that is not contained in a source such as a book or periodical, identify the visual in your text and then cite it using the first element in the works cited entry: the photographer's or artist's name or the title of the work. (See item 69 on p. 165.)

> Photographs such as *Woman Aircraft Worker* (Bransby) and *Women Welders* (Parks) demonstrate the US government's attempt to document the contributions of women on the home front during World War II.

21. E-mail, letter, or personal interview   Cite e-mail messages, personal letters, and personal interviews by the name listed in the works cited entry, as for any other source. Identify the type of source in your text if you feel it is necessary. (See item 53 on p. 160 and items 83 and 84 on pp. 169 and 170.)

22. Web site or other electronic source   Your in-text citation for an electronic source should follow the same guidelines as for other sources. If the source lacks page numbers but has numbered paragraphs, sections, or divisions, use those numbers with the appropriate abbreviation in your in-text citation: "par.," "sec.," "ch.," "pt.," and so on. Do not add such numbers if the source itself does not use them. In that case, simply give the author or title in your in-text citation.

> Julian Hawthorne points out profound differences between his father and Ralph Waldo Emerson but concludes that, in their lives and their writing, "together they met the needs of nearly all that is worthy in human nature" (ch. 4).

23. Indirect source (source quoted in another source)   When a writer's or a speaker's quoted words appear in a source written by someone else, begin the parenthetical citation with the abbreviation "qtd. in."

> Researchers Botan and McCreadie point out that "workers are objects of information collection without participating in the process of exchanging the information . . ." (qtd. in Kizza and Ssanyu 14).

Literary works and sacred texts

Literary works and sacred texts are usually available in a variety of editions. Your list of works cited will specify which edition you are using, and your in-text citation will usually consist of a page number from the edition you consulted (see item 24). When possible, give enough information—such as book parts, play divisions, or line numbers—so that readers can locate the cited passage in any edition of the work (see items 25–27).

24. Literary work without parts or line numbers   Many literary works, such as most short stories and many novels and plays, do not have parts or line numbers. In such cases, simply cite the page number.

> At the end of Kate Chopin's "The Story of an Hour," Mrs. Mallard drops dead upon learning that her husband is alive. In the final irony of the story, doctors report that she has died of a "joy that kills" (25).

25. Verse play or poem   For verse plays, give act, scene, and line numbers that can be located in any edition of the work. Use arabic numerals and separate the numbers with periods.

> In Shakespeare's *King Lear*, Gloucester, blinded for suspected treason, learns a profound lesson from his tragic experience: "A man may see how this world goes / with no eyes" (4.2.148-49).

For a poem, cite the part, stanza, and line numbers, if it has them, separated by periods.

> The Green Knight claims to approach King Arthur's court "because the praise of you, prince, is puffed so high, / And your manor and your men are considered so magnificent" (1.12.258-59).

For poems that are not divided into numbered parts or stanzas, use line numbers. For a first reference, use the word "lines": (lines 5-8). Thereafter use just the numbers: (12-13).

26. Novel with numbered divisions   When a novel has numbered divisions, put the page number first, followed by a semicolon, and then the book, part, or chapter in which the passage may be found. Use abbreviations such as "pt." and "ch."

> One of Kingsolver's narrators, teenager Rachel, pushes her vocabulary beyond its limits. For example, Rachel complains that being forced to live in the Congo with her missionary family is "a sheer tapestry of justice" because her chances of finding a boyfriend are "dull and void" (117; bk. 2, ch. 10).

27. Sacred text   When citing a sacred text such as the Bible or the Qur'an, name the edition you are using in your works cited entry (see item 19 on p. 144). In your parenthetical citation, give the book, chapter, and verse (or their equivalent), separated by periods. Common abbreviations for books of the Bible are acceptable.

> Consider the words of Solomon: "If your enemy is hungry, give him bread to eat; and if he is thirsty, give him water to drink" (*Oxford Annotated Bible*, Prov. 25.21).

The title of a sacred work is italicized when it refers to a specific edition of the work, as in the preceding example. If you refer to the book in a general sense in your text, neither italicize it nor put it in quotation marks: "The Bible and the Qur'an provide allegories that help readers understand how to lead a moral life."

Directory to MLA works cited models

MLA list of works cited

An alphabetized list of works cited, which appears at the end of your research paper, gives publication information for each of the sources you have cited in the paper. Include only sources that you have quoted, summarized, or paraphrased. (For information about preparing the list, see p. 174; for a sample list of works cited, see p. 181.)

General guidelines for works cited in MLA style

In an MLA works cited entry, the first author's name is inverted (the last name comes first, followed by a comma and the first name), and all other names are in normal order. In titles of works, all words are capitalized except articles (*a*, *an*, *the*), prepositions (*to*, *from*, *between*, and so on), coordinating conjunctions (*and*, *but*, *or*, *nor*, *for*, *so*, *yet*), and the *to* in infinitives—unless they are the first or last word of the title or subtitle. Titles of periodical articles and other short works, such as brief documents from Web sites, are put in quotation marks; titles of books and other long works, such as entire Web sites, are italicized.

The city of publication is given without a state name. Publishers' names are shortened, usually to the first principal word ("Wiley" for "John Wiley and Sons," for instance), and "University" and "Press" are abbreviated "U" and "P" in the names of university publishers: UP of Florida. The date of publication is the date on the title page or the most recent date on the copyright page.

All works cited entries must include the medium in which a work was published, produced, or delivered. The medium usually appears at the end of the entry, capitalized but neither italicized nor in quotation marks. Typical designations for the medium are "Print," "Web," "Radio," "Television," "CD," "Audiocassette," "Film," "Videocassette," "DVD," "Photograph," "Performance," "Lecture," "MP3 file," and "PDF file." (See specific items throughout this section.)

Listing authors (print and online)

Alphabetize entries in the list of works cited by authors' last names (or by title if a work has no author). The author's name is important because citations in the text of the paper refer to it and readers will be looking for it at the beginning of an entry in the alphabetized list.

NAME CITED IN TEXT

According to Nancy Flynn, . . .

BEGINNING OF WORKS CITED ENTRY

Flynn, Nancy.

1. Single author

author: last
name first   title (book)   city of
publication   publisher   date   medium

Wood, James. *How Fiction Works*. New York: Farrar, 2008. Print.

2. Two or three authors

first author:
last name first   second author:
in normal order   title (book)   city of
publication

Gourevitch, Philip, and Errol Morris. *Standard Operating Procedure*. New York:

publisher   date   medium

Penguin, 2008. Print.

first author:
last name first   other authors:
in normal order   title (newspaper article)

Farmer, John, John Azzarello, and Miles Kara. "Real Heroes, Fake Stories."

newspaper title   date of
publication   page   medium

New York Times 14 Sept. 2008: WK10. Print.

3. Four or more authors Name all the authors or name the first author followed by "et al." (Latin for "and others"). In an in-text citation, use the same form for the authors' names as you use in the works cited entry. See item 7 on page 124.

first author:
last name first   other authors:
in normal order   title (book)

Harris, Shon, Allen Harper, Chris Eagle, and Jonathan Ness. *Gray Hat Hacking*.

edition
number   city of
publication   publisher   date   medium

2nd ed. New York: McGraw, 2007. Print.

4. Organization as author

author: organization name,
not abbreviated   title (book)

National Wildlife Federation. *Rain Check: Conservation Groups Monitor Mercury*

city of
publication   publisher,
with common abbreviations   date

Levels in Milwaukee's Rain. Ann Arbor: Natl. Wildlife Federation, 2001.

medium

Print.

For a publication by a government agency, see item 73. Your in-text citation should also treat the organization as the author (see item 8 on p. 124).

5. Unknown author

Article or other short work

   title (newspaper article)   label   newspaper title date of publication page

"Poverty, by Outdated Numbers." Editorial. *Boston Globe* 20 Sept. 2008: A16.

  medium

Print.

title (TV title (TV   city of   date of
episode) program)   producer network station broadcast broadcast

"Heat." *Frontline*. Prod. Martin Smith. PBS. KTWU,Topeka. 21 Oct. 2008.

   medium

Television.

For other examples of an article with no author and a television program, see items 31 and 65, respectively.

Book, entire Web site, or other long work

          city of
   title (book)   publication publisher date medium

New Concise World Atlas. New York: Oxford UP, 2007. Print.

            title (Web site)

Women of Protest: Photographs from the Records of the National Woman's Party.

       no
 sponsor of site date medium date of access

Lib. of Cong., n.d. Web. 29 Sept. 2008.

Before concluding that the author of an online source is unknown, check carefully (see the tip on p. 122). Also remember that an organization or a government may be the author (see items 4 and 73).

6. Two or more works by the same author If your list of works cited includes two or more works by the same author, first alphabetize the works by title (ignoring the article *A*, *An*, or *The* at the beginning of a title). Use the author's name for the first entry only; for subsequent entries, use three hyphens followed by a period. The three hyphens must stand for exactly the same name or names as in the first entry.

Knopp, Lisa. *Field of Vision*. Iowa City: U of Iowa P, 1996. Print.

---. *The Nature of Home: A Lexicon and Essays*. Lincoln: U of Nebraska P,
      2002. Print.

Books (print)

Items 7–24 apply to print books. For online books, see items 41 and 42. For an illustrated citation of a print book, see page 138.

7. Basic format for a book

author: last
name first · · · · · · · · book title · · · · · · · · · · city of publication · · publisher

Sacks, Oliver. *Musicophilia: Tales of Music and the Brain*. New York: Knopf,

date · medium

2007. Print.

Take the information about the book from its title page and copyright page. Use a short form of the publisher's name; omit terms such as "Press," "Inc.," and "Co." except when naming university presses ("Harvard UP," for example). If the copyright page lists more than one date, use the most recent one.

8. Book with an author and an editor

author: last
name first · · · · · · book title · · · · · · editor's name: in normal order · · city of publication

Plath, Sylvia. *The Unabridged Journals of Sylvia Plath*. Ed. Karen V. Kukil. New York:

imprint-publisher · · date · medium

Anchor-Doubleday, 2000. Print.

The abbreviation "Ed." means "Edited by," so it is the same for one or multiple editors.

Citation at a glance | Book (MLA)

To cite a print book in MLA style, include the following elements:

1 Author
2 Title and subtitle
3 City of publication
4 Publisher
5 Date of publication
6 Medium

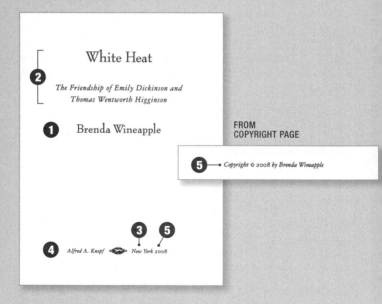

WORKS CITED ENTRY FOR A PRINT BOOK

```
         1               2
Wineapple, Brenda. White Heat: The Friendship of Emily Dickinson and
                              3       4     5     6
    Thomas Wentworth Higginson. New York: Knopf, 2008. Print.
```

For more on citing print books in MLA style, see pages 137–46.

9. Book with an author and a translator   "Trans." means "Translated by," so it is the same for one or multiple translators.

Scirocco, Alfonso. *Garibaldi: Citizen of the World*. Trans. Allan Cameron.
     Princeton: Princeton UP, 2007. Print.

10. Book with an editor   Begin with the editor's name. For one editor, use "ed." (for "editor") after the name; for multiple editors, use "eds." (for "editors").

Lago, Mary, Linda K. Hughes, and Elizabeth MacLeod Walls, eds. *The BBC Talks of
     E. M. Forster, 1929-1960*. Columbia: U of Missouri P, 2008. Print.

11. Graphic narrative or illustrated book   For a book that combines text and illustrations, begin your citation with the person you wish to emphasize (writer, illustrator, artist) and list any other contributors after the title of the book. Use the abbreviation "illus." and other common labels to identify contributors. If the writer and illustrator are the same person, cite the work as you would a book, with no labels.

Weaver, Dustin, illus. *The Tenth Circle*. By Jodi Picoult. New York: Washington
     Square, 2006. Print.

Moore, Alan. *V for Vendetta*. Illus. David Lloyd. New York: Vertigo-DC Comics,
     2008. Print.

Thompson, Craig. *Blankets*. Marietta: Top Shelf, 2005.

12. Book with an author using a pseudonym   Give the author's name as it appears on the title page (the pseudonym), and follow it with the author's real name in brackets.

Dinesen, Isak [Karen Blixen]. *Winter's Tales*. 1942. New York: Vintage, 1993.
     Print.

13. Book in a language other than English   If your readers are not familiar with the language of the book, include a translation of the title in brackets. Capitalize the title according to the conventions of the book's language, and give the original publication information.

Nemtsov, Boris, and Vladimir Milov. *Putin. Itogi. Nezavisimyi Ekspertnyi Doklad* [*Putin. The Results: An Independent Expert Report*]. Moscow: Novaya Gazeta, 2008. Print.

14. Entire anthology An anthology is a collection of works on a common theme, often with different authors for the selections and usually with an editor for the entire volume. The abbreviation "eds." is for multiple editors. If the book has only one editor, use the singular "ed." after the editor's name.

Dumanis, Michael, and Cate Marvin, eds. *Legitimate Dangers: American Poets of the New Century*. Louisville: Sarabande, 2006. Print.

15. One or more selections from an anthology

One selection from anthology

author of selection:
last name first   title of selection   title of anthology

Brouwer, Joel. "The Spots." *Legitimate Dangers: American Poets of the*

editor(s) of anthology: city of
name(s) in normal order   publication   publisher

New Century. Ed. Michael Dumanis and Cate Marvin. Louisville: Sarabande,

pages of
date   selection   medium

2006. 51-52. Print.

The abbreviation "Ed." means "Edited by," so it is the same for one or multiple editors. For an illustrated citation of a selection from an anthology, see pages 142–43.

If you use two or more works from the same anthology in your paper, provide an entry for the entire anthology (see item 14) and give a shortened entry for each selection. Cross-reference the editor(s) of the anthology and give the page number(s) on which the selection appears. Use the medium only in the entry for the complete anthology. Alphabetize the entries in the list of works cited by authors' or editors' last names, as shown on the next page.

Two or more selections, with separate anthology entry

		editor(s) of anthology: last name(s) only	pages of selection
author of selection	title of selection		

Brouwer, Joel. "The Spots." Dumanis and Marvin 51-52.

editor(s) of anthology	title of anthology

Dumanis, Michael, and Cate Marvin, eds. *Legitimate Dangers: American Poets of the*

	city of publication	publisher	date	medium

New Century. Louisville: Sarabande, 2006. Print.

author of selection	title of selection	editor(s) of anthology: last name(s) only	pages of selection

Keith, Sally. "Orphean Song." Dumanis and Marvin 195-96.

16. Edition other than the first   Include the number of the edition (1st, 2nd, 3rd, and so on). If the book has a translator or an editor in addition to the author, give the name of the translator or editor before the edition number, using the abbreviation "Trans." for "Translated by" (see item 9) or "Ed." for "Edited by" (see item 10).

Auletta, Ken. *The Underclass*. 2nd ed. Woodstock: Overlook, 2000. Print.

17. Multivolume work   Include the total number of volumes before the city and publisher, using the abbreviation "vols." If the volumes were published over several years, give the inclusive dates of publication. The abbreviation "Ed." means "Edited by," so it is the same for one or multiple editors.

author: last name first	title	editor's name: in normal order	total volumes	city of publication	publisher

Stark, Freya. *Letters*. Ed. Lucy Moorehead. 8 vols. Salisbury: Compton,

inclusive dates	medium

1974-82. Print.

If you cite only one of the volumes in your paper, include the volume number before the city and publisher and give the date of publication for that volume. After the date, give the medium of publication followed by the total number of volumes. See the example on page 144.

Citation at a glance | Selection from an anthology (MLA)

To cite a selection from an anthology in MLA style, include the following elements:

1 Author of selection
2 Title of selection
3 Title and subtitle of anthology
4 Editor(s) of anthology
5 City of publication

6 Publisher
7 Date of publication
8 Page numbers of selection
9 Medium

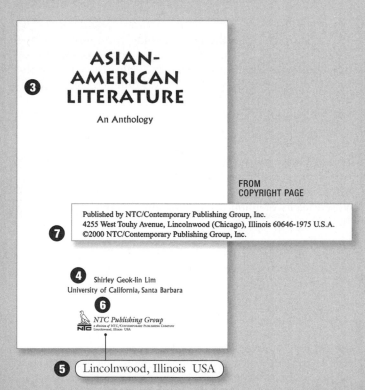

3 ASIAN-AMERICAN LITERATURE

An Anthology

FROM
COPYRIGHT PAGE

7 Published by NTC/Contemporary Publishing Group, Inc.
4255 West Touhy Avenue, Lincolnwood (Chicago), Illinois 60646-1975 U.S.A.
©2000 NTC/Contemporary Publishing Group, Inc.

4 Shirley Geok-lin Lim
University of California, Santa Barbara

6 NTC Publishing Group
a division of NTC/CONTEMPORARY PUBLISHING COMPANY
Lincolnwood, Illinois USA

5 Lincolnwood, Illinois USA

FIRST PAGE OF SELECTION

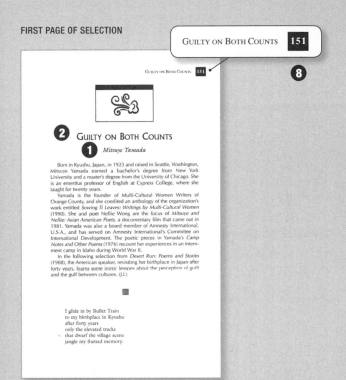

8

GUILTY ON BOTH COUNTS   151

2 GUILTY ON BOTH COUNTS

1 *Mitsuye Yamada*

Born in Kyushu, Japan, in 1923 and raised in Seattle, Washington, Mitsuye Yamada earned a bachelor's degree from New York University and a master's degree from the University of Chicago. She is an emeritus professor of English at Cypress College, where she taught for twenty years.

Yamada is the founder of Multi-Cultural Women Writers of Orange County, and she coedited an anthology of the organization's work entitled *Sowing Ti Leaves: Writings by Multi-Cultural Women* (1990). She and poet Nellie Wong are the focus of *Mitsuye and Nellie: Asian American Poets*, a documentary film that came out in 1981. Yamada was also a board member of Amnesty International, U.S.A., and has served on Amnesty International's Committee on International Development. The poetic pieces in Yamada's *Camp Notes and Other Poems* (1976) recount her experiences in an internment camp in Idaho during World War II.

In the following selection from *Desert Run: Poems and Stories* (1988), the American speaker, revisiting her birthplace in Japan after forty years, learns some ironic lessons about the perception of guilt and the gulf between cultures. (J.J.)

I glide in by Bullet Train
to my birthplace in Kyushu
after forty years
only the elevated tracks
that dwarf the village scene
jangle my framed memory.

WORKS CITED ENTRY FOR A SELECTION FROM AN ANTHOLOGY

┌─── 1 ───┐ ┌─────── 2 ───────┐ ┌─────── 3 ───────┐
Yamada, Mitsuye. "Guilty on Both Counts." *Asian-American Literature: An*

┌─────── 4 ───────┐ ┌─── 5 ───┐ ┌ 6 ┐┌ 7 ┐ ┌─ 8 ─┐
Anthology. Ed. Shirley Geok-lin Lim. Lincolnwood: NTC, 2000. 151-54.

┌─ 9 ─┐
Print.

For more on citing selections from anthologies in MLA style, see pages 140–41.

author: last
name first | title | editor: in normal order | volume cited | city of publication | publisher | date of volume

Stark, Freya. *Letters*. Ed. Lucy Moorehead. Vol. 5. Salisbury: Compton, 1978.

medium | total volumes

Print. 8 vols.

18. Encyclopedia or dictionary entry List the author of the entry (if there is one), the title of the entry, the title of the reference work, the edition number (if any), the date of the edition, and the medium. Volume and page numbers are not necessary because the entries in the source are arranged alphabetically and are therefore easy to locate.

Posner, Rebecca. "Romance Languages." *The Encyclopaedia Britannica: Macropaedia*. 15th ed. 1987. Print.

"Sonata." *The American Heritage Dictionary of the English Language*. 4th ed. 2000. Print.

19. Sacred text Give the title of the edition of the sacred text (taken from the title page), italicized; the editor's or translator's name (if any); publication information; and the medium. Add the name of the version, if there is one.

The Oxford Annotated Bible with the Apocrypha. Ed. Herbert G. May and Bruce M. Metzger. New York: Oxford UP, 1965. Print. Rev. Standard Vers.

The Qur'an: Translation. Trans. Abdullah Yusuf Ali. Elmhurst: Tahrike, 2000. Print.

20. Foreword, introduction, preface, or afterword

author of foreword: last name first | book part | book title

Bennett, Hal Zina. Foreword. *Shimmering Images: A Handy Little Guide to Writing*

author of book: in normal order | city of publication | imprint-publisher | date

Memoir. By Lisa Dale Norton. New York: Griffin-St. Martin's, 2008.

pages of foreword | medium

xiii-xvi. Print.

If the book part has a title, include it in quotation marks immediately after the author's name and before the label for the book part.

Ozick, Cynthia. "Portrait of the Essay as a Warm Body." Introduction. *The Best American Essays 1998*. Ed. Ozick. Boston: Houghton, 1998. xv-xxi. Print.

21. Book with a title in its title   If the book title contains a title normally italicized, neither italicize the internal title nor place it in quotation marks.

Woodson, Jon. *A Study of Joseph Heller's* Catch-22: *Going Around Twice*. New York: Lang, 2001. Print.

If the title within the title is normally put in quotation marks, retain the quotation marks and italicize the entire book title.

Millás, Juan José. *"Personality Disorders" and Other Stories*. Trans. Gregory B. Kaplan. New York: MLA, 2007. Print. MLA Texts and Trans.

22. Book in a series   After the publication information, give the medium of publication and then the series name as it appears on the title page, followed by the series number, if any.

Douglas, Dan. *Assessing Languages for Specific Purposes*. Cambridge: Cambridge UP, 2000. Print. Cambridge Applied Linguistics Ser.

23. Republished book   After the title of the book, give the original publication date, followed by the current publication information. If the republished book contains new material, such as an introduction or afterword, include information about the new material after the original date.

Trilling, Lionel. *The Liberal Imagination*. 1950. Introd. Louis Menand. New York: New York Review of Books, 2008. Print.

24. Publisher's imprint   If a book was published by an imprint (a division) of a publishing company, give the name of the imprint, a hyphen, and the name of the publisher.

Ackroyd, Peter. *The Fall of Troy*. New York: Talese-Doubleday, 2007. Print.

Articles in periodicals (print)

This section shows how to prepare works cited entries for articles in print magazines, journals, and newspapers. See "General guidelines" and "Listing authors" on pages 133 and 134 for how to handle basic parts of the entries. See also "Online sources" on page 150 for articles from Web sites and articles accessed through a library's database.

For articles appearing on consecutive pages, provide the range of pages (see items 25 and 26). When an article does not appear on consecutive pages, give the number of the first page followed by a plus sign: 32+. For dates requiring a month, abbreviate all but May, June, and July. For an illustrated citation of an article in a periodical, see pages 148–49.

25. Article in a journal (paginated by volume or by issue)

author: last name first   article title

Blackburn, Robin. "Economic Democracy: Meaningful, Desirable, Feasible?"

                volume,
journal title   issue   year   page range   medium

      Daedalus 136.3 (2007): 36-45. Print.

26. Article in a monthly magazine

author: last   magazine
name first   article title   title   date: month(s) + year

Lanting, Frans. "Life: A Journey through Time." *Audubon* Nov.-Dec. 2006:

     page
     range   medium

     48-52. Print.

27. Article in a weekly magazine

                             magazine   date: day +   page
author: last name first   article title   title   month + year   range   medium

von Drehle, David. "The Ghosts of Memphis." *Time* 7 Apr. 2008: 34-37. Print.

28. Article in a daily newspaper   Give the page range of the article. If the article does not appear on consecutive pages, use a plus sign (+) after the first page number. If the city of publication is not obvious from the title of the newspaper, include the city in brackets after the name of the newspaper.

If sections are identified by letter, include the section letter as part of the page number. If sections are numbered, include the section number between the date and the page number, using the abbreviation "sec.": 14 Sept. 2009, sec. 2: 21.

Page number with section letter

Include the section letter as part of the page number.

author: last name first   article title   newspaper title   date: day + month + year
McKenna, Phil. "It Takes Just One Village." *New York Times* 23 Sept. 2008,

name of edition   page medium
New England ed.: D1. Print.

Page number with section number

Include the section number immediately after the date, using the abbreviation "sec."

author: last name first   article title   newspaper title   city of publication
Knox, David Blake. "Lord Archer, Storyteller." *Sunday Independent* [Dublin]

date: inverted   section page medium
14 Sept. 2008, sec. 2: 9. Print.

29. Abstract of a journal article   Include the word "Abstract" after the title of the article.

Walker, Joyce. "Narratives in the Database: Memorializing September 11th
     Online." Abstract. *Computers and Composition* 24.2 (2007): 121. Print.

30. Article with a title in its title   Use single quotation marks around a title or another quoted term that appears in an article title. Italicize a title or term normally italicized.

Shen, Min. "'Quite a Moon!' The Archetypal Feminine in *Our Town*." *American
     Drama* 16.2 (2007): 1-14. Print.

Citation at a glance | Article in a periodical (MLA)

To cite an article in a print periodical in MLA style, include the following elements:

1 Author of article
2 Title and subtitle of article
3 Title of periodical
4 Volume and issue number (for scholarly journal)
5 Date or year of publication
6 Page numbers of article
7 Medium

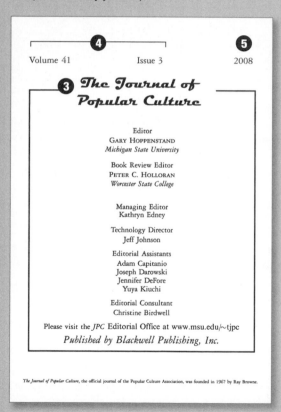

4 Volume 41   Issue 3   **5** 2008

3 *The Journal of Popular Culture*

Editor
GARY HOPPENSTAND
Michigan State University

Book Review Editor
PETER C. HOLLORAN
Worcester State College

Managing Editor
Kathryn Edney

Technology Director
Jeff Johnson

Editorial Assistants
Adam Capitanio
Joseph Darowski
Jennifer DeFore
Yuya Kiuchi

Editorial Consultant
Christine Birdwell

Please visit the *JPC* Editorial Office at www.msu.edu/~tjpc

Published by Blackwell Publishing, Inc.

The Journal of Popular Culture, the official journal of the Popular Culture Association, was founded in 1967 by Ray Browne.

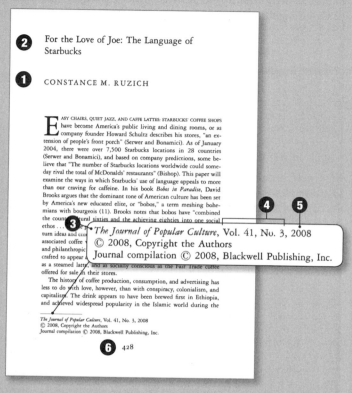

2 For the Love of Joe: The Language of
Starbucks

1 CONSTANCE M. RUZICH

EASY CHAIRS, QUIET JAZZ, AND CAFFE LATTES: STARBUCKS' COFFEE SHOPS
have become America's public living and dining rooms, or as
company founder Howard Schultz describes his stores, "an extension of people's front porch" (Serwer and Bonamici). As of January
2004, there were over 7,500 Starbucks locations in 28 countries
(Serwer and Bonamici), and based on company predictions, some believe that "The number of Starbucks locations worldwide could some-
day rival the total of McDonald's' restaurants" (Bishop). This paper will
examine the ways in which Starbucks' use of language appeals to more
than our craving for caffeine. In his book *Bobos in Paradise*, David
Brooks argues that the dominant tone of American culture has been set
by America's new educated elite, or "bobos," a term meshing bohe-
mians with bourgeois (11). Brooks notes that bobos have "combined
the count... rural sixties and the achieving eighties into one social
ethos ... **3** turn ideas and em... associated coffee ... and philanthropic ... crafted to appear ... as a steamed latte, and as socially conscious as the Fair Trade coffee
offered for sale in their stores.
The history of coffee production, consumption, and advertising has
less to do with love, however, than with conspiracy, colonialism, and
capitalism. The drink appears to have been brewed first in Ethiopia,
and achieved widespread popularity in the Islamic world during the

4 **5** *The Journal of Popular Culture*, Vol. 41, No. 3, 2008
© 2008, Copyright the Authors
Journal compilation © 2008, Blackwell Publishing, Inc.

The Journal of Popular Culture, Vol. 41, No. 3, 2008
© 2008, Copyright the Authors
Journal compilation © 2008, Blackwell Publishing, Inc.

6 428

├——— 1 ———┤ ├——————— 2 ———————┤
Ruzich, Constance M. "For the Love of Joe: The Language of Starbucks."

├————— 3 —————┤ ┌ 4 ┐ ┌ 5 ┐ ┌ 6 ┐ ┌ 7 ┐
Journal of Popular Culture 41.3 (2008): 428-42. Print.

For more on citing print periodical articles in MLA style, see
pages 146–50.

31. Editorial or other unsigned article   Begin with the article title and alphabetize the entry by title in the list of works cited.

"Getting the Message: Communicating Electronically with Doctors Can Spur
    Honesty from Young Patients." Editorial. *Columbus* [OH] *Dispatch* 19
    June 2008: 10A. Print.

32. Letter to the editor

Morris, David. "Fiercely Proud." Letter. *Progressive* Feb. 2008: 6. Print.

33. Book or film review   Name the reviewer and the title of the review, if any, followed by "Rev. of" and the title and author or director of the work reviewed. Add the publication information for the periodical in which the review appears. If the review has no author and no title, begin with "Rev. of" and alphabetize the entry by the first principal word in the title of the work reviewed.

Dodge, Chris. Rev. of *The Radical Jack London: Writings on War and
    Revolution*, ed. Jonah Raskni. *Utne Reader* Sept.-Oct. 2008: 35.
    Print.

Lane, Anthony. "Dream On." Rev. of *The Science of Sleep* and *Renaissance*, dir.
    Michel Gondry. *New Yorker* 25 Sept. 2006: 155-57. Print.

Online sources

MLA guidelines assume that readers can locate most online sources by entering the author, title, or other identifying information in a search engine or a database. Consequently, the *MLA Handbook* does not require a Web address (URL) in citations for online sources. Some instructors may require a URL; for an example, see the note at the end of item 34.

   MLA style calls for a sponsor or a publisher for most online sources. If a source has no sponsor or publisher, use the abbreviation "N.p." (for "No publisher") in the sponsor position. If there is no date of publication or update, use "n.d." (for "no date") after the sponsor. For an article in an online journal or an article from a database, give page numbers if they are available; if they are not, use the abbreviation "n. pag." (See item 37.)

34. Entire Web site

Web site with author

author: last name first   title of Web site   sponsor of site (personal page)   update   medium

Peterson, Susan Lynn. *The Life of Martin Luther.* Susan Lynn Peterson, 2005. Web.

date of access: inverted

24 Jan. 2009.

Web site with organization (group) as author

organization name: not abbreviated   title of Web site   sponsor: abbreviated

American Library Association. *American Library Association.* ALA,

update   medium   date of access: inverted

2008. Web. 14 Jan. 2009.

Web site with no author

title of Web site   sponsor of site   update   medium

Margaret Sanger Papers Project. History Dept., New York U, 18 Oct. 2000. Web.

date of access: inverted

6 Jan. 2009.

Web site with editor

See item 10 (p. 139) for listing the name(s) of editor(s).

Halsall, Paul, ed. *Internet Modern History Sourcebook.* Fordham U, 22 Sept. 2001. Web. 19 Jan. 2009.

Web site with no title

Use the label "Home page" or another appropriate description in place of a title.

Yoon, Mina. Home page. Oak Ridge Natl. Laboratory, 28 Dec. 2006. Web. 12 Jan. 2009.

NOTE: If your instructor requires a URL for Web sources, include the URL, enclosed in angle brackets, at the end of the entry. When a URL in a works cited entry must be divided at the end of a line, break it after a slash. Do not insert a hyphen.

Peterson, Susan Lynn. *The Life of Martin Luther.* Susan Lynn Peterson, 2005.
    Web. 24 Jan. 2009. <http://www.susanlynnpeterson.com/index_files/
    luther.htm>.

35. Short work from a Web site   Short works include articles, poems, and other documents that are not book length or that appear as internal pages on a Web site. For an illustrated citation of a short work from a Web site, see page 154.

Short work with author

author: last name first	title of short work	title of Web site	sponsor	no update date

Shiva, Vandana. "Bioethics: A Third World Issue." *NativeWeb.* NativeWeb, n.d.

medium	date of access: inverted

Web. 22 Jan. 2009.

Short work with no author

title of short work	title of Web site	sponsor of site	update	medium	date of access: inverted

"Sister Aimee." *American Experience.* PBS Online, 2 Apr. 2007. Web. 30 Oct. 2009.

36. Web site with an author using a pseudonym   Begin the entry with the pseudonym and add the author's or creator's real name, if known, in brackets. Follow with the information required for a Web site or a short work from a Web site (see item 34 or 35).

Grammar Girl [Mignon Fogarty]. "What Is the Plural of 'Mouse'?" *Grammar Girl:
    Quick and Dirty Tips for Better Writing.* Holtzbrinck, 16 Sept. 2008. Web.
    10 Nov. 2009.

37. Article in an online scholarly journal

author: last name first — article title

Mason, John Edwin. "'Mannenberg': Notes on the Making of an Icon and Anthem."

journal title — volume, issue year — not paginated medium — date of access: inverted

African Studies Quarterly 9.4 (2007): n. pag. Web. 23 Sept. 2009.

38. Article in an online magazine   Give the author; the title of the article, in quotation marks; the title of the magazine, italicized; the sponsor or publisher of the site (use "N.p." if there is none); the date of publication; the medium; and your date of access.

Burton, Robert. "The Certainty Epidemic." *Salon.com*. Salon Media Group,
   29 Feb. 2008. Web. 18 Jan. 2009.

39. Article in an online newspaper   Give the author, the title of the article, in quotation marks; the title of the newspaper, italicized; the sponsor or publisher of the site (use "N.p." if there is none); the date of publication; the medium; and your date of access.

Smith, Andrew D. "Poll: More than 70% of US Workers Use Internet on the
   Job." *Dallasnews.com*. Dallas Morning News, 25 Sept. 2008. Web.
   29 Oct. 2009.

40. Work from a database   For a source retrieved from a library's subscription database, first list the publication information for the source (see items 25–33) and then provide information about the database. For an illustrated citation of an article from a database, see page 156.

author of source: last name first — title of article — journal title — volume, issue year — page numbers

Heyen, William. "Sunlight." *American Poetry Review* 36.2 (2007): 55-56. *Expanded*

database name — medium — date of access: inverted

Academic ASAP. Web. 24 Sept. 2009.

Citation at a glance | Short work from a Web site (MLA)

To cite a short work from a Web site in MLA style, include the following elements:

1 Author of short work (if any)

2 Title of short work

3 Title of Web site

4 Sponsor of Web site ("N.p." if none)

5 Update date ("n.d." if none)

6 Medium

7 Date of access

INTERNAL PAGE OF WEB SITE

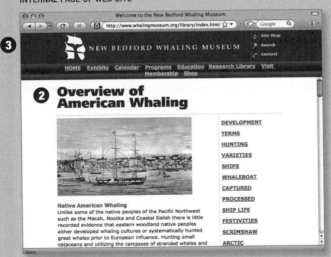

FOOTER ON HOME PAGE

the local area. It houses the most extensive collection of art, artifacts, and manuscripts pertaining to American whaling in the age of sail - late eighteenth century to the early twentieth, when sailing ships dominated merchant trade and whaling.

18 Johnny Cake Hill | New Bedford, MA | 02740-6398 | Tel. (508) 997-0046
Fax: (508) 997-0018 | Library Fax: (508) 207-1064

©Copyright 2006 Old Dartmouth Historical Society / New Bedford Whaling Museum

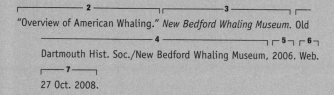

"Overview of American Whaling." *New Bedford Whaling Museum.* Old
Dartmouth Hist. Soc./New Bedford Whaling Museum, 2006. Web.
27 Oct. 2008.

For more on citing sources from Web sites in MLA style, see pages 150–53 and 155–60.

Barrera, Rebeca María. "A Case for Bilingual Education." *Scholastic Parent and Child* Nov.-Dec. 2004: 72-73. *Academic Search Premier.* Web. 1 Feb. 2009.

Williams, Jeffrey J. "Why Today's Publishing World Is Reprising the Past." *Chronicle of Higher Education* 13 June 2008: 8+. *LexisNexis Academic.* Web. 29 May 2009.

41. Online book-length work Cite a book or a book-length work, such as a play or a long poem, as you would a short work from a Web site (see item 35), but italicize the title of the work.

author: last
name first title of long poem title of Web site sponsor of site update
Milton, John. *Paradise Lost: Book I. Poetryfoundation.org.* Poetry Foundation, 2008.

medium date of access:
inverted
Web. 14 Dec. 2009.

Give the print publication information for the work, if available (see items 7–24), followed by the title of the Web site, the medium, and your date of access. See the example on page 157.

Citation at a glance | Article from a database (MLA)

To cite an article from a database in MLA style, include the following elements:

1. Author of article
2. Title of article
3. Title of periodical
4. Volume and issue numbers (for scholarly journal)
5. Date or year of publication
6. Page numbers of article ("n. pag." if there are none)
7. Name of database
8. Medium
9. Date of access

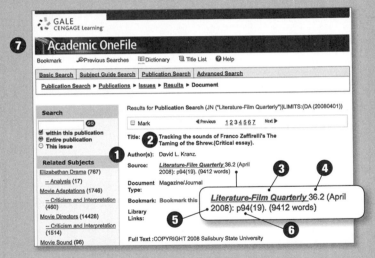

WORKS CITED ENTRY FOR AN ARTICLE FROM A DATABASE

Kranz, David L. "Tracking the Sounds of Franco Zeffirelli's *The Taming of the Shrew*." *Literature-Film Quarterly* 36.2 (2008): 94-112. *Academic OneFile*. Web. 28 Oct. 2008.

For more on citing articles from a database in MLA style, see

pages 153–55.

author: last
name first   book title

Jacobs, Harriet A. *Incidents in the Life of a Slave Girl: Written by Herself*. Ed.

editor of   city of
original book publication year   title of Web site   medium

L. Maria Child. Boston, 1861. *Documenting the American South*. Web.

date of access:
inverted

3 Feb. 2009.

42. Part of an online book   Begin as for a part of a print book (see item 20 on p. 144). If the online book part has no page numbers, use "N. pag." following the publication information. End with the Web site on which the work is found, the medium, and your date of access.

Adams, Henry. "Diplomacy." *The Education of Henry Adams*. Boston: Houghton,
    1918. N. pag. *Bartleby.com: Great Books Online*. Web. 8 Jan. 2009.

43. Digital archives   Digital archives are online collections of documents or records—books, letters, photographs, data—that have been converted to digital form. Cite publication information for the original document, if it is available, using the models throughout this section. Then give the location of the document, if any, neither italicized nor in quotation marks; the name of the archive, italicized; the medium ("Web"); and your date of access.

Fiore, Mark. *Shockwaves*. 18 Oct. 2001. *September 11 Digital Archive*. Web.
    3 Apr. 2009.

Oblinger, Maggie. Letter to Charlie Thomas. 31 Mar. 1895. Nebraska State
    Hist. Soc. *Prairie Settlement: Nebraska Photographs and Family Letters,
    1862-1912*. Web. 3 Apr. 2009.

WPA Household Census for 1047 W. 50th Street, Los Angeles County. 1939. USC
    Lib. Spec. Collections. *USC Libraries Digital Archive*. Web. 12 Mar. 2009.

44. Entry in an online reference work   Give the title of the entry, in quotation marks; the title of the site; the sponsor and update date (use "n.d." if there is none); the medium; and your date of access.

"Native American Church." *Britannica*. Encyclopaedia Britannica, 2008. Web.
29 Jan. 2009.

45. Online poem   Cite as you would a short work from a Web site (item 35) or part of an online book (item 42).

Bell, Acton [Anne Brontë]. "Mementos." *Poems by Currer, Ellis, and Acton Bell*.
London, 1846. N. pag. *A Celebration of Women Writers*. Web. 18 Sept. 2009.

46. Entire Weblog (blog)   Cite a blog as you would an entire Web site (see item 34).

Gristmill. Grist Magazine, 2008. Web. 19 Jan. 2009.

47. Entry or comment in a Weblog (blog)   Cite an entry or a comment (a response to an entry) in a blog as you would a short work from a Web site (see item 35). If the comment or entry has no title, use the label "Weblog entry" or "Weblog comment." Follow with the remaining information as for an entire blog in item 46.

"Social Media: Facebook and MySpace as University Curricula." *Open
Education*. Open Education.net, n.d. Web. 19 Sept. 2008.

Cindy. Weblog comment. *Open Education*. Open Education.net, 5 Sept. 2008.
Web. 14 Aug. 2009.

48. Academic course or department home page   Cite as you would a short work from a Web site (see item 35). For a course home page, begin with the name of the instructor and the title of the course or title of the page (use "Course home page" if there is no other title). For a department home page, begin with the name of the department and the label "Dept. home page."

Marrone, Carole. "355:301: College Writing and Research." *Rutgers School
of Arts and Sciences*. Writing Program, Rutgers U, 2008. Web. 19 Sept.
2008.

Comparative Media Studies. Dept. home page. *Massachusetts Institute of Technology*. MIT, 2006. Web. 6 Oct. 2009.

49. Online video clip   Cite as you would a short work from a Web site (see item 35).

author: last
name first   video title   title of
                                         Web site   sponsor   update

Murphy, Beth. "Tips for a Good Profile Piece." *YouTube*. YouTube, 7 Sept. 2008.

          date of access:
medium   inverted

Web. 19 Apr. 2009.

50. Online abstract   Cite as you would an abstract of a journal article (see item 29), giving whatever print information is available, followed by the medium and your date of access. If you found the abstract in an online periodical database, include the name of the database after the print publication information (see item 40).

Turner, Fred. "Romantic Automatism: Art, Technology, and Collaborative Labor in Cold War America." Abstract. *Journal of Visual Culture* 7.1 (2008): 5. Web. 25 Oct. 2009.

51. Online editorial or letter to the editor   Cite as you would an editorial or a letter to the editor in a print publication (see item 31 or 32), adding information for a short work from a Web site (see item 35).

"Compromise Is Key with Religion at Work." Editorial. *StarTribune.com*. Star Tribune, 18 June 2008. Web. 25 June 2009.

52. Online review   Begin the entry as you would for a review in a magazine or newspaper (see item 33). If the review is published in print as well as online, add publication information as for an article in a periodical (see items 25–28), the Web site on which the review appears, the medium, and your date of access. If the review is published only on the Web, add information as for a short work from a Web site (see item 35). If you found the review in a database, cite as in item 40.

Greer, W. R. "Who's the Fairest One of All?" Rev. of *Mirror, Mirror*, by Gregory
    Maguire. *Reviewsofbooks.com*. Reviewsofbooks.com, 2003. Web. 26 Oct.
    2009.

53. E-mail message   Begin with the writer's name and the subject line. Then write "Message to" followed by the name of the recipient. End with the date of the message and the medium ("E-mail").

Lowe, Walter. "Review Questions." Message to the author. 15 Mar. 2009. E-mail.

54. Posting to an online discussion list   When possible, cite archived versions of postings. If you cannot locate an archived version, keep a copy of the posting for your records. Begin with the author's name, followed by the title or subject line, in quotation marks (use the label "Online posting" if the posting has no title). Then proceed as for a short work from a Web site (see item 35).

Fainton, Peter. "Re: Backlash against New Labour." *Media Lens Message
    Board*. Media Lens, 7 May 2008. Web. 2 June 2008.

55. Entry in a wiki   A wiki is an online reference that is openly edited by its users. Treat an entry in a wiki as you would a short work from a Web site (see item 35). Because wiki content is, by definition, collectively edited and can be updated frequently, do not include an author. Give the title of the entry; the name of the wiki, italicized; the sponsor or publisher of the wiki (use "N.p." if there is none); the date of the last update; the medium; and your date of access.

"Hip Hop Music." *Wikipedia*. Wikimedia Foundation, 26 Sept. 2008. Web.
    18 Mar. 2009.

"Negation in Languages." *UniLang.org*. UniLang, 25 Oct. 2004. Web.
    9 June 2009.

Audio and visual sources (including online versions)

56. Digital file   A digital file is any document or image that exists in digital form, independent of a Web site. To cite a digital file, begin with information required for the source (such as a photograph, a report, a sound recording, or a radio program), following the guidelines for the specific source. Then for the medium, indicate the type of file: "JPEG file," "PDF file," "MP3 file," and so on.

photographer   photograph title   date of composition   location of photograph

Hine, Lewis W. *Girl in Cherryville Mill*. 1908. Prints and Photographs Div., Lib. of

medium: file type

Cong. JPEG file.

"Scenes from a Recession." *This American Life*. Narr. Ira Glass. NPR, 30 Mar.
2009. MP3 file.

National Institute of Mental Health. *What Rescue Workers Can Do*.
Washington: US Dept. of Health and Human Services, 2006. PDF file.

57. Podcast   If you view or listen to a podcast online, cite it as you would a short work from a Web site (see item 35). If you download the podcast and view or listen to it on a computer or portable player, cite it as a digital file (see item 56).

Podcast online

"Calculating the Demand for Charter Schools." Narr. David Guenthner. *Texas
PolicyCast*. Texas Public Policy Foundation, 28 Aug. 2008. Web. 10 Jan.
2009.

Podcast downloaded as digital file

"Calculating the Demand for Charter Schools." Narr. David Guenthner. *Texas
PolicyCast*. Texas Public Policy Foundation, 28 Aug. 2008. MP3 file.

58. Musical score   For both print and online versions, begin with the composer's name; the title of the work, italicized (unless it is named by form, number, and key); and the date of composition. For a print source, give the place of publication; the name of the publisher and date of publication; and the medium. For an online source, give the title of the Web site; the publisher or sponsor of the site; the date of Web publication; the medium; and your date of access.

Handel, G. F. *Messiah: An Oratorio*. N.d. *CCARH Publications: Scores and Parts*.
Center for Computer Assisted Research in the Humanities, 2003. Web.
5 Jan. 2009.

59. Sound recording   Begin with the name of the person you want to emphasize: the composer, conductor ("Cond."), or performer ("Perf."). For a long work, give the title, italicized (unless it is named by form, number, and key); the names of pertinent artists (such as performers, readers, or musicians); and the orchestra and conductor, if relevant. End with the manufacturer, the date, and the medium ("CD," "Audiocassette").

Bizet, Georges. *Carmen*. Perf. Jennifer Laramore, Thomas Moser, Angela
Gheorghiu, and Samuel Ramey. Bavarian State Orch. and Chorus. Cond.
Giuseppe Sinopoli. Warner, 1996. CD.

For a song, put the title in quotation marks. If you include the name of the album or CD, italicize it.

Blige, Mary J. "Be without You." *The Breakthrough*. Geffen, 2005. CD.

60. Film   Typically, begin with the title, italicized, followed by the director ("Dir.") and lead actors ("Perf.") or narrator ("Narr."); the distributor; the year of the film's release; and the medium ("Film," "Videocassette"). If your paper emphasizes a person involved with the film, you may begin with that person, as in the first example in item 61.

movie title   director   major performers
Frozen River. Dir. Courtney Hunt. Perf. Melissa Leo, Charlie McDermott, and Misty

                       release
        distributor   date   medium
        Upham. Sony, 2008. Film.

61. DVD Cite as you would a film, giving "DVD" as the medium. To cite the film as a whole, begin with the film's title, as in item 60. If your paper emphasizes a particular person, begin with that person's name and title, as shown here.

Forster, Marc, dir. *Finding Neverland*. Perf. Johnny Depp, Kate Winslet, Julie
    Christie, Radha Mitchell, and Dustin Hoffman. Miramax, 2004. DVD.

For any other work on DVD, such as an educational work or a game, cite as you would a film, giving information about the author, director, distributor, and so on.

Across the Drafts: Students and Teachers Talk about Feedback. Harvard
    Expository Writing Program, 2005. DVD.

62. Special feature on a DVD Begin with the title of the feature, in quotation marks, and the names of any important contributors, as for films or DVDs (item 60 or 61). End with information about the DVD, as in item 61.

"Sweeney's London." Prod. Eric Young. *Sweeney Todd: The Demon Barber of
    Fleet Street*. Dir. Tim Burton. DreamWorks, 2007. DVD. Disc 2.

63. CD-ROM Treat a CD-ROM as you would any other source, but add the medium ("CD-ROM").

"Pimpernel." *The American Heritage Dictionary of the English Language*.
    4th ed. Boston: Houghton, 2000. CD-ROM.

64. Computer software or video game List the developer or author of the software (if any); the title, italicized; the distributor and date of publication; and the platform or medium.

Firaxis Games. *Sid Meier's Civilization Revolution*. Take-Two Interactive, 2008.
    Xbox 360.

65. Radio or television program Begin with the title of the radio segment or television episode (if any), in quotation marks. Then give the title of the program or series, italicized; information about the program, such as the writer ("By"), director ("Dir."), performers ("Perf."), or narrator ("Narr.");

the network; the local station (if any) and location; the broadcast date; and the medium ("Television," "Radio"). For a program accessed online, after the program information give the network, the original broadcast date, the title of the Web site, the medium ("Web"), and your date of access.

"Machines of the Gods." *Ancient Discoveries*. History Channel. 14 Oct. 2008.
    Television.

"Elif Shafak: Writing under a Watchful Eye." *Fresh Air*. Narr. Terry Gross. Natl.
    Public Radio, 6 Feb. 2007. *NPR.org*. Web. 22 Feb. 2009.

66. Radio or television interview   Begin with the name of the person who was interviewed, followed by the word "Interview" and the interviewer's name, if relevant. End with information about the program as in item 65.

De Niro, Robert, Barry Levinson, and Art Linson. Interview by Charlie Rose.
    Charlie Rose. PBS. WGBH, Boston, 13 Oct. 2008. Television.

67. Live performance   For a live performance of a concert, a play, a ballet, or an opera, begin with the title of the work performed, italicized. Then give the author or composer of the work ("By"); relevant information such as the director ("Dir."), the choreographer ("Chor."), the conductor ("Cond."), or the major performers ("Perf."); the theater, ballet, or opera company, if any; the theater and location; the date of the performance; and the label "Performance."

The Brothers Size. By Tarell Alvin McCraney. Dir. Bijan Sheibani. Young Vic
    Theatre, London. 15 Oct. 2008. Performance.

Symphony no. 4 in G. By Gustav Mahler. Cond. Mark Wigglesworth. Perf.
    Juliane Banse and Boston Symphony Orch. Symphony Hall, Boston.
    17 Apr. 2009. Performance.

68. Lecture or public address   Begin with the speaker's name, followed by the title of the lecture (if any), in quotation marks; the organization sponsoring the lecture; the location; the date; and a label such as "Lecture" or "Address."

Wellbery, David E. "On a Sentence of Franz Kafka." Franke Inst. for the
Humanities. Gleacher Center, Chicago. 1 Feb. 2006. Lecture.

69. Work of art Cite the artist's name; the title of the artwork, italicized; the date of composition; the medium of composition (for instance, "Lithograph on paper," "Photograph," "Charcoal on paper"); and the institution and city in which the artwork is located. For artworks found online, omit the medium of composition and include the title of the Web site, the medium ("Web"), and your date of access.

Constable, John. *Dedham Vale*. 1802. Oil on canvas. Victoria and Albert
Museum, London.

Hessing, Valjean. *Caddo Myth*. 1976. Joslyn Art Museum, Omaha. *Joslyn Art
Museum*. Web. 19 Apr. 2009.

70. Cartoon Give the cartoonist's name; the title of the cartoon, if it has one, in quotation marks; the label "Cartoon" or "Comic strip"; publication information; and the medium. To cite an online cartoon, instead of publication information give the title of the Web site, the sponsor or publisher, the medium, and your date of access.

Keefe, Mike. "Content of Character." Cartoon. *Denverpost.com*. Denver Post,
28 Aug. 2008. Web. 12 Dec. 2008.

71. Advertisement Name the product or company being advertised, followed by the word "Advertisement." Give publication information for the source in which the advertisement appears.

Truth by Calvin Klein. Advertisement. *Vogue* Dec. 2000: 95-98. Print.

Arbella Insurance. Advertisement. *Boston.com*. NY Times, n.d. Web. 3 June
2009.

72. Map or chart   Cite a map or a chart as you would a book or a short work within a longer work. Use the word "Map" or "Chart" following the title. Add the medium and, for an online source, the sponsor or publisher and the date of access.

Joseph, Lori, and Bob Laird. "Driving While Phoning Is Dangerous." Chart.
    USA Today 16 Feb. 2001: 1A. Print.

"Serbia." Map. *Syrena Maps*. Syrena, 2 Feb. 2001. Web. 17 Mar. 2009.

Other sources (including online versions)

This section includes a variety of sources not covered elsewhere. For online sources, consult the appropriate model in this section and also see items 34–55.

73. Government document   Treat the government agency as the author, giving the name of the government followed by the name of the department and the agency, if any. For print sources, add the medium at the end of the entry. For online sources, follow the model for an entire Web site (item 34) or a short work from a Web site (item 35).

government   department   agency

United States. Dept. of the Interior. Office of Inspector General. "Excessive

document title

Indulgences: Personal Use of the Internet at the Department of the Interior."

Web site title   publisher/sponsor   publication date   medium

Office of Inspector General. Dept. of the Interior, Sept. 1999. Web.

date of access: inverted

20 May 2009.

Canada. Minister of Indian Affairs and Northern Dev. *Gathering Strength:*
    Canada's Aboriginal Action Plan. Ottawa: Minister of Public Works and
    Govt. Services Can., 2000. Print.

74. Historical document To cite a historical document, such as the US Constitution or the Canadian Charter of Rights and Freedoms, begin with the document author, if it has one, and then give the document title, neither italicized nor in quotation marks, and the document date. For a print version, continue as for a selection in an anthology (see item 15) or for a book (with the title not italicized). For an online version, cite as a short work from a Web site (see item 35).

Jefferson, Thomas. First Inaugural Address. 1801. *The American Reader.*
    Ed. Diane Ravitch. New York: Harper, 1990. 42-44. Print.

The Virginia Declaration of Rights. 1776. *A Chronology of US
    Historical Documents.* U of Oklahoma Coll. of Law, 2008. Web.
    23 Feb. 2009.

75. Legal source

Legislative act (law)
Begin with the name of the act, neither italicized nor in quotation marks. Then provide the act's Public Law number; its Statutes at Large volume and page numbers; its date of enactment; and the medium of publication.

Electronic Freedom of Information Act Amendments of 1996. Pub. L.
    104-231. 110 Stat. 3048. 2 Oct. 1996. Print.

Court case
Name the first plaintiff and the first defendant. Then give the volume, name, and page number of the law report; the court name; the year of the decision; and publication information. Do not italicize the name of the case. (In the text of the paper, the name of the case is italicized; see item 19 on p. 128.)

Utah v. Evans. 536 US 452. Supreme Court of the US. 2002. *Supreme Court
    Collection.* Legal Information Inst., Cornell U Law School, n.d. Web.
    30 Apr. 2008.

76. Pamphlet or brochure Cite as you would a book (see items 7–24).

Commonwealth of Massachusetts. Dept. of Jury Commissioner. *A Few Facts
    about Jury Duty*. Boston: Commonwealth of Massachusetts, 2004.
    Print.

77. Unpublished dissertation   Begin with the author's name,
followed by the dissertation title in quotation marks; the abbreviation "Diss."; the name of the institution; the year the dissertation was accepted; and the medium of the dissertation.

Jackson, Shelley. "Writing Whiteness: Contemporary Southern Literature in
    Black and White." Diss. U of Maryland, 2000. Print.

78. Published dissertation   For dissertations that have been
published in book form, italicize the title. After the title and
before the book's publication information, give the abbreviation "Diss.," the name of the institution, and the year the dissertation was accepted. Add the medium of publication at the
end.

Damberg, Cheryl L. *Healthcare Reform: Distributional Consequences of an
    Employer Mandate for Workers in Small Firms*. Diss. Rand Graduate
    School, 1995. Santa Monica: Rand, 1996. Print.

79. Abstract of a dissertation   Cite an abstract as you would an
unpublished dissertation. After the dissertation date, give the
abbreviation *DA* or *DAI* (for *Dissertation Abstracts* or *Dissertation Abstracts International*), followed by the volume and issue
numbers; the year of publication; inclusive page numbers or,
if the abstract is not numbered, the item number; and the
medium of publication. For an abstract accessed in an online
database, give the item number in place of the page number,
followed by the name of the database, the medium, and your
date of access.

Chen, Shu-Ling. "Mothers and Daughters in Morrison, Tan, Marshall, and
    Kincaid." Diss. U of Washington, 2000. *DAI* 61.6 (2000): AAT9975963.
    ProQuest Dissertations and Theses. Web. 22 Feb. 2009.

80. Published proceedings of a conference   Cite as you would a book, adding the name, date, and location of the conference after the title.

Urgo, Joseph R., and Ann J. Abadie, eds. *Faulkner and Material Culture*.
Proc. of Faulkner and Yoknapatawpha Conf., 25-29 July 2004, U of
Mississippi. Jackson: UP of Mississippi, 2007. Print.

81. Paper in conference proceedings   Cite as you would a selection in an anthology (see item 15), giving information about the conference after the title and editors of the conference proceedings (see item 80).

Henninger, Katherine R. "Faulkner, Photography, and a Regional Ethics of
Form." *Faulkner and Material Culture*. Ed. Joseph R. Urgo and Ann
J. Abadie. Proc. of Faulkner and Yoknapatawpha Conf., 25-29 July
2004, U of Mississippi. Jackson: UP of Mississippi, 2007. 121-38.
Print.

82. Published interview   Name the person interviewed, followed by the title of the interview (if there is one). If the interview does not have a title, include the word "Interview" after the interviewee's name. Give publication information for the work in which the interview was published.

Armstrong, Lance. "Lance in France." *Sports Illustrated* 28 June 2004: 46+.
Print.

If the name of the interviewer is relevant, include it after the name of the interviewee.

Prince. Interview by Bilge Ebiri. *Yahoo! Internet Life* 7.6 (2001): 82-85. Print.

83. Personal interview   To cite an interview that you conducted, begin with the name of the person interviewed. Then write "Personal interview" or "Telephone interview," followed by the date of the interview.

Akufo, Dautey. Personal interview. 11 Apr. 2009.

84. Personal letter   To cite a letter that you received, begin with the writer's name and add the phrase "Letter to the author," followed by the date. Add the medium ("MS" for "manuscript," or a handwritten letter; "TS" for "typescript," or a typed letter).

Primak, Shoshana. Letter to the author. 6 May 2009. TS.

85. Published letter   Begin with the writer of the letter, the words "Letter to" and the recipient, and the date of the letter (use "N.d." if the letter is undated). Then add the title of the collection and proceed as for a selection in an anthology (see item 15).

Wharton, Edith. Letter to Henry James. 28 Feb. 1915. *Henry James and Edith
     Wharton: Letters, 1900-1915*. Ed. Lyall H. Powers. New York: Scribner's,
     1990. 323-26. Print.

86. Manuscript   Give the author, a title or a description of the manuscript, and the date of composition, followed by the abbreviation "MS" for "manuscript" (handwritten) or "TS" for "typescript." Add the name and location of the institution housing the material. For a manuscript found online, give the preceding information but omit "MS" or "TS." Then list the title of the Web site, the medium ("Web"), and your date of access.

Arendt, Hannah. *Between Past and Present*. N.d. 1st draft. Hannah Arendt
     Papers. MS Div., Lib. of Cong. *Manuscript Division, Library of Congress*.
     Web. 24 Apr. 2009.

MLA information notes (optional)

Researchers who use the MLA system of parenthetical documentation may also use information notes for one of two purposes:

  1. to provide additional material that is important but might interrupt the flow of the paper

2. to refer to several sources or to provide comments on sources

Information notes may be either footnotes or endnotes. Footnotes appear at the foot of the page; endnotes appear on a separate page at the end of the paper, just before the list of works cited. For either style, the notes are numbered consecutively throughout the paper. The text of the paper contains a raised arabic numeral that corresponds to the number of the note.

TEXT

In the past several years, employees have filed a number of lawsuits against employers because of online monitoring practices.[1]

NOTE

1. For a discussion of federal law applicable to electronic surveillance in the workplace, see Kesan 293.

MLA manuscript format

The following guidelines are consistent with advice given in the *MLA Handbook for Writers of Research Papers*, 7th ed. (New York: MLA, 2009), and with typical requirements for student papers. For a sample MLA paper, see pages 176–81.

Formatting the paper

Papers written in MLA style should be formatted as follows.

Materials and font   Use good-quality 8½″ × 11″ white paper. Avoid a font that is unusual or hard to read.

Title and identification   MLA does not require a title page. On the first page of your paper, place your name, your instructor's name, the course title, and the date on separate lines against the left margin. Then center your title. (See p. 176 for a sample first page.)

If your instructor requires a title page, ask for formatting guidelines. A format similar to the one on page 219 may be acceptable.

Pagination   Put the page number preceded by your last name in the upper right corner of each page, one-half inch below the top edge. Use arabic numerals (1, 2, 3, and so on).

Margins, line spacing, and paragraph indents   Leave margins of one inch on all sides of the page. Left-align the text.

Double-space throughout the paper. Do not add extra space above or below the title of the paper or between paragraphs.

Indent the first line of each paragraph one-half inch from the left margin.

Capitalization and italics   In titles of works, capitalize all words except articles (*a, an, the*), prepositions (*to, from, between,* and so on), coordinating conjunctions (*and, but, or, nor, for, so, yet*), and the *to* in infinitives—unless they are the first or last word of the title or subtitle. Follow these guidelines in your paper even if the title appears in all capital or all lowercase letters in the source.

In the text of an MLA paper, when a complete sentence follows a colon, lowercase the first word following the colon unless the sentence is a well-known expression or principle.

Italicize the titles of books and other long works, such as Web sites. Use quotation marks around the titles of periodical articles, short stories, poems, and other short works. (Some instructors may prefer underlining for the titles of long works. Be consistent throughout your paper.)

Long quotations   When a quotation is longer than four typed lines of prose or three lines of verse, set it off from the text by indenting the entire quotation one inch from the left margin. Double-space the indented quotation, and do not add extra space above or below it.

Quotation marks are not needed when a quotation has been set off from the text by indenting. See pages 176–77 for an example.

Web addresses   When a Web address (URL) mentioned in the text of your paper must be divided at the end of a line, break it only after a slash and do not insert a hyphen. For MLA rules on dividing Web addresses in your list of works cited, see page 174.

Headings   MLA neither encourages nor discourages the use of headings and provides no guidelines for their use. If you would like to insert headings in a long essay or research paper, check first with your instructor.

Visuals   MLA classifies visuals as tables and figures (figures include graphs, charts, maps, photographs, and drawings). Label each table with an arabic numeral ("Table 1," "Table 2," and so on) and provide a clear caption that identifies the subject. Capitalize the caption as you would a title; do not italicize the label and caption or place them in quotation marks. The label and caption should appear on separate lines above the table, flush with the left margin.

For a table that you have borrowed or adapted, give the source below the table in a note like the following:

Source: David N. Greenfield and Richard A. Davis; "Lost in Cyberspace: The Web @ Work"; *CyberPsychology and Behavior* 5.4 (2002): 349; print.

For each figure, place the figure number (using the abbreviation "Fig.") and a caption below the figure, flush left.

Capitalize the caption as you would a sentence; include source information following the caption. (When referring to the figure in your paper, use the abbreviation "fig." in parenthetical citations; otherwise spell out the word.) See page 179 for an example of a figure in a paper.

Place visuals in the text, as close as possible to the sentences that relate to them, unless your instructor prefers them in an appendix.

Preparing the list of works cited

Begin the list of works cited on a new page at the end of the paper. Center the title Works Cited about one inch from the top of the page. Double-space throughout. See page 181 for a sample list of works cited.

Alphabetizing the list   Alphabetize the list by the last names of the authors (or editors); if a work has no author or editor, alphabetize by the first word of the title other than *A*, *An*, or *The*.

If your list includes two or more works by the same author, use the author's name for the first entry only. For subsequent entries, use three hyphens followed by a period. List the titles in alphabetical order. (See item 6 on page 136.)

Indenting   Do not indent the first line of each works cited entry, but indent any additional lines one-half inch. This technique highlights the names of the authors, making it easy for readers to scan the alphabetized list. See page 181.

Web addresses   If you need to include a Web address (URL) in a works cited entry, do not insert a hyphen when dividing it at the end of a line. Break the URL only after a slash. Insert angle brackets around the URL. (See the note following item 34 on p. 151.) If your word processing program automatically turns Web addresses into links (by underlining them and changing the color), turn off this feature.

Sample research paper: MLA style

On the following pages is a research paper on the topic of electronic surveillance in the workplace, written by Anna Orlov, a student in a composition class. Orlov's paper is documented with in-text citations and a list of works cited in MLA style.

Orlov 1

Anna Orlov

Professor Willis

English 101

17 March 2009

Online Monitoring:

A Threat to Employee Privacy in the Wired Workplace

As the Internet has become an integral tool of businesses,
company policies on Internet usage have become as common as
policies regarding vacation days or sexual harassment. A 2005 study by
the American Management Association and ePolicy Institute found that
76% of companies monitor employees' use of the Web, and the number
of companies that block employees' access to certain Web sites has
increased 27% since 2001 (1). Unlike other company rules, however,
Internet usage policies often include language authorizing companies
to secretly monitor their employees, a practice that raises questions
about rights in the workplace. Although companies often have
legitimate concerns that lead them to monitor employees' Internet
usage—from expensive security breaches to reduced productivity—the
benefits of electronic surveillance are outweighed by its costs to
employees' privacy and autonomy.

While surveillance of employees is not a new phenomenon,
electronic surveillance allows employers to monitor workers with
unprecedented efficiency. In his book *The Naked Employee*, Frederick
Lane describes offline ways in which employers have been permitted
to intrude on employees' privacy for decades, such as drug testing,
background checks, psychological exams, lie detector tests, and in-store
video surveillance. The difference, Lane argues, between these old
methods of data gathering and electronic surveillance involves quantity:

> Technology makes it possible for employers to gather
> enormous amounts of data about employees, often far

Title is centered.

*Summary and
long quotation are
introduced with
a signal phrase
naming the author.*

*Long quotation is
set off from the
text; quotation
marks are omitted.*

Marginal annotations indicate MLA-style formatting.

> beyond what is necessary to satisfy safety or productivity
> concerns. And the trends that drive technology—faster,
> smaller, cheaper—make it possible for larger and larger
> numbers of employers to gather ever-greater amounts of
> personal data. (3-4)

In an age when employers can collect data whenever employees use
their computers—when they send e-mail, surf the Web, or even arrive
at or depart from their workstations—the challenge for both employers
and employees is to determine how much is too much.

Another key difference between traditional surveillance and
electronic surveillance is that employers can monitor workers' computer
use secretly. One popular monitoring method is keystroke logging, which is
done by means of an undetectable program on employees' computers. The
Web site of a vendor for Spector Pro, a popular keystroke logging program,
explains that the software can be installed to operate in "Stealth" mode
so that it "does not show up as an icon, does not appear in the Windows
system tray, . . . [and] cannot be uninstalled without the Spector Pro
password which YOU specify" ("Automatically"). As Lane explains, these
programs record every key entered into the computer in hidden directories
that can later be accessed or uploaded by supervisors; the programs can
even scan for keywords tailored to individual companies (128-29).

Some experts have argued that a range of legitimate concerns
justifies employer monitoring of employee Internet usage. As *PC World*
columnist Daniel Tynan points out, companies that don't monitor
network traffic can be penalized for their ignorance: "Employees could
accidentally (or deliberately) spill confidential information . . . or allow
worms to spread throughout a corporate network." The ePolicy
Institute, an organization that advises companies about reducing risks
from technology, reported that breaches in computer security cost

Page numbers
are given in
parentheses after
the final period.

Source with an
unknown author
is cited by a
shortened title.

Orlov 3

institutions $100 million in 1999 alone (Flynn). Companies also are
held legally accountable for many of the transactions conducted on
their networks and with their technology. Legal scholar Jay Kesan
points out that the law holds employers liable for employees' actions
such as violations of copyright laws, the distribution of offensive or
graphic sexual material, and illegal disclosure of confidential
information (312).

These kinds of concerns should give employers, in certain
instances, the right to monitor employee behavior. But employers
rushing to adopt surveillance programs might not be adequately
weighing the effect such programs can have on employee morale.
Employers must consider the possibility that employees will perceive
surveillance as a breach of trust that can make them feel like
disobedient children, not responsible adults who wish to perform their
jobs professionally and autonomously.

Yet determining how much autonomy workers should be given
is complicated by the ambiguous nature of productivity in the wired
workplace. On the one hand, computers and Internet access give
employees powerful tools to carry out their jobs; on the other hand,
the same technology offers constant temptations to avoid work. As a
2005 study by *Salary*.com and *America Online* indicates, the Internet
ranked as the top choice among employees for ways of wasting time
on the job; it beat talking with co-workers—the second most
popular method—by a margin of nearly two to one (Frauenheim). Chris
Gonsalves, an editor for *eWeek.com*, argues that the technology has
changed the terms between employers and employees: "While bosses
can easily detect and interrupt water-cooler chatter," he writes, "the
employee who is shopping at Lands' End or IMing with fellow fantasy
baseball managers may actually appear to be working." The gap
between behaviors that are observable to managers and the employee's

No page number
is available for this
Web source.

Orlov 4

Fig. 1. This "Dilbert" comic strip suggests that personal Internet usage is widespread in the workplace (Adams 106).

Illustration has figure number, caption, and source information.

actual activities when sitting behind a computer has created additional motivations for employers to invest in surveillance programs. "Dilbert," a popular cartoon that spoofs office culture, aptly captures how rampant recreational Internet use has become in the workplace (see fig. 1).

But monitoring online activities can have the unintended effect of making employees resentful. As many workers would be quick to point out, Web surfing and other personal uses of the Internet can provide needed outlets in the stressful work environment; many scholars have argued that limiting and policing these outlets can exacerbate tensions between employees and managers. Kesan warns that "prohibiting personal use can seem extremely arbitrary and can seriously harm morale. . . . Imagine a concerned parent who is prohibited from checking on a sick child by a draconian company policy" (315-16). As this analysis indicates, employees can become disgruntled when Internet usage policies are enforced to their full extent.

Orlov uses a brief signal phrase to move from her argument to the words of a source.

Additionally, many experts disagree with employers' assumption that online monitoring can increase productivity. Employment law attorney Joseph Schmitt argues that, particularly for employees who are paid a salary rather than an hourly wage, "a company shouldn't care whether employees spend one or 10 hours on the Internet as long as they are getting their jobs done—and provided that they are not accessing inappropriate sites" (qtd. in Verespej). Other experts even argue that time spent on personal Internet browsing can actually be productive for companies. According to Bill Coleman, an executive at *Salary.com*, "Personal Internet use and casual office conversations often turn into new business ideas or suggestions for gaining operating efficiencies" (qtd. in Frauenheim). Employers, in other words, may benefit from showing more faith in their employees' ability to exercise their autonomy.

> Orlov cites an indirect source: words quoted in another source.

Employees' right to privacy and autonomy in the workplace, however, remains a murky area of the law. Although evaluating where to draw the line between employee rights and employer powers is often a duty that falls to the judicial system, the courts have shown little willingness to intrude on employers' exercise of control over their computer networks. Federal law provides few guidelines related to online monitoring of employees, and only Connecticut and Delaware require companies to disclose this type of surveillance to employees (Tam et al.). "It is unlikely that we will see a legally guaranteed zone of privacy in the American workplace," predicts Kesan (293). This reality leaves employees and employers to sort the potential risks and benefits of technology in contract agreements and terms of employment. With continuing advances in technology, protecting both employers and employees will require greater awareness of these programs, better disclosure to employees, and a more public discussion about what types of protections are necessary to guard individual freedoms in the wired workplace.

Orlov 6

Works Cited

Adams, Scott. *Dilbert and the Way of the Weasel*. New York: Harper, 2002. Print.

American Management Association and ePolicy Institute. "2005 Electronic Monitoring and Surveillance Survey." *American Management Association*. Amer. Management Assn., 2005. Web. 15 Feb. 2009.

"Automatically Record Everything They Do Online! Spector Pro 5.0 FAQ's." *Netbus.org*. Netbus.Org, n.d. Web. 17 Feb. 2009.

Flynn, Nancy. "Internet Policies." *ePolicy Institute*. ePolicy Inst., n.d. Web. 15 Feb. 2009.

Frauenheim, Ed. "Stop Reading This Headline and Get Back to Work." *CNET News.com*. CNET Networks, 11 July 2005. Web. 17 Feb. 2009.

Gonsalves, Chris. "Wasting Away on the Web." *eWeek.com*. Ziff Davis Enterprise Holdings, 8 Aug. 2005. Web. 16 Feb. 2009.

Kesan, Jay P. "Cyber-Working or Cyber-Shirking? A First Principles Examination of Electronic Privacy in the Workplace." *Florida Law Review* 54.2 (2002): 289-332. Print.

Lane, Frederick S., III. *The Naked Employee: How Technology Is Compromising Workplace Privacy*. New York: Amer. Management Assn., 2003. Print.

Tam, Pui-Wing, et al. "Snooping E-mail by Software Is Now a Workplace Norm." *Wall Street Journal* 9 Mar. 2005: B1+. Print.

Tynan, Daniel. "Your Boss Is Watching." *PC World*. PC World Communications, 6 Oct. 2004. Web. 17 Feb. 2009.

Verespej, Michael A. "Inappropriate Internet Surfing." *Industry Week*. Penton Media, 7 Feb. 2000. Web. 16 Feb. 2009.

Heading is centered.

List is alphabetized by authors' last names (or by title when a work has no author).

Abbreviation "n.d." indicates that the online source has no update date.

First line of each entry is at the left margin; extra lines are indented ½".

Double-spacing is used throughout.

A work with four authors is listed by the first author's name and the abbreviation "et al." (for "and others").

APA Style: The Social Sciences

In most social science classes, you will be asked to use the APA system for documenting sources, which is set forth in the *Publication Manual of the American Psychological Association*, 6th ed. (Washington: APA, 2010). APA recommends in-text citations that refer readers to a list of references.

An in-text citation gives the author of the source (often in a signal phrase), the year of publication, and at times a page number in parentheses. At the end of the paper, a list of references provides publication information about the source (see p. 228 for a sample list of references).

IN-TEXT CITATION

Yanovski and Yanovski (2002) reported that "the current state of the treatment for obesity is similar to the state of the treatment of hypertension several decades ago" (p. 600).

ENTRY IN THE LIST OF REFERENCES

Yanovski, S. Z., & Yanovski, J. A. (2002). Drug therapy: Obesity. *The New England Journal of Medicine, 346,* 591-602.

For a reference list that includes this entry, see page 228.

APA in-text citations

APA's in-text citations provide at least the author's last name and the year of publication. For direct quotations and some paraphrases, a page number is given as well.

NOTE: APA style requires the use of the past tense or the present perfect tense in signal phrases introducing cited material: *Smith (2005) reported; Smith (2005) has argued.*

1. Basic format for a quotation   Ordinarily, introduce the quotation with a signal phrase that includes the author's last name

Directory to APA in-text citation models

followed by the year of publication in parentheses. Put the page number preceded by "p." (or "pp." for more than one page) in parentheses after the quotation.

> Critser (2003) noted that despite growing numbers of overweight Americans, many health care providers still "remain either in ignorance or outright denial about the health danger to the poor and the young" (p. 5).

If the author is not named in the signal phrase, place the author's name, the year, and the page number in parentheses after the quotation: (Critser, 2003, p. 5).

NOTE: APA style requires the year of publication in an in-text citation. Do not include a month, even if the entry in the reference list includes the month.

2. Basic format for a summary or a paraphrase Include the author's last name and the year either in a signal phrase introducing the material or in parentheses following it. Give a page number to help readers find the passage. For online sources without page numbers, see "No page numbers" on page 187.

Yanovski and Yanovski (2002) explained that sibutramine suppresses appetite by blocking the reuptake of the neurotransmitters serotonin and norepinephrine in the brain (p. 594).

Sibutramine suppresses appetite by blocking the reuptake of the neurotransmitters serotonin and norepinephrine in the brain (Yanovski & Yanovski, 2002, p. 594).

3. Work with two authors Name both authors in the signal phrase or the parentheses each time you cite the work. In the parentheses, use "&" between the authors' names; in the signal phrase, use "and."

According to Sothern and Gordon (2003), "Environmental factors may contribute as much as 80% to the causes of childhood obesity" (p. 104).

Obese children often engage in limited physical activity (Sothern & Gordon, 2003, p. 104).

4. Work with three to five authors Identify all authors in the signal phrase or the parentheses the first time you cite the source.

In 2003, Berkowitz, Wadden, Tershakovec, and Cronquist concluded, "Sibutramine . . . must be carefully monitored in adolescents, as in adults, to control increases in [blood pressure] and pulse rate" (p. 1811).

In subsequent citations, use the first author's name followed by "et al." in either the signal phrase or the parentheses.

As Berkowitz et al. (2003) advised, "Until more extensive safety and efficacy data are available, . . . weight-loss medications should be used only on an experimental basis for adolescents" (p. 1811).

5. Work with six or more authors Use the first author's name followed by "et al." in the signal phrase or the parentheses.

McDuffie et al. (2002) tested 20 adolescents, aged 12-16, over a three-month period and found that orlistat, combined with behavioral therapy, produced an average weight loss of 4.4 kg, or 9.7 pounds (p. 646).

6. Work with unknown author   If the author is unknown, mention the work's title in the signal phrase or give the first word or two of the title in the parenthetical citation. Titles of articles and chapters are put in quotation marks; titles of books and reports are italicized. (For online sources with no author, see p. 187.)

> Children struggling to control their weight must also struggle with the pressures of television advertising that, on the one hand, encourages the consumption of junk food and, on the other, celebrates thin celebrities ("Television," 2002).

NOTE: In the rare case when "Anonymous" is specified as the author, treat it as if it were a real name: (Anonymous, 2001). In the list of references, also use the name Anonymous as author.

7. Organization as author   If the author is a government agency or another organization, name the organization in the signal phrase or in the parenthetical citation the first time you cite the source.

> Obesity puts children at risk for a number of medical complications, including type 2 diabetes, hypertension, sleep apnea, and orthopedic problems (Henry J. Kaiser Family Foundation, 2004, p. 1).

If the organization has a familiar abbreviation, you may include it in brackets the first time you cite the source and use the abbreviation alone in later citations.

FIRST CITATION   (Centers for Disease Control and Prevention [CDC], 2009)

LATER CITATIONS   (CDC, 2009)

8. Authors with the same last name   To avoid confusion, use initials with the last names if your reference list includes two or more authors with the same last name.

> Research by E. Smith (1989) revealed that . . .

9. Two or more works by the same author in the same year   When your list of references includes more than one work by the same author in the same year, use lowercase letters ("a," "b," and so on) with the year to order the entries in the reference list. (See item 6 on p. 192.) Use those same letters with the year in the in-text citation.

> Research by Durgin (2003b) has yielded new findings about the role of counseling in treating childhood obesity.

10. Two or more works in the same parentheses   When your parenthetical citation names two or more works, put them in the same order that they appear in the reference list, separated with semicolons.

> Researchers have indicated that studies of pharmacological treatments for childhood obesity are inconclusive (Berkowitz et al., 2003; McDuffie et al., 2002).

11. Personal communication   Personal interviews, memos, letters, e-mail, and similar unpublished communications should be cited in the text only, not in the reference list. (Use the first initial with the last name in parentheses.)

> One of Atkinson's colleagues, who has studied the effect of the media on children's eating habits, has contended that advertisers for snack foods will need to design ads responsibly for their younger viewers (F. Johnson, personal communication, October 20, 2009).

12. Electronic source   When possible, cite electronic sources, including online sources, as you would any other source, giving the author and the year.

> Atkinson (2001) found that children who spent at least four hours a day watching TV were less likely to engage in adequate physical activity during the week.

Electronic sources sometimes lack authors' names, dates, or page numbers.

Unknown author

If no author is named, mention the title of the source in the signal phrase or give the first word or two of the title in the parentheses (see also item 6). (If an organization serves as the author, see item 7.)

> The body's basal metabolic rate, or BMR, is a measure of its at-rest energy requirement ("Exercise," 2003).

Unknown date

When the date is unknown, use the abbreviation "n.d." (for "no date").

> Attempts to establish a definitive link between television programming and children's eating habits have been problematic (Magnus, n.d.).

No page numbers

APA ordinarily requires page numbers for quotations, summaries, and paraphrases. When an electronic source lacks stable numbered pages, include paragraph numbers or headings to help readers locate the passage being cited.

If the source has numbered paragraphs, use the paragraph number preceded by the abbreviation "para.": (Hall, 2008, para. 5). If the source contains headings, cite the appropriate heading in parentheses; you may also indicate the paragraph under the heading that you are referring to, even if the paragraphs are not numbered.

> Hoppin and Taveras (2004) pointed out that several other medications were classified by the Drug Enforcement Administration as having the "potential for abuse" (Weight-Loss Drugs section, para. 6).

NOTE: Electronic files in portable document format (PDF) often have stable page numbers. For such sources, give the page number in the parenthetical citation.

13. Indirect source If you use a source that was cited in another source (a secondary source), name the original source in your signal phrase. List the secondary source in your reference list and include it in your parenthetical citation, preceded by the words "as cited in." In the following example, Satcher is the original source, and Critser is the secondary source, given in the reference list.

> Former surgeon general Dr. David Satcher described "a nation of young people seriously at risk of starting out obese and dooming themselves to the difficult task of overcoming a tough illness" (as cited in Critser, 2003, p. 4).

14. Sacred or classical text Identify the text, the version or edition you used, and the relevant part (chapter, verse, line). It is not necessary to include the source in the reference list.

> Peace activists have long cited the biblical prophet's vision of a world without war: "And they shall beat their swords into plowshares, and their spears into pruning hooks; nation shall not lift up sword against nation, neither shall they learn war any more" (Isaiah 2:4, Revised Standard Version).

APA list of references

In APA style, the alphabetical list of works cited, which appears at the end of the paper, is titled "References." For advice on preparing the reference list, see pages 216–18. For a sample reference list, see page 228.

Alphabetize entries in the list of references by authors' last names; if a work has no author, alphabetize it by its title. The first element of each entry is important because citations in the text of the paper refer to it and readers will be looking for it in the alphabetized list. The date of publication appears immediately after the first element of the citation.

In APA style, titles of books are italicized; titles of articles are neither italicized nor put in quotation marks. (For rules on capitalization of titles, see p. 215.)

Directory to APA references (bibliographic entries)

→

> ## Directory to APA references (bibliographic entries) (*continued*)
>
> **Other sources (including online versions)**
>
> 51. Dissertation from a database, 209
> 52. Unpublished dissertation, 209
> 53. Government document, 210
> 54. Report from a private organization, 210
> 55. Legal source, 210
> 56. Conference proceedings, 210
> 57. Paper presented at a meeting or symposium (unpublished), 210
> 58. Poster session at a conference, 211
>
> 59. Map or chart, 211
> 60. Advertisement, 211
> 61. Published interview, 211
> 62. Lecture, speech, or address, 211
> 63. Work of art or photograph, 211
> 64. Brochure, pamphlet, or fact sheet, 211
> 65. Presentation slides, 212
> 66. Film or video (motion picture), 212
> 67. Television program, 212
> 68. Sound recording, 213
> 69. Computer software or video game, 213

General guidelines for listing authors (print and online)

In APA style, all authors' names are inverted (the last name comes first), and initials only are used for all first and middle names.

NAME AND DATE CITED IN TEXT

Duncan (2008) has reported that . . .

BEGINNING OF ENTRY IN THE LIST OF REFERENCES

Duncan, B. (2008).

1. Single author

author: last name
+ initial(s) year   title (book)

Egeland, J. (2008). *A billion lives: An eyewitness report from the frontlines of*

place of publication publisher

humanity. New York, NY: Simon & Schuster.

2. Multiple authors List up to seven authors by last names followed by initials. Use an ampersand (&) before the name of the last author. If there are more than seven authors, list the first six followed by three ellipsis dots and the last author's name. (See p. 184 for citing works with multiple authors in your paper.)

Two to seven authors

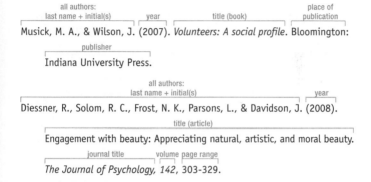

all authors:
last name + initial(s)   year   title (book)   place of publication

Musick, M. A., & Wilson, J. (2007). *Volunteers: A social profile.* Bloomington:

publisher

Indiana University Press.

all authors:
last name + initial(s)   year

Diessner, R., Solom, R. C., Frost, N. K., Parsons, L., & Davidson, J. (2008).

title (article)

Engagement with beauty: Appreciating natural, artistic, and moral beauty.

journal title   volume page range

The Journal of Psychology, 142, 303-329.

Eight or more authors

Mulvaney, S. A., Mudasiru, E., Schlundt, D. G., Baughman, C. L., Fleming,
    M., VanderWoude, A., . . . Rothman, R. (2008). Self-management in
    Type 2 diabetes: The adolescent perspective. *The Diabetes Educator,*
    34, 118-127.

3. Organization as author

author:
organization name   year   title (book)

American Psychiatric Association. (1994). *Diagnostic and statistical manual of*

edition   place   organization as author
number   of publication   and publisher

mental disorders (4th ed.). Washington, DC: Author.

If the publisher is not the same as the author, give the publisher's name as you would for any other source.

4. Unknown author   Begin the entry with the work's title.

| | | place of | |
| title (book) | year | publication | publisher |

New concise world atlas. (2007). New York, NY: Oxford University Press.

| | year + date | | volume, | page |
| title (article) | (for weekly publication) | journal title | issue | range |

Order in the jungle. (2008, March 15). *The Economist, 386*(8571), 83-85.

5. Two or more works by the same author   Use the author's name for all entries. List the entries by year, the earliest first.

Barry, P. (2007, December 8). Putting tumors on pause. *Science News, 172*, 365.

Barry, P. (2008, August 2). Finding the golden genes. *Science News, 174*, 16-21.

6. Two or more works by the same author in the same year   List the works alphabetically by title. In the parentheses, following the year add "a," "b," and so on. Use these same letters when giving the year in the in-text citation. (See also p. 217.)

Elkind, D. (2008a, Spring). Can we play? *Greater Good, 4*(4), 14-17.

Elkind, D. (2008b, June 27). The price of hurrying children [Web log post]. Retrieved from http://blogs.psychologytoday.com/blog/digital-children

Articles in periodicals (print)

Periodicals include scholarly journals, magazines, and newspapers. For a journal or a magazine, give only the volume number if the publication is paginated continuously through each volume; give the volume and issue numbers if each issue of the volume begins on page 1. Italicize the volume number and put the issue number, not italicized, in parentheses.

For all periodicals, when an article appears on consecutive pages, provide the range of pages. When an article does not appear on consecutive pages, give all page numbers: A1, A17. (See also "Online sources" beginning on p. 200 for on-line articles and articles accessed through a library's database.) For an illustrated citation of an article in a periodical, see page 194.

7. Article in a journal

author: last name
+ initial(s)   year   article title
Zhang, L.-F. (2008). Teachers' styles of thinking: An exploratory study. *The Journal*

                            page
    journal title   volume   range
    of Psychology, 142, 37-55.

8. Article in a magazine   Cite as a journal article, but give the year and the month for monthly magazines; add the day for weekly magazines.

McKibben, B. (2007, October). Carbon's new math. *National Geographic, 212*(4), 32-37.

9. Article in a newspaper

author: last name   year + month + day
+ initial(s)   (for daily publication)   article title
Svoboda, E. (2008, October 21). Deep in the rain forest, stalking the next

                            page
            newspaper title   number
    pandemic. *The New York Times*, p. D5.

Give the year, month, and day for daily and weekly newspapers. Use "p." or "pp." before page numbers.

10. Article with three to seven authors

Ungar, M., Brown, M., Liebenberg, L., Othman, R., Kwong, W. M., Armstrong, M., & Gilgun, J. (2007). Unique pathways to resilience across cultures. *Adolescence, 42*, 287-310.

Citation at a glance | Article in a periodical (APA)

To cite an article in a print periodical in APA style, include the following elements:

1 Author
2 Year of publication
3 Title of article
4 Name of periodical

5 Volume number; issue number, if required (see p. 192)
6 Page numbers of article

REFERENCE LIST ENTRY FOR AN ARTICLE IN A PRINT PERIODICAL

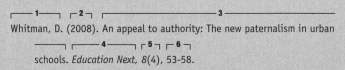

Whitman, D. (2008). An appeal to authority: The new paternalism in urban

schools. *Education Next, 8*(4), 53-58.

For variations on citing articles in print periodicals in APA style, see pages 192–96.

11. Article with eight or more authors List the first six authors followed by three ellipsis dots and the last author.

Krippner, G., Granovetter, M., Block, F., Biggart, N., Beamish, T., Hsing, Y.,
     . . . O'Riain, S. (2004). Polanyi Symposium: A conversation on
     embeddedness. *Socio-Economic Review, 2,* 109-135.

12. Abstract of a journal article

Lahm, K. (2008). Inmate-on-inmate assault: A multilevel examination of
     prison violence [Abstract]. *Criminal Justice and Behavior, 35*(1),
     120-137.

13. Letter to the editor Letters to the editor appear in journals, magazines, and newspapers. Follow the appropriate model (see items 7–9), and insert the words "Letter to the editor" in brackets after the title of the letter. If the letter has no title, use the bracketed words as the title.

Park, T. (2008, August). Defining the line [Letter to the editor]. *Scientific
     American, 299*(2), 10.

14. Editorial or other unsigned article

The global justice movement [Editorial]. (2005). *Multinational Monitor,
     26*(7/8), 6.

15. Newsletter article

Setting the stage for remembering. (2006, September). *Mind, Mood, and
     Memory, 2*(9), 4-5.

16. Review Give the author and title of the review (if any) and, in brackets, the type of work, the title, and the author for a book or the year for a motion picture. If the review has no author or title, use the material in brackets as the title.

Applebaum, A. (2008, February 14). A movie that matters [Review of the
     motion picture *Katyn,* 2007]. *The New York Review of Books, 55*(2), 13-15.

Agents of change. (2008, February 2). [Review of the book *The power of unreasonable people: How social entrepreneurs create markets that change the world,* by J. Elkington & P. Hartigan]. *The Economist, 386*(8565), 94.

Books (print)

Items 17–29 apply to print books. For online books, see items 36 and 37. For an illustrated citation of a print book, see page 198.

Take the information about a book from its title page and copyright page. If more than one place of publication is listed, use only the first. Give the city and state (abbreviated) for all US cities or the city and the country (not abbreviated) for all non-US cities; also include the province (not abbreviated) for Canadian cities. Do not give a state if the publisher's name includes it (as in many university presses, for example).

17. Basic format for a book

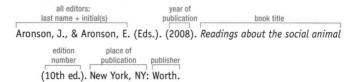

author: last
name + initial(s)   year of publication   book title

McKenzie, F. R. (2008). *Theory and practice with adolescents: An applied approach.*

place of publication   publisher

Chicago, IL: Lyceum Books.

18. Book with an editor

all editors:
last name + initial(s)   year of publication   book title

Aronson, J., & Aronson, E. (Eds.). (2008). *Readings about the social animal*

edition
number   place of publication   publisher

(10th ed.). New York, NY: Worth.

The abbreviation "Eds." is for multiple editors. If the book has one editor, use "Ed."

19. Book with an author and an editor

author: last name + initial(s)   year of publication   book title   name(s) of editor(s): in normal order

McLuhan, M. (2003). *Understanding me: Lectures and interviews* (S. McLuhan

place of publication (city, province, country)   publisher

& D. Staine, Eds.). Toronto, Ontario, Canada: McClelland & Stewart.

The abbreviation "Eds." is for multiple editors. If the book has one editor, use "Ed."

20. Book with an author and a translator   After the title, name the translator, followed by "Trans.," in parentheses. Add the original date of publication at the end of the entry.

Steinberg, M. D. (2003). *Voices of revolution, 1917* (M. Schwartz, Trans.). New Haven, CT: Yale University Press. (Original work published 2001)

21. Edition other than the first

O'Brien, J. A. (Ed.). (2006). *The production of reality: Essays and readings on social interaction* (4th ed.). Thousand Oaks, CA: Pine Forge Press.

22. Article or chapter in an edited book or an anthology

author of chapter: last name + initial(s)   year of publication   title of chapter

Denton, N. A. (2006). Segregation and discrimination in housing. In R. G.

book editor(s): in normal order   book title

Bratt, M. E. Stone, & C. Hartman (Eds.), *A right to housing: Foundation of*

page range for chapter   place of publication   publisher

a new social agenda (pp. 61-81). Philadelphia, PA: Temple University Press.

The abbreviation "Eds." is for multiple editors. If the book has one editor, use "Ed."

Citation at a glance | Book (APA)

To cite a print book in APA style, include the following elements:

1. Author
2. Year of publication
3. Title and subtitle
4. Place of publication
5. Publisher

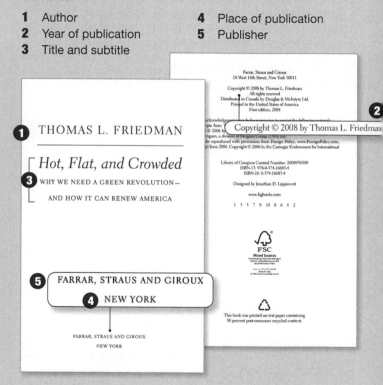

1 THOMAS L. FRIEDMAN

Hot, Flat, and Crowded
3 WHY WE NEED A GREEN REVOLUTION—
AND HOW IT CAN RENEW AMERICA

5 FARRAR, STRAUS AND GIROUX
4 NEW YORK

FARRAR, STRAUS AND GIROUX
NEW YORK

Farrar, Straus and Giroux
18 West 18th Street, New York 10011

Copyright © 2008 by Thomas L. Friedman
All rights reserved
Distributed in Canada by Douglas & McIntyre Ltd.
Printed in the United States of America
First edition, 2008

2 Copyright © 2008 by Thomas L. Friedman

Library of Congress Control Number: 2008930589
ISBN-13: 978-0-374-16685-4
ISBN-10: 0-374-16685-4

Designed by Jonathan D. Lippincott

www.fsgbooks.com

1 3 5 7 9 10 8 6 4 2

This book was printed on text paper containing
30 percent post-consumer recycled content.

REFERENCE LIST ENTRY FOR A PRINT BOOK

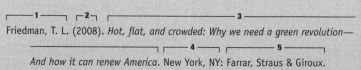

┌──1──┐ ┌─2─┐ ┌────────────────────────3────────────────────────
Friedman, T. L. (2008). *Hot, flat, and crowded: Why we need a green revolution—*

──────────────────────┐ ┌──4──┐ ┌───────5───────┐
And how it can renew America. New York, NY: Farrar, Straus & Giroux.

For more on citing print books in APA style, see pages 196–99.

23. Multivolume work   Give the number of volumes after the title.

Luo, J. (Ed.). (2005). *China today: An encyclopedia of life in the People's Republic* (Vols. 1-2). Westport, CT: Greenwood Press.

24. Introduction, preface, foreword, or afterword

Gore, A. (2000). Foreword. In B. Katz (Ed.), *Reflections on regionalism* (pp. ix-x). Washington, DC: Brookings Institution Press.

25. Dictionary or other reference work

Leong, F. T. L. (Ed.). (2008). *Encyclopedia of counseling* (Vols. 1-4). Thousand Oaks, CA: Sage.

26. Article in a reference work

Konijn, E. A. (2008). Affects and media exposure. In W. Donsbach (Ed.), *The international encyclopedia of communication* (Vol. 1, pp. 123-129). Malden, MA: Blackwell.

27. Republished book

Mailer, N. (2008). *Miami and the siege of Chicago: An informal history of the Republican and Democratic conventions of 1968*. New York, NY: New York Review Books. (Original work published 1968)

28. Book with a title in its title   If the book title contains another book title or an article title, neither italicize the internal title nor place it in quotation marks.

Marcus, L. (Ed.). (1999). *Sigmund Freud's* The interpretation of dreams: *New interdisciplinary essays*. Manchester, England: Manchester University Press.

29. Sacred or classical text   It is not necessary to list sacred works such as the Bible or the Qur'an or classical Greek and Roman works in your reference list. See item 14 on page 188 for how to cite these sources in the text of your paper.

Online sources

When citing an online article, include publication information as for a print periodical (see items 7–16) and add information about the online version (see items 30–35).

Online articles and books sometimes include a DOI (digital object identifier). APA uses the DOI, when available, in place of a URL in reference list entries.

Use a retrieval date for an online source only if the content is likely to change. Most of the examples in this section do not show a retrieval date because the content of the sources is stable; if you are unsure about whether to use a retrieval date, include the date or consult your instructor.

If you must break a DOI or a URL at the end of a line, break it after a double slash or before any other mark of punctuation; do not add a hyphen. Do not put a period at the end of the entry.

30. Article in an online journal

author: last
name + initial(s) | year of publication | article title | journal title

Whitmeyer, J. M. (2000). Power through appointment. *Social Science Research,*

volume page range | DOI

  29, 535-555. doi:10.1006/ssre.2000.0680

If there is no DOI, include the URL for the journal's home page.

Ashe, D. D., & McCutcheon, L. E. (2001). Shyness, loneliness, and attitude
    toward celebrities. *Current Research in Social Psychology, 6*, 124-133.
    Retrieved from http://www.uiowa.edu/~grpproc/crisp/crisp.html

31. Article in an online magazine   Treat as an article in a print magazine (see item 8), adding whatever publication information is available. Give the URL for the magazine's home page.

Rupley, S. (2010, February 26). The myth of the benign monopoly. *Salon*.
    Retrieved from http://www.salon.com/

32. Article in an online newspaper   Treat as an article in a print newspaper (see item 9), adding the URL for the newspaper's home page.

Watson, P. (2008, October 19). Biofuel boom endangers orangutan habitat.
   Los Angeles Times. Retrieved from http://www.latimes.com/

33. Article published only online   If an article in a journal, magazine, or newspaper appears only online, give whatever publication information is available in the source and add the description "Supplemental material" in brackets following the article title.

Samuel, T. (2009, March 27). Mind the wage gap [Supplemental material].
   The American Prospect. Retrieved from http://www.prospect.org/

34. Article from a database   Start with the publication information for the source (see items 7–16). If the database entry includes a DOI for the article, use the DOI number at the end. For an illustrated citation of a work from a database, see page 202.

```
            all authors:
            last name + initial(s)      year                        article title
┌──────────────────────────────┐  ┌──────┐  ┌──────────────────────────────────────────┐
Eskritt, M., & McLeod, K. (2008). Children's note taking as a mnemonic tool.
                                                        page
                  journal title                volume  range       DOI
┌──────────────────────────────────────────┐  ┌──┐  ┌─────┐  ┌──────────┐
Journal of Experimental Child Psychology, 101, 52-74. doi:10.1016
┌──────────────────────────┐
/jecp.2008.05.007
```

If there is no DOI, include the URL for the home page of the journal.

Howard, K. R. (2007). Childhood overweight: Parental perceptions and
   readiness for change. *The Journal of School Nursing, 23,* 73-79.
   Retrieved from http://jsn.sagepub.com/

Citation at a glance | Article from a database (APA)

To cite an article from a database in APA style, include the following elements:

1 Author(s)
2 Date of publication
3 Title of article
4 Name of periodical
5 Volume number; issue number, if required (see p. 192)

6 Page range
7 DOI (digital object identifier)
8 URL for journal's home page (if there is no DOI)

ON-SCREEN VIEW OF DATABASE RECORD

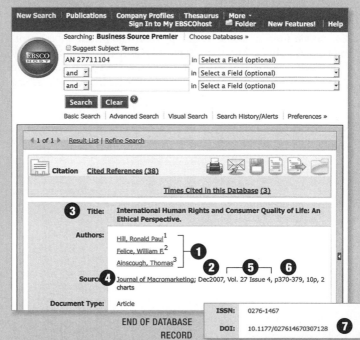

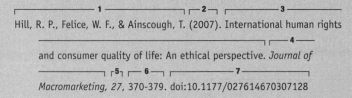

For more on citing articles from a database in APA style, see item 34.

35. Abstract for an online article

Brockerhoff, E. G., Jactel, H., Parrotta, J. A., Quine, C. P., & Sayer, J. (2008). Plantation forests and biodiversity: Oxymoron or opportunity? [Abstract]. *Biodiversity and Conservation, 17*, 925-951. doi:10.1007/s10531-008-9380-x

36. Online book

Adams, B. (2004). *The theory of social revolutions*. Retrieved from http://www.gutenberg.org/catalog/world/readfile?fk_files=44092 (Original work published 1913)

37. Chapter in an online book

Clinton, S. J. (1999). What can be done to prevent childhood obesity? In *Understanding childhood obesity* (pp. 81-98). Retrieved from http://www.questia.com/

38. Online reference work

Swain, C. M. (2004). Sociology of affirmative action. In N. J. Smelser & P. B. Baltes (Eds.), *International encyclopedia of the social and behavioral sciences*. Retrieved from http://www.sciencedirect.com/science/referenceworks/9780080430768

Use a retrieval date only if the content of the work is likely to change.

39. Document from a Web site   List as many of the following elements as are available: author's name, publication date (or "n.d." if there is no date), title (in italics), and URL. Give your retrieval date only if the content of the source is likely to change.

Source with date

all authors: online publication
last name + initial(s)   date: year + month   document title

Cain, A., & Burris, M. (1999, April). *Investigation of the use of mobile*

URL

phones while driving. Retrieved from http://www.cutr.usf.edu/pdf

/mobile_phone.PDF

Source with no date

Archer, D. (n.d.). *Exploring nonverbal communication*. Retrieved from http://
    nonverbal.ucsc.edu

Source with no author

If a source has no author, begin with the title and follow it with the date in parentheses.

What causes Alzheimer's disease? (2008). Retrieved from http://
    www.memorystudy.org/alzheimers_causes.htm

40. Section in a Web document

            author (organization)   year   title of section

National Institute on Media and the Family. (2009). Mobile networking.

        title of Web document

In *Guide to social networking: Risks*. Retrieved from http://www

URL

.mediafamily.org/network_pdf/MediaWise_Guide_to_Social

_Networking_Risks_09.pdf

For an illustrated citation of a section in a Web document, see page 206.

41. Document from a university Web site or government agency   Name the organization or agency in your retrieval statement.

Cosmides, L., & Tooby, J. (1997). *Evolutionary psychology: A primer.*
Retrieved from University of California, Santa Barbara, Center for
Evolutionary Psychology website: http://www.psych.ucsb.edu
/research/cep/primer.html

42. Article in an online newsletter   Cite as an online article (see items 30–32), giving the title of the newsletter and whatever other information is available, including volume and issue numbers.

In the face of extinction. (2008, May). *NSF Current.* Retrieved from http://
www.nsf.gov/news/newsletter/may_08/index.jsp

43. Podcast

organization as producer   date of posting
National Academies (Producer). (2007, June 6). Progress in preventing

podcast title   descriptive label
childhood obesity: How do we measure up? [Audio podcast].

series title   URL
The sounds of science podcast. Retrieved from http://media.nap.edu

/podcasts/

writer/
presenter   date of posting   podcast title
Chesney, M. (2007, September 13). Gender differences in the use of

podcast number   descriptive label
complementary and alternative medicine (No. 12827) [Audio podcast].

Web site hosting podcast
Retrieved from University of California Television website:

URL
http://www.uctv.tv/ondemand

Citation at a glance | Section in a Web document (APA)

To cite a section in a Web document in APA style, include the following elements:

1. Author
2. Date of publication or most recent update
3. Title of section
4. Title of document
5. URL of section or of document

2003 Minnesota Health Statistics Annual Summary - Minneso... http://www.health.state.mn.us/divs/chs/03annsum/index.html

Minnesota Department of Health
Protecting, maintaining and improving the health of all Minnesotans

MDH

Minnesota Center for Health Statistics
- Home
- General statistics
  - Minnesota Vital Statistics Interactive Queries
  - Minnesota Vital Signs
  - Minnesota County Health Tables
  - Mini Profiles
  - Minnesota Health Statistics Annual Summary
  - Population Health Assessment Quarterly
- Topic-specific statistics
  - Induced Abortions in Minnesota Reports
  - Populations of Color Health Status Report
  - Tobacco Reports

2003 Minnesota Health Statistics Annual Summary ④

The Minnesota "Annual Summary" or "Minnesota Health Statistics" is a report published yearly. The most recent version of this report is *2003 Minnesota Health Statistics*, published February 2005. This report provides statistical data on the following seven subjects for the state of Minnesota.

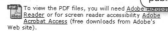
published February 2005. ②

To view the PDF files, you will need Adobe Acrobat Reader or for screen reader accessibility Adobe Acrobat Access (free downloads from Adobe's Web site).

- **Overview of 2003 Annual Summary (PDF: 251KB/11 pages)**
- **Live Births (PDF: 608KB/21 pages)**
- **Fertility (PDF: 80KB/2 pages)** ◄ ③
- **Infant Mortality and Fetal Deaths (PDF: 414KB/15 pages)**
- **General Mortality (PDF: 581KB/40 pages)**
- **Marriage (PDF: 83KB/4 pages)**
- **Divorce (PDF: 62KB/3 pages)**
- **Population (PDF: 29KB/12 pages)**

Note: Induced abortion statistics previously reported in this publication are now published separately.
See > Report to the Legislature: Induced Abortions in Minnesota

See also> Minnesota Health Statistics Annual Summary Main Page

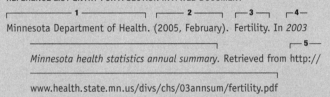

Fertility Table 1
Total Reported Pregnancies by Outcome and Rate
Minnesota Residents, 1980 - 2003

Year	Total Reported Pregnancies*	Live Births	Induced Abortions	Fetal Deaths	Female Population Ages 15-44	Pregnancy Rate**
1980	*http://www.health.state.mn.us/divs/chs/03annsum/fertility.pdf*					
1981	84,934	68,652	15,821	461	967,087	87.8
1982	84,500	68,512	15,559	429	977,905	86.4
1983	80,530	65,559	14,514	457	981,287	82.1
1984	82,736	66,715	15,556	465	985,608	83.9
1985	83,853	67,412	16,002	439	994,249	84.3
1986	81,882	65,766	15,716	400	997,501	82.1
1987	81,318	65,168	15,746	404	1,004,801	80.9
1988	83,335	66,745	16,124	466	1,020,209	81.7
1989	83,426	67,490	15,506	430	1,024,576	81.4
1990	83,714	67,985	15,280	449	1,025,919	81.6

REFERENCE LIST ENTRY FOR A SECTION IN A WEB DOCUMENT

┌──────────1──────────┐ ┌────2────┐ ┌─3─┐ ┌─4─┐

Minnesota Department of Health. (2005, February). Fertility. In *2003*

┌──────────────────────────────────────┐ ┌──5──┐

Minnesota health statistics annual summary. Retrieved from http://

www.health.state.mn.us/divs/chs/03annsum/fertility.pdf

For more on citing documents from Web sites in APA style,
see pages 204–09.

44. Weblog (blog) post Give the writer's name, the date of the post, the subject, the label "Web log post," and the URL. For a response to a post, use the label "Web log comment."

Kellermann, M. (2007, May 23). Disclosing clinical trials [Web log post]. Retrieved from http://www.iq.harvard.edu/blog/sss /archives/2007/05

45. Online audio or video file Give the medium or a description of the source file in brackets following the title.

Chomsky, N. (n.d.). The new imperialism [Audio file]. Retrieved from http:// www.rhapsody.com/noamchomsky

Zakaria, F. (Host), & McCullough, C. (Writer). (2007, March 6). In focus: American teens, Rwandan truths [Video file]. Retrieved from http:// www.pulitzercenter.org/showproject.cfm?id=26

46. Entry in a wiki Begin with the title of the entry and the date of posting (use "n.d." for "no date" if the entry does not have a date). Then add your retrieval date and the URL for the wiki entry. Include the date of retrieval because the content of a wiki is often not stable. If an author or an editor is identified, include that name at the beginning of the entry.

Ethnomethodology. (n.d.). Retrieved August 22, 2008, from http:// en.stswiki.org/index.php/Ethnomethodology

47. Data set or graphic representation Give information about the type of source in brackets following the title. If there is no title, give a brief description of the content of the source in brackets in place of the title.

U.S. Department of Agriculture, Economic Research Service. (2009). *Eating and health module (ATUS): 2007 data* [Data set]. Retrieved from http:// www.ers.usda.gov/Data/ATUS/Data/2007/2007data.htm

Gallup. (2008, October 23). *No increase in proportion of first-time voters*
    [Graphs]. Retrieved from http://www.gallup.com/poll/111331
    /No-Increase-Proportion-First-Time-Voters.aspx

48. Conference hearing

Carmona, R. H. (2004, March 2). *The growing epidemic of childhood obesity*.
    Testimony before the Subcommittee on Competition, Foreign Commerce,
    and Infrastructure of the U.S. Senate Committee on Commerce, Science,
    and Transportation. Retrieved from http://www.hhs.gov/asl/testify
    /t040302.html

49. E-mail   E-mail messages, letters, and other personal communications are not included in the list of references. (See
p. 186 for citing these sources in the text of your paper.)

50. Online posting   If an online posting is not archived, cite
it as a personal communication in the text of your paper and
do not include it in the list of references. If the posting is
archived, give the URL and the name of the discussion list if
the name is not part of the URL.

McKinney, J. (2006, December 19). Adult education-healthcare
    partnerships [Electronic mailing list message]. Retrieved from http://
    www.nifl.gov/pipermail/healthliteracy/2006/000524.html

Other sources (including online versions)

51. Dissertation from a database

Hymel, K. M. (2009). *Essays in urban economics* (Doctoral dissertation). Available
    from ProQuest Dissertations and Theses database. (AAT 3355930)

52. Unpublished dissertation

Mitchell, R. D. (2007). *The Wesleyan Quadrilateral: Relocating the conversa-
    tion* (Unpublished doctoral dissertation). Claremont School of Theology,
    Claremont, CA.

53. Government document

U.S. Census Bureau. (2006). *Statistical abstract of the United States*.
Washington, DC: Government Printing Office.

U.S. Census Bureau, Bureau of Economic Analysis. (2008, August). *U.S.
international trade in goods and services* (Report No. CB08-121,
BEA08-37, FT-900). Retrieved from http://www.census.gov
/foreign-trade/Press-Release/2008pr/06/ftdpress.pdf

54. Report from a private organization If the publisher and
the author are the same, begin with the publisher. For a print
source, use "Author" as the publisher at the end of the entry
(see item 3 on p. 191); for an online source, give the URL. If
the report has a number, put it in parentheses following the
title.

Ford Foundation. (n.d.). *Helping citizens to understand and influence state
budgets*. Retrieved from http://www.fordfound.org/pdfs/impact
/evaluations/state_fiscal_initiative.pdf

55. Legal source

Sweatt v. Painter, 339 U.S. 629 (1950). Retrieved from Cornell University Law
School, Legal Information Institute website: http://www.law.cornell
.edu/supct/html/historics/USSC_CR_0339_0629_ZS.html

56. Conference proceedings

Stahl, G. (Ed.). (2002). *Proceedings of CSCL '02: Computer support for
collaborative learning*. Hillsdale, NJ: Erlbaum.

57. Paper presented at a meeting or symposium (unpublished)

Anderson, D. N. (2008, May). *Cab-hailing and the micropolitics of gesture*.
Paper presented at the Arizona Linguistics and Anthropology
Symposium, Tucson, AZ.

58. Poster session at a conference

Wang, Z., & Keogh, T. (2008, June). *A click away: Student response to clickers*. Poster session presented at the annual conference of the American Library Association, Anaheim, CA.

59. Map or chart

Ukraine [Map]. (2008). Retrieved from the University of Texas at Austin Perry-Castañeda Library Map Collection website: http://www.lib.utexas .edu/maps/cia08/ukraine_sm_2008.gif

60. Advertisement

Xbox 360 [Advertisement]. (2007, February). *Wired, 15*(2), 71.

61. Published interview

Murphy, C. (2007, June 22). As the Romans did [Interview by G. Hahn]. Retrieved from http://www.theatlantic.com/

62. Lecture, speech, or address

Fox, V. (2008, March 5). *Economic growth, poverty, and democracy in Latin America: A president's perspective*. Address at the Freeman Spogli Institute, Stanford University, Stanford, CA.

63. Work of art or photograph

Weber, J. (1992). *Toward freedom* [Outdoor mural]. Sherman Oaks, CA.

Newkirk, K. (2006). *Gainer (part II)*. Museum of Contemporary Art, Chicago, IL.

64. Brochure, pamphlet, or fact sheet

National Council of State Boards of Nursing. (n.d.). *Professional boundaries* [Brochure]. Retrieved from https://www.ncsbn.org/Professional _Boundaries_2007_Web.pdf

World Health Organization. (2007, October). *Health of indigenous peoples*
(No. 326) [Fact sheet]. Retrieved from http://www.who.int/mediacentre
/factsheets/fs326/en/index.html

65. Presentation slides

Boeninger, C. F. (2008, August). *Web 2.0 tools for reference and
instructional services* [Presentation slides]. Retrieved from http://
libraryvoice.com/archives/2008/08/04/opal-20-conference
-presentation-slides/

66. Film or video (motion picture)   Give the director, producer,
and other relevant contributors, followed by the year of
the film's release, the title, the description "Motion picture"
in brackets, the country where the film was made, and the
studio. If you viewed the film on videocassette or DVD, indicate that medium in brackets in place of "Motion picture."
If the original release date and the date of the DVD or videocassette are different, add "Original release" and that date in
parentheses at the end of the entry. If the motion picture
would be difficult for your readers to find, include instead the
name and address of its distributor.

Guggenheim, D. (Director), & Bender, L. (Producer). (2006). *An inconvenient
truth* [DVD]. United States: Paramount Home Entertainment.

Spurlock, M. (Director). (2004). *Super size me* [Motion picture].
Available from IDP Films, 1133 Broadway, Suite 926, New York,
NY 10010

67. Television program   List the producer and the date the
program was aired. Give the title, followed by "Television
broadcast" in brackets, the city, and the television network
or service.

Pratt, C. (Executive producer). (2008, October 5). *Face the nation* [Television
broadcast]. Washington, DC: CBS News.

For a television series, use the year in which the series was produced, and follow the title with "Television series" in brackets. For an episode in a series, list the writer and director and the year. After the episode title, put "Television series episode" in brackets. Follow with information about the series.

Fanning, D. (Executive producer). (2008). *Frontline* [Television series]. Boston, MA: WGBH.

Smith, M. (Writer/producer). (2008). Heat [Television series episode]. In D. Fanning (Executive producer), *Frontline*. Boston, MA: WGBH.

68. Sound recording

Thomas, G. (1996). Breath. On *Didgeridoo: Ancient sound of the future* [CD]. Oxnard, CA: Aquarius International Music.

69. Computer software or video game   Add the words "Computer software" (neither italicized nor in quotation marks) in brackets after the title of the program.

Sims 2 [Computer software]. (2005). New York, NY: Maxis.

APA manuscript format

The American Psychological Association makes a number of recommendations for formatting a paper and preparing a list of references. The following guidelines are consistent with advice given in the *Publication Manual of the American Psychological Association*, 6th ed. (Washington: APA, 2010), and typical requirements for undergraduate papers.

The APA manual provides guidelines for papers prepared for publication in a scholarly journal; it does not provide separate guidelines for papers prepared for undergraduate classes. The formatting guidelines in this section and the sample paper on pages 219–28 can be used for either type of paper. If you are in doubt about the specific format preferred or required in your course, ask your instructor.

Formatting the paper

Many instructors in the social sciences require students to follow APA guidelines for formatting a paper.

Materials and font Use good-quality 8½" × 11" white paper. Avoid a font that is unusual or hard to read.

Title page Begin at the top left with the words "Running head," followed by a colon and a short form of the title of your paper. The short form should be no more than fifty characters and should be typed in all capital letters. Flush with the right margin, put the page number 1.

About halfway down the page, center the full title of your paper (capitalizing all words of four letters or more), your name, and your school's name. At the bottom of the page, you may add the heading "Author Note," centered, followed by a brief paragraph that lists specific information about the course or department or provides acknowledgments or contact information. See page 219 for a sample title page.

Some instructors may instead require a title page like the one on page 229. If in doubt about the requirements in your course, check with your instructor.

Page numbers and running head Number all pages with arabic numerals (1, 2, 3, and so on) in the upper right corner about one-half inch from the top of the page. The title page should be numbered 1.

On every page, in the upper left corner on the same line as the page number, place a running head. The running head consists of a short form of the title of the paper (no more than fifty characters) in all capital letters. (On the title page only, include the words "Running head" followed by a colon before the shortened title.) See pages 219–28.

Margins, line spacing, and paragraph indents   Use margins of one inch on all sides of the page. Left-align the text.

Double-space throughout the paper. Indent the first line of each paragraph one-half inch.

Capitalization, italics, and quotation marks   Capitalize all words of four letters or more in titles of works and in headings that appear in the text of the paper. Capitalize the first word after a colon if the word begins a complete sentence.

Italicize the titles of books and other long works, such as Web sites. Use quotation marks around the titles of periodical articles, short stories, poems, and other short works.

NOTE: APA has different requirements for titles in the reference list. See page 217.

Long quotations and footnotes   When a quotation is longer than forty words, set it off from the text by indenting it one-half inch from the left margin. Double-space the quotation. Do not use quotation marks around a quotation that has been set off from the text. See page 227 for an example.

Place each footnote, if any, at the bottom of the page on which the text reference occurs. Double-space between the last line of text on the page and the footnote. Double-space the footnote and indent the first line one-half inch. Begin the note with the superscript arabic numeral that corresponds to the number in the text. See page 221 for an example.

Abstract   If your instructor requires an abstract, include it immediately after the title page. Center the word Abstract one inch from the top of the page; double-space the abstract as you do the body of your paper.

An abstract is a 100-to-150-word paragraph that provides readers with a quick overview of your essay. It should express your main idea and your key points; it might also briefly suggest any implications or applications of the research you discuss in the paper. See page 220 for an example.

Headings Although headings are not always necessary, their use is encouraged in the social sciences. For most undergraduate papers, one level of heading will usually be sufficient.

In APA style, major headings are centered and boldface. Capitalize the first word of the heading, along with all words except articles, short prepositions, and coordinating conjunctions. See the sample paper on pages 219–28.

Visuals APA classifies visuals as tables and figures (figures include graphs, charts, drawings, and photographs). Keep visuals as simple as possible.

Label each table with an arabic numeral (Table 1, Table 2, and so on) and provide a clear title. The label and title should appear on separate lines above the table, flush left and double-spaced.

Below the table, give its source in a note. If any data in the table require an explanatory footnote, use a superscript lowercase letter in the body of the table and in a footnote following the source note. Double-space source notes and footnotes and do not indent the first line of each note. See page 224 for an example of a table in a student paper.

For each figure, place a label and a caption below the figure, flush left and double-spaced. The label and caption need not appear on separate lines.

In the text of your paper, discuss the most significant features of each visual. Place the visual as close as possible to the sentences that relate to it unless your instructor prefers it in an appendix.

Preparing the list of references

Begin your list of references on a new page at the end of the paper. Center the title References one inch from the top of the page. Double-space throughout. For a sample reference list, see page 228.

Indenting entries   Use a hanging indent in the reference list: Type the first line of each entry flush left and indent any additional lines one-half inch, as shown on page 228.

Alphabetizing the list   Alphabetize the reference list by the last names of the authors (or editors); when a work has no author or editor, alphabetize by the first word of the title other than *A*, *An*, or *The*.

If your list includes two or more works by the same author, arrange the entries by year, the earliest first. If your list includes two or more works by the same author in the same year, arrange the works alphabetically by title. Add the letters "a," "b," and so on within the parentheses after the year. Use only the year and the letter for articles in journals: (2002a). Use the full date and the letter for articles in magazines and newspapers in the reference list: (2005a, July 7). Use only the year and the letter in the in-text citation.

Authors' names   Invert all authors' names and use initials instead of first names. With two or more authors, use an ampersand (&) before the last author's name. Separate the names with commas. Include names for the first seven authors; if there are eight or more authors, give the first six authors, three ellipsis dots, and the last author (see p. 191).

Titles of books and articles   Italicize the titles and subtitles of books. Do not use quotation marks around the titles of articles. Capitalize only the first word of the title and subtitle (and all proper nouns) of books and articles. Capitalize names of periodicals as you would capitalize them normally.

Abbreviations for page numbers   Abbreviations for "page" and "pages" ("p." and "pp.") are used before page numbers of newspaper articles and articles in edited books (see item 9 on p. 193 and item 22 on p. 197) but not before page numbers of articles in magazines and scholarly journals (see items 7 and 8 on p. 193).

Breaking a URL   When a URL or a DOI (digital object identifier) must be divided, break it after a double slash or before any other mark of punctuation. Do not insert a hyphen, and do not add a period at the end.

For information about the exact format of each entry in your list, consult the models on pages 190–213.

Sample research paper: APA style

On the following pages is a research paper on the effectiveness of treatments for childhood obesity, written by Luisa Mirano, a student in a psychology class. Mirano's assignment was to write a literature review paper documented with APA-style citations and references.

See the guidelines on page 213 for a discussion of formatting differences in APA-style student papers and papers prepared for scholarly publication.

Running head: CAN MEDICATION CURE OBESITY IN CHILDREN?   1

A running head, which will be used in the printed journal article, consists of a shortened title in all capital letters. On the title page, it is preceded by the label "Running head." Page numbers appear in the upper right corner.

Can Medication Cure Obesity in Children?

A Review of the Literature

Luisa Mirano

Northwest-Shoals Community College

Full title, writer's name, and school name are centered halfway down the page.

Author Note

This paper was prepared for Psychology 108, Section B, taught by Professor Kang.

An author's note lists specific information about the course or department and can provide acknowledgments and contact information.

Marginal annotations indicate APA-style formatting.

Abstract

In recent years, policymakers and medical experts have expressed alarm about the growing problem of childhood obesity in the United States. While most agree that the issue deserves attention, consensus dissolves around how to respond to the problem. This literature review examines one approach to treating childhood obesity: medication. The paper compares the effectiveness for adolescents of the only two drugs approved by the Food and Drug Administration (FDA) for long-term treatment of obesity, sibutramine and orlistat. This examination of pharmacological treatments for obesity points out the limitations of medication and suggests the need for a comprehensive solution that combines medical, social, behavioral, and political approaches to this complex problem.

Can Medication Cure Obesity in Children?

A Review of the Literature

In March 2004, U.S. Surgeon General Richard Carmona called attention to a health problem in the United States that, until recently, has been overlooked: childhood obesity. Carmona said that the "astounding" 15% child obesity rate constitutes an "epidemic." Since the early 1980s, that rate has "doubled in children and tripled in adolescents." Now more than nine million children are classified as obese.[1] While the traditional response to a medical epidemic is to hunt for a vaccine or a cure-all pill, childhood obesity is more elusive. The lack of success of recent initiatives suggests that medication might not be the answer for the escalating problem. This literature review considers whether the use of medication is a promising approach for solving the childhood obesity problem by responding to the following questions:

1. What are the implications of childhood obesity?

2. Is medication effective at treating childhood obesity?

3. Is medication safe for children?

4. Is medication the best solution?

Understanding the limitations of medical treatments for children highlights the complexity of the childhood obesity problem in the United States and underscores the need for physicians, advocacy groups, and policymakers to search for other solutions.

What Are the Implications of Childhood Obesity?

Obesity can be a devastating problem from both an individual and a societal perspective. Obesity puts children at risk for a number of

[1]Obesity is measured in terms of body-mass index (BMI): weight in kilograms divided by square of height in meters. A child or an adolescent with a BMI in the 95th percentile for his or her age and gender is considered obese.

Full title, centered.

Headings, centered, help readers follow the organization.

Mirano uses a footnote to define an essential term that would be cumbersome to define within the text.

CAN MEDICATION CURE OBESITY IN CHILDREN? 4

medical complications, including type 2 diabetes, hypertension, sleep apnea, and orthopedic problems (Henry J. Kaiser Family Foundation, 2004, p. 1). Researchers Hoppin and Taveras (2004) have noted that obesity is often associated with psychological issues such as depression, anxiety, and binge eating (Table 4).

Obesity also poses serious problems for a society struggling to cope with rising health care costs. The cost of treating obesity currently totals $117 billion per year—a price, according to the surgeon general, "second only to the cost of [treating] tobacco use" (Carmona, 2004). And as the number of children who suffer from obesity grows, long-term costs will only increase.

Is Medication Effective at Treating Childhood Obesity?

The widening scope of the obesity problem has prompted medical professionals to rethink old conceptions of the disorder and its causes. As researchers Yanovski and Yanovski (2002) have explained, obesity was once considered "either a moral failing or evidence of underlying psychopathology" (p. 592). But this view has shifted: Many medical professionals now consider obesity a biomedical rather than a moral condition, influenced by both genetic and environmental factors. Yanovski and Yanovski have further noted that the development of weight-loss medications in the early 1990s showed that "obesity should be treated in the same manner as any other chronic disease . . . through the long-term use of medication" (p. 592).

The search for the right long-term medication has been complicated. Many of the drugs authorized by the Food and Drug Administration (FDA) in the early 1990s proved to be a disappointment. Two of the medications—fenfluramine and dexfenfluramine—were withdrawn from the market because of severe side effects (Yanovski & Yanovski, 2002, p. 592), and several others were classified by the Drug Enforcement Administration as having the "potential for abuse" (Hoppin & Taveras, 2004, Weight-Loss Drugs section, para. 6). Currently only two medications have been approved by the FDA for long-term treatment of obesity: sibutramine (marketed as Meridia) and orlistat (marketed as Xenical). This section compares studies on the effectiveness of each.

> In a parenthetical citation, an ampersand links the names of two authors.

Sibutramine suppresses appetite by blocking the reuptake of the neurotransmitters serotonin and norepinephrine in the brain (Yanovski & Yanovski, 2002, p. 594). Though the drug won FDA approval in 1998, experiments to test its effectiveness for younger patients came considerably later. In 2003, University of Pennsylvania researchers Berkowitz, Wadden, Tershakovec, and Cronquist released the first double-blind placebo study testing the effect of sibutramine on adolescents, aged 13-17, over a 12-month period. Their findings are summarized in Table 1.

After 6 months, the group receiving medication had lost 4.6 kg (about 10 pounds) more than the control group. But during the second half of the study, when both groups received sibutramine, the results were more ambiguous. In months 6-12, the group that continued to take sibutramine gained an average of 0.8 kg, or roughly 2 pounds; the control group, which switched from placebo to sibutramine, lost 1.3 kg, or roughly 3 pounds (p. 1808). Both groups received behavioral therapy covering diet, exercise, and mental health.

These results paint a murky picture of the effectiveness of the medication: While initial data seemed promising, the results after one year raised questions about whether medication-induced weight loss could be sustained over time. As Berkowitz et al. (2003) advised, "Until more extensive safety and efficacy data are available, . . . weight-loss medications should be used only on an experimental basis for adolescents" (p. 1811).

CAN MEDICATION CURE OBESITY IN CHILDREN? 6

Table 1

Effectiveness of Sibutramine and Orlistat in Adolescents

Medication	Subjects	Treatment[a]	Side effects	Average weight loss/gain
Sibutramine	Control	0-6 mos.: placebo 6-12 mos.: sibutramine	Mos. 6-12: increased blood pressure; increased pulse rate	After 6 mos.: loss of 3.2 kg (7 lb) After 12 mos.: loss of 4.5 kg (9.9 lb)
	Medicated	0-12 mos.: sibutramine	Increased blood pressure; increased pulse rate	After 6 mos.: loss of 7.8 kg (17.2 lb) After 12 mos.: loss of 7.0 kg (15.4 lb)
Orlistat	Control	0-12 mos.: placebo	None	Gain of 0.67 kg (1.5 lb)
	Medicated	0-12 mos.: orlistat	Oily spotting; flatulence; abdominal discomfort	Loss of 1.3 kg (2.9 lb)

Note. The data on sibutramine are adapted from "Behavior Therapy and Sibutramine for the Treatment of Adolescent Obesity," by R. I. Berkowitz, T. A. Wadden, A. M. Tershakovec, & J. L. Cronquist, 2003, *Journal of the American Medical Association, 289*, pp. 1807-1809. The data on orlistat are adapted from *Xenical (Orlistat) Capsules: Complete Product Information*, by Roche Laboratories, December 2003, retrieved from http://www .rocheusa.com/products/xenical/pi.pdf

[a]The medication and/or placebo were combined with behavioral therapy in all groups over all time periods.

A note gives the source of the data.

A content note explains data common to all subjects.

A study testing the effectiveness of orlistat in adolescents showed similarly ambiguous results. The FDA approved orlistat in 1999 but did not authorize it for adolescents until December 2003. Roche Laboratories (2003), maker of orlistat, released results of a one-year study testing the drug on 539 obese adolescents, aged 12-16. The drug, which promotes weight loss by blocking fat absorption in the large intestine, showed some effectiveness in adolescents: an average loss of 1.3 kg, or roughly 3 pounds, for subjects taking orlistat for one year, as opposed to an average gain of 0.67 kg, or 1.5 pounds, for the control group (pp. 8-9). See Table 1.

Short-term studies of orlistat have shown slightly more dramatic results. Researchers at the National Institute of Child Health and Human Development tested 20 adolescents, aged 12-16, over a three-month period and found that orlistat, combined with behavioral therapy, produced an average weight loss of 4.4 kg, or 9.7 pounds (McDuffie et al., 2002, p. 646). The study was not controlled against a placebo group; therefore, the relative effectiveness of orlistat in this case remains unclear.

Is Medication Safe for Children?

While modest weight loss has been documented for both medications, each carries risks of certain side effects. Sibutramine has been observed to increase blood pressure and pulse rate. In 2002, a consumer group claimed that the medication was related to the deaths of 19 people and filed a petition with the Department of Health and Human Services to ban the medication (Hilts, 2002). The sibutramine study by Berkowitz et al. (2003) noted elevated blood pressure as a side effect, and dosages had to be reduced or the medication discontinued in 19 of the 43 subjects in the first six months (p. 1809).

The main side effects associated with orlistat were abdominal discomfort, oily spotting, fecal incontinence, and nausea (Roche

For a source with six or more authors, the first author's surname followed by "et al." is used for the first and subsequent references.

When this article was first cited, all four authors were named. In subsequent citations of a work with three to five authors, "et al." is used after the first author's name.

Laboratories, 2003, p. 13). More serious for long-term health is the concern that orlistat, being a fat-blocker, would affect absorption of fat-soluble vitamins, such as vitamin D. However, the study found that this side effect can be minimized or eliminated if patients take vitamin supplements two hours before or after administration of orlistat (p. 10). With close monitoring of patients taking the medication, many of the risks can be reduced.

Is Medication the Best Solution?

The data on the safety and efficacy of pharmacological treatments of childhood obesity raise the question of whether medication is the best solution for the problem. The treatments have clear costs for individual patients, including unpleasant side effects, little information about long-term use, and uncertainty that they will yield significant weight loss.

In purely financial terms, the drugs cost more than $3 a day on average (Duenwald, 2004). In each of the clinical trials, use of medication was accompanied by an expensive regime of behavioral therapies, including counseling, nutritional education, fitness advising, and monitoring. As journalist Greg Critser (2003) noted in his book *Fat Land,* use of weight-loss drugs is unlikely to have an effect without the proper "support system"—one that includes doctors, facilities, time, and money (p. 3). For some, this level of care is prohibitively expensive.

A third complication is that the studies focused on adolescents aged 12-16, but obesity can begin at a much younger age. Little data exist to establish the safety or efficacy of medication for treating very young children.

While the scientific data on the concrete effects of these medications in children remain somewhat unclear, medication is not the only avenue for addressing the crisis. Both medical experts and

CAN MEDICATION CURE OBESITY IN CHILDREN?   9

policymakers recognize that solutions might come not only from a
laboratory but also from policy, education, and advocacy. A handbook
designed to educate doctors on obesity called for "major changes in
some aspects of western culture" (Hoppin & Taveras, 2004,
Conclusion section, para. 1). Cultural change may not be the typical
realm of medical professionals, but the handbook urged doctors to
be proactive and "focus [their] energy on public policies and
interventions" (Conclusion section, para. 1).

Brackets indicate
a word not in the
original source.

The solutions proposed by a number of advocacy groups
underscore this interest in political and cultural change. A report by
the Henry J. Kaiser Family Foundation (2004) outlined trends that may
have contributed to the childhood obesity crisis, including food
advertising for children as well as

> a reduction in physical education classes and after-school
> athletic programs, an increase in the availability of sodas
> and snacks in public schools, the growth in the number of
> fast-food outlets . . . , and the increasing number of highly
> processed high-calorie and high-fat grocery products. (p. 1)

A quotation longer
than forty words is
indented without
quotation marks.

Addressing each of these areas requires more than a doctor armed
with a prescription pad; it requires a broad mobilization not just of
doctors and concerned parents but of educators, food industry
executives, advertisers, and media representatives.

The barrage of possible approaches to combating childhood
obesity—from scientific research to political lobbying—indicates both
the severity and the complexity of the problem. While none of the
medications currently available is a miracle drug for curing the nation's
9 million obese children, research has illuminated some of the
underlying factors that affect obesity and has shown the need for
a comprehensive approach to the problem that includes behavioral,
medical, social, and political change.

228 Sample research paper: APA style

CAN MEDICATION CURE OBESITY IN CHILDREN?   10

List of references
begins on a new
page. Heading is
centered.

List is
alphabetized
by authors'
last names. All
authors' names
are inverted.

The first line of
an entry is at
the left margin;
subsequent lines
indent ½".

Double-spacing is
used throughout.

References

Berkowitz, R. I., Wadden, T. A., Tershakovec, A. M., & Cronquist, J. L.
(2003). Behavior therapy and sibutramine for the treatment of
adolescent obesity. *Journal of the American Medical Association*,
289, 1805-1812.

Carmona, R. H. (2004, March 2). *The growing epidemic of childhood
obesity*. Testimony before the Subcommittee on Competition,
Foreign Commerce, and Infrastructure of the U.S. Senate
Committee on Commerce, Science, and Transportation. Retrieved
from http://www.hhs.gov/asl/testify/t040302.html

Critser, G. (2003). *Fat land*. Boston, MA: Houghton Mifflin.

Duenwald, M. (2004, January 6). Slim pickings: Looking beyond ephedra.
The New York Times, p. F1. Retrieved from http://nytimes.com/

Henry J. Kaiser Family Foundation. (2004, February). *The role of media
in childhood obesity*. Retrieved from http://www.kff.org
/entmedia/7030.cfm

Hilts, P. J. (2002, March 20). Petition asks for removal of diet drug
from market. *The New York Times*, p. A26. Retrieved from http://
nytimes.com/

Hoppin, A. G., & Taveras, E. M. (2004, June 25). Assessment and
management of childhood and adolescent obesity. *Clinical Update*.
Retrieved from http://www.medscape.com/viewarticle/481633

McDuffie, J. R., Calis, K. A., Uwaifo, G. I., Sebring, N. G., Fallon, E. M.,
Hubbard, V. S., & Yanovski, J. A. (2002). Three-month tolerability
of orlistat in adolescents with obesity-related comorbid
conditions. *Obesity Research*, *10*, 642-650.

Roche Laboratories. (2003, December). *Xenical (orlistat) capsules:
Complete product information*. Retrieved from http://www
.rocheusa.com/products/xenical/pi.pdf

Yanovski, S. Z., & Yanovski, J. A. (2002). Drug therapy: Obesity. *The New
England Journal of Medicine*, *346*, 591-602.

ALTERNATIVE APA TITLE PAGE

Obesity in Children 1

Can Medication Cure Obesity in Children?

A Review of the Literature

Luisa Mirano

Psychology 108, Section B

Professor Kang

October 31, 2004

Short title and page number in the upper right corner on all pages.

Full title, centered.

Writer's name, course, instructor's name, and date, all centered at the bottom of the page.

ALTERNATIVE APA RUNNING HEAD

Obesity in Children 5

were classified by the Drug Enforcement Administration as having the "potential for abuse" (Hoppin & Taveras, 2004, Weight-Loss Drugs section, para. 6). Currently only two medications have been approved by the FDA for long-term treatment of obesity: sibutramine (marketed

Marginal annotations indicate APA-style formatting.

Chicago Style: History

In history and some humanities courses, you may be required to use the documentation system set forth in *The Chicago Manual of Style*, 16th ed. (Chicago: U of Chicago P, 2010). Most assignments in history and other humanities classes are based to some extent on reading. At times you will be asked to respond to one or two readings, such as essays or historical documents. At other times you may be asked to write a research paper that draws on a wide variety of sources.

Chicago documentation style

In *Chicago* style, superscript numbers in the text of the paper refer readers to notes with corresponding numbers either at the foot of the page (footnotes) or at the end of the paper (endnotes). A bibliography is often required as well; it appears at the end of the paper and gives publication information for all the works cited in the notes.

TEXT

A Union soldier, Jacob Thompson, claimed to have seen Forrest order the killing, but when asked to describe the six-foot-two general, he called him "a little bit of a man."[12]

FOOTNOTE OR ENDNOTE

12. Brian Steel Wills, *A Battle from the Start: The Life of Nathan Bedford Forrest* (New York: HarperCollins, 1992), 187.

BIBLIOGRAPHY ENTRY

Wills, Brian Steel. *A Battle from the Start: The Life of Nathan Bedford Forrest*. New York: HarperCollins, 1992.

First and subsequent notes for a source

The first time you cite a source, the note should include publication information for that work as well as the page number on which the passage being cited may be found.

> 1. Peter Burchard, *One Gallant Rush: Robert Gould Shaw and His Brave Black Regiment* (New York: St. Martin's, 1965), 85.

For subsequent references to a source you have already cited, you may simply give the author's last name, a short form of the title, and the page or pages cited. A short form of the title of a book is italicized; a short form of the title of an article is put in quotation marks.

> 4. Burchard, *One Gallant Rush*, 31.

When you have two consecutive notes from the same source, you may use "Ibid." (meaning "in the same place") and the page number for the second note. Use "Ibid." alone if the page number is the same.

> 5. Jack Hurst, *Nathan Bedford Forrest: A Biography* (New York: Knopf, 1993), 8.

> 6. Ibid., 174.

Chicago-*style bibliography*

A bibliography, which appears at the end of your paper, lists every work you have cited in your notes; in addition, it may include works that you consulted but did not cite. For advice on constructing the list, see page 247. A sample bibliography appears on page 256.

NOTE: If you include a bibliography, *The Chicago Manual of Style* suggests that you shorten all notes, including the first reference to a source, as described on this page. Check with your instructor, however, to see whether using an abbreviated note for a first reference to a source is acceptable.

Model notes and bibliography entries

The following models are consistent with guidelines set forth in *The Chicago Manual of Style*, 16th ed. For each type of source, a model note appears first, followed by a model bibliography entry. The note shows the format you should use when citing

a source for the first time. For subsequent citations of a source, use shortened notes (see p. 231).

Some online sources, typically periodical articles, use a permanent locator called a digital object identifier (DOI). Use the DOI, when it is available, in place of a URL in your citations of online sources.

When a URL (Web address) or a DOI must break across lines, do not insert a hyphen or break at a hyphen if the URL or DOI contains one. Instead, break after a colon or a double slash or before any other mark of punctuation.

Books (print and online)

1. Basic format for a print book

1. Mary N. Woods, *Beyond the Architect's Eye: Photographs and the American Built Environment* (Philadelphia: University of Pennsylvania Press, 2009).

Woods, Mary N. *Beyond the Architect's Eye: Photographs and the American Built Environment*. Philadelphia: University of Pennsylvania Press, 2009.

2. Basic format for an online book

2. John Dewey, *Democracy and Education* (1916; ILT Digital Classics, 1994), chap. 4, http://ilt.columbia.edu/publications/dewey.html.

Dewey, John. *Democracy and Education*. 1916. ILT Digital Classics, 1994. http://ilt.columbia.edu/publications/dewey.html.

3. Basic format for an e-book (electronic book)

3. Leo Tolstoy, *War and Peace*, trans. Richard Pevear and Larissa Volokhonsky (New York: Knopf, 2007), Kindle edition, vol. 1, pt. 1, chap. 3.

Tolstoy, Leo. *War and Peace*. Translated by Richard Pevear and Larissa Volokhonsky. New York: Knopf, 2007. Kindle edition.

4. Two or more authors   For a work with two or three authors, give all authors' names in both the note and the bibliography entry. For a work with four or more authors, in the note give the first author's name followed by "et al." (for "and others"); in the bibliography entry, list all authors' names.

Directory to *Chicago*-style notes and bibliography entries

4. Chris Stringer and Peter Andrews, *The Complete World of Human Evolution* (London: Thames and Hudson, 2005), 45.

Stringer, Chris, and Peter Andrews. *The Complete World of Human Evolution*. London: Thames and Hudson, 2005.

4. Lynn Hunt et al., *The Making of the West: Peoples and Cultures*, 3rd ed. (Boston: Bedford/St. Martin's, 2009), 541.

Hunt, Lynn, Thomas R. Martin, Barbara H. Rosenwein, R. Po-chia Hsia, and Bonnie G. Smith. *The Making of the West: Peoples and Cultures*. 3rd ed. Boston: Bedford/St. Martin's, 2009.

5. Organization as author

5. Dormont Historical Society, *Images of America: Dormont* (Charleston, SC: Arcadia Publishing, 2008), 24.

Dormont Historical Society. *Images of America: Dormont*. Charleston, SC: Arcadia Publishing, 2008.

6. Unknown author

6. *The Men's League Handbook on Women's Suffrage* (London, 1912), 23.

The Men's League Handbook on Women's Suffrage. London, 1912.

7. Multiple works by the same author In the bibliography, use six hyphens in place of the author's name in the second and subsequent entries. Arrange the entries alphabetically by title or by date; be consistent throughout the bibliography.

Harper, Raymond L. *A History of Chesapeake, Virginia*. Charleston, SC: History Press, 2008.

------. *South Norfolk, Virginia, 1661-2005*. Charleston, SC: History Press, 2005.

8. Edited work without an author

8. Jack Beatty, ed., *Colossus: How the Corporation Changed America* (New York: Broadway Books, 2001), 127.

Beatty, Jack, ed. *Colossus: How the Corporation Changed America*. New York: Broadway Books, 2001.

9. Edited work with an author

9. Ted Poston, *A First Draft of History,* ed. Kathleen A. Hauke (Athens: University of Georgia Press, 2000), 46.

Poston, Ted. *A First Draft of History*. Edited by Kathleen A. Hauke. Athens: University of Georgia Press, 2000.

10. Translated work

10. Tonino Guerra, *Abandoned Places*, trans. Adria Bernardi (Barcelona: Guernica, 1999), 71.

Guerra, Tonino. *Abandoned Places*. Translated by Adria Bernardi. Barcelona: Guernica, 1999.

11. Edition other than the first

11. Arnoldo DeLeon, *Mexican Americans in Texas: A Brief History*, 3rd ed. (Wheeling, IL: Harlan Davidson, 2009), 34.

DeLeon, Arnoldo. *Mexican Americans in Texas: A Brief History*. 3rd ed. Wheeling, IL: Harlan Davidson, 2009.

12. Volume in a multivolume work

12. Charles Reagan Wilson, ed., *Myth, Manner, and Memory*, vol. 4 of *The New Encyclopedia of Southern Culture* (Chapel Hill: University of North Carolina Press, 2006), 198.

Wilson, Charles Reagan, ed. *Myth, Manner, and Memory*. Vol. 4 of *The New Encyclopedia of Southern Culture*. Chapel Hill: University of North Carolina Press, 2006.

13. Work in an anthology

13. Zora Neale Hurston, "From *Dust Tracks on a Road*," in *The Norton Book of American Autobiography*, ed. Jay Parini (New York: Norton, 1999), 336.

Hurston, Zora Neale. "From *Dust Tracks on a Road*." In *The Norton Book of American Autobiography*, edited by Jay Parini, 333-43. New York: Norton, 1999.

14. Introduction, preface, foreword, or afterword

14. Nelson DeMille, foreword to *Flag: An American Biography*, by Marc Leepson (New York: Thomas Dunne, 2005), xii.

DeMille, Nelson. Foreword to *Flag: An American Biography*, by Marc Leepson, xi–xiv. New York: Thomas Dunne, 2005.

15. Republished book

15. Garry Wills, *Inventing America: Jefferson's Declaration of Independence* (1978; repr., Boston: Houghton Mifflin, 2002), 86.

Wills, Garry. *Inventing America: Jefferson's Declaration of Independence*. 1978. Reprint, Boston: Houghton Mifflin, 2002.

16. Work with a title in its title Use quotation marks around any title within an italicized title.

16. Gary Schmidgall, ed., *Conserving Walt Whitman's Fame: Selections from Horace Traubel's "Conservator," 1890-1919* (Iowa City: University of Iowa Press, 2006), 165.

Schmidgall, Gary, ed. *Conserving Walt Whitman's Fame: Selections from Horace Traubel's "Conservator," 1890-1919*. Iowa City: University of Iowa Press, 2006.

17. Letter in a published collection Use the day-month-year form for the date of the letter. If the letter writer's name is part of the book title, begin the note with only the last name but begin the bibliography entry with the full name.

17. Mitford to Esmond Romilly, 29 July 1940, in *Decca: The Letters of Jessica Mitford*, ed. Peter Y. Sussman (New York: Knopf, 2006), 55-56.

Mitford, Jessica. *Decca: The Letters of Jessica Mitford*. Edited by Peter Y. Sussman. New York: Knopf, 2006.

18. Work in a series

18. R. Keith Schoppa, *The Columbia Guide to Modern Chinese History*, Columbia Guides to Asian History (New York: Columbia University Press, 2000), 256-58.

Schoppa, R. Keith. *The Columbia Guide to Modern Chinese History*. Columbia Guides to Asian History. New York: Columbia University Press, 2000.

19. Encyclopedia or dictionary entry

19. *Encyclopaedia Britannica*, 15th ed., s.v. "Monroe Doctrine."

19. Bryan A. Garner, *Garner's Modern American Usage* (Oxford: Oxford University Press, 2003), s.v. "brideprice."

Garner, Bryan A. *Garner's Modern American Usage*. Oxford: Oxford University Press, 2003.

The abbreviation "s.v." is for the Latin *sub verbo* ("under the word").

Well-known reference works such as encyclopedias do not require publication information and are usually not included in the bibliography.

20. Sacred text

20. Matt. 20:4-9 (Revised Standard Version).

20. Qur'an 18:1-3.

Sacred texts are usually not included in the bibliography.

21. Source quoted in another source

21. Ron Grossman and Charles Leroux, "A Local Outpost of Democracy," *Chicago Tribune*, March 5, 1996, quoted in William Julius Wilson and Richard P. Taub, *There Goes the Neighborhood: Racial, Ethnic, and Class Tensions in Four Chicago Neighborhoods and Their Meaning for America* (New York: Knopf, 2006), 18.

Grossman, Ron, and Charles Leroux. "A Local Outpost of Democracy." *Chicago Tribune*, March 5, 1996. Quoted in William Julius Wilson and Richard P. Taub, *There Goes the Neighborhood: Racial, Ethnic, and Class Tensions in Four Chicago Neighborhoods and Their Meaning for America* (New York: Knopf, 2006), 18.

Articles in periodicals (print and online)

22. Article in a print journal   Include the volume and issue numbers and the date; end the bibliography entry with the page range of the article.

22. T. H. Breen, "Will American Consumers Buy a Second American Revolution?," *Journal of American History* 93, no. 2 (2006): 405.

Breen, T. H. "Will American Consumers Buy a Second American Revolution?" *Journal of American History* 93, no. 2 (2006): 404-8.

23. Article in an online journal   Give the DOI if the article has one; if there is no DOI, give the URL for the article. For an unpaginated online article, in your note you may include locators, such as numbered paragraphs (if the article has them), or headings from the article.

23. Brian Lennon, "New Media Critical Homologies," *Postmodern Culture* 19, no. 2 (2009), http://pmc.iath.virginia.edu/text-only /issue.109/19.2lennon.txt.

Lennon, Brian. "New Media Critical Homologies." *Postmodern Culture* 19, no. 2 (2009). http://pmc.iath.virginia.edu/text-only/issue.109 /19.2lennon.txt.

24. Journal article from a database   Give whatever identifying information is available in the database listing: a DOI for the article; the name of the database and the number assigned by the database; or a "stable" or "persistent" URL for the article.

24. Constant Leung, "Language and Content in Bilingual Education," *Linguistics and Education* 16, no. 2 (2005): 239, doi:10.1016/j.linged .2006.01.004.

Leung, Constant. "Language and Content in Bilingual Education." *Linguistics and Education* 16, no. 2 (2005): 238-52. doi:10.1016 /j.linged.2006.01.004.

25. Article in a print magazine   Provide a page number in the note and a page range in the bibliography.

25. Tom Bissell, "Improvised, Explosive, and Divisive," *Harper's*, January 2006, 42.

Bissell, Tom. "Improvised, Explosive, and Divisive." *Harper's*, January 2006, 41-54.

26. Article in an online magazine   Include the URL for the article.

26. Katharine Mieszkowski, "A Deluge Waiting to Happen," *Salon*, July 3, 2008, http://www.salon.com/news/feature/2008/07/03/floods /index.html.

Mieszkowski, Katharine. "A Deluge Waiting to Happen." *Salon*, July 3, 2008.
    http://www.salon.com/news/feature/2008/07/03/floods/index.html.

27. Magazine article from a database   Give whatever identifying information is available in the database listing: a DOI for the article; the name of the database and the number assigned by the database; or a "stable" or "persistent" URL for the article.

27. "Facing Facts in Afghanistan," *National Review*, November 2, 2009, 14, Expanded Academic ASAP (A209905060).

"Facing Facts in Afghanistan." *National Review*, November 2, 2009, 14.
    Expanded Academic ASAP (A209905060).

28. Article in a print newspaper   Page numbers are not necessary; a section letter or number, if available, is sufficient.

28. Randal C. Archibold, "These Neighbors Are Good Ones without a New Fence," *New York Times*, October 22, 2008, sec. A.

Archibold, Randal C. "These Neighbors Are Good Ones without a New Fence."
    New York Times, October 22, 2008, sec. A.

29. Article in an online newspaper   Include the URL for the article; if the URL is very long, use the URL for the newspaper's home page. Omit page numbers, even if the source provides them.

29. Doyle McManus, "The Candor War," *Chicago Tribune*, July 29, 2010, http://www.chicagotribune.com/.

McManus, Doyle. "The Candor War." *Chicago Tribune*, July 29, 2010. http://
    www.chicagotribune.com/.

30. Newspaper article from a database   Give whatever identifying information is available in the database listing: a DOI for the article; the name of the database and the number assigned by the database; or a "stable" or "persistent" URL for the article.

30. Clifford J. Levy, "In Kyrgyzstan, Failure to Act Adds to Crisis," *New York Times*, June 18, 2010, General OneFile (A229196045).

Levy, Clifford J. "In Kyrgyzstan, Failure to Act Adds to Crisis." *New York Times*, June 18, 2010. General OneFile (A229196045).

31. Unsigned newspaper article

31. "Renewable Energy Rules," *Boston Globe*, August 11, 2003, sec. A.

Boston Globe. "Renewable Energy Rules." August 11, 2003, sec. A.

32. Book review

32. Benjamin Wittes, "Remember the Titan," review of *Louis D. Brandeis: A Life*, by Melvin T. Urofsky, *Wilson Quarterly* 33, no. 4 (2009): 100.

Wittes, Benjamin. "Remember the Titan." Review of *Louis D. Brandeis: A Life*, by Melvin T. Urofsky. *Wilson Quarterly* 33, no. 4 (2009): 100-101.

33. Letter to the editor   Do not use the letter's title, even if the publication gives one.

33. David Harlan, letter to the editor, *New York Review of Books*, October 9, 2008.

Harlan, David. Letter to the editor. *New York Review of Books*, October 9, 2008.

Online sources

For most Web sites, include an author if a site has one, the title of the site, the sponsor, the date of publication or modified date (date of most recent changes), and the site's URL. Do not italicize a Web site unless the site is an online book or periodical. Use quotation marks for the titles of sections or pages in a Web site. If a site does not have a date of publication or modified date, give the date you accessed the site ("accessed January 3, 2010").

34. Web site

34. Chesapeake and Ohio Canal National Historical Park, National Park Service, last modified April 9, 2010, http://www.nps.gov/choh/index.htm.

Chesapeake and Ohio Canal National Historical Park. National Park Service.
  Last modified April 9, 2010. http://www.nps.gov/choh/index.htm.

35. Short work from a Web site   Place the title of the short
work in quotation marks.

  35. George P. Landow, "Victorian and Victorianism," Victorian Web, last
modified August 2, 2009, http://victorianweb.org/vn/victor4.html.

Landow, George P. "Victorian and Victorianism." Victorian Web. Last modified
  August 2, 2009. http://victorianweb.org/vn/victor4.html.

36. Online posting or e-mail   If an online posting has been
archived, include a URL. E-mails that are not part of an online discussion are treated as personal communications (see
item 42). Online postings and e-mails are not included in the
bibliography.

  36. Susanna J. Sturgis to Copyediting-L discussion list, July 17, 2010,
http://listserv.indiana.edu/archives/copyediting-l.html.

37. Weblog (blog) post   Treat as a short work from a Web site
(see item 35). Put the title of the post in quotation marks, and
italicize the name of the blog. Insert "blog" in parentheses
after the name if the word *blog* is not part of the name.

  37. Miland Brown, "The Flawed Montevideo Convention of 1933,"
World History Blog, http://www.worldhistoryblog.com/2008/05/flawed
-montevideo-convention-of-1933.html.

Brown, Miland. "The Flawed Montevideo Convention of 1933." World
  History Blog. http://www.worldhistoryblog.com/2008/05/flawed
  -montevideo-convention-of-1933.html.

38. Podcast   Treat as a short work from a Web site (see item
35), including the following, if available: the author's (or
speaker's) name; the title of the podcast, in quotation marks;
an identifying number, if any; the title of the site on which
it appears; the sponsor of the site; and the URL. Identify the
type of podcast or file format and the date of posting or your
date of access before the URL.

38. Paul Tiyambe Zeleza, "Africa's Global Past," Episode 40, Africa Past and Present, African Online Digital Library, podcast audio, April 29, 2010, http://afripod.aodl.org/.

Zeleza, Paul Tiyambe. "Africa's Global Past." Episode 40. Africa Past and Present. African Online Digital Library. Podcast audio, April 29, 2010. http://afripod.aodl.org/

39. Online audio or video   Cite as a short work from a Web site (see item 35). If the source is a downloadable file, identify the file format or medium before the URL.

39. Richard B. Freeman, "Global Capitalism, Labor Markets, and Inequality," Institute of International Studies, University of California at Berkeley, http://www.youtube.com/watch?v=cgNCFsXGUa0.

Freeman, Richard B. "Global Capitalism, Labor Markets, and Inequality." Institute of International Studies, University of California at Berkeley. http://www.youtube.com/watch?v=cgNCFsXGUa0.

Other sources (including online versions)

40. Government document

40. U.S. Department of State, *Foreign Relations of the United States: Diplomatic Papers, 1943* (Washington, DC: GPO, 1965), 562.

U.S. Department of State. *Foreign Relations of the United States: Diplomatic Papers, 1943*. Washington, DC: GPO, 1965.

41. Unpublished dissertation

41. Stephanie Lynn Budin, "The Origins of Aphrodite" (PhD diss., University of Pennsylvania, 2000), 301-2, ProQuest (AAT 9976404).

Budin, Stephanie Lynn. "The Origins of Aphrodite." PhD diss., University of Pennsylvania, 2000. ProQuest (AAT 9976404).

42. Personal communication

42. Sara Lehman, e-mail message to author, August 13, 2009.

Personal communications are not included in the bibliography.

43. Published or broadcast interview

43. Robert Downey Jr., interview by Graham Norton, *The Graham Norton Show*, BBC America, December 14, 2009.

Downey, Robert, Jr. Interview by Graham Norton. *The Graham Norton Show*. BBC America, December 14, 2009.

44. Published proceedings of a conference

44. Julie Kimber, Peter Love, and Phillip Deery, eds., *Labour Traditions: Proceedings of the Tenth National Labour History Conference*, University of Melbourne, Carlton, Victoria, Australia, July 4-6, 2007 (Melbourne: Australian Society for the Study of Labour History, 2007), 5.

Kimber, Julie, Peter Love, and Phillip Deery, eds. *Labour Traditions: Proceedings of the Tenth National Labour History Conference*. University of Melbourne, Carlton, Victoria, Australia, July 4-6, 2007. Melbourne: Australian Society for the Study of Labour History, 2007.

45. Video or DVD

45. *The Secret of Roan Inish*, directed by John Sayles (1993; Culver City, CA: Columbia TriStar Home Video, 2000), DVD.

The Secret of Roan Inish. Directed by John Sayles. 1993; Culver City, CA: Columbia TriStar Home Video, 2000. DVD.

46. Sound recording

46. Gustav Holst, *The Planets*, Royal Philharmonic Orchestra, conducted by André Previn, Telarc 80133, compact disc.

Holst, Gustav. *The Planets*. Royal Philharmonic Orchestra. Conducted by André Previn. Telarc 80133, compact disc.

47. Musical score or composition

47. Antonio Vivaldi, *L'Estro armonico*, op. 3, ed. Eleanor Selfridge-Field (Mineola, NY: Dover, 1999).

Vivaldi, Antonio. *L'Estro armonico*, op. 3. Edited by Eleanor Selfridge-Field. Mineola, NY: Dover, 1999.

48. Work of art

48. Aaron Siskind, *Untitled (The Most Crowded Block)*, gelatin silver print, 1939, Kemper Museum of Contemporary Art, Kansas City, MO.

Siskind, Aaron. *Untitled (The Most Crowded Block)*. Gelatin silver print, 1939. Kemper Museum of Contemporary Art, Kansas City, MO.

49. Performance

49. Robert Schenkkan, *The Kentucky Cycle*, directed by Richard Elliott, Willows Theatre, Concord, CA, August 31, 2007.

Schenkkan, Robert. *The Kentucky Cycle*. Directed by Richard Elliott. Willows Theatre, Concord, CA, August 31, 2007.

Chicago manuscript format

The following guidelines for formatting a *Chicago*-style paper and preparing its endnotes and bibliography are based on *The Chicago Manual of Style*, 16th ed. (Chicago: U of Chicago P, 2010). For a sample *Chicago* paper, see pages 248–56.

Formatting the paper

Materials and font   Use good-quality 8½″ × 11″ white paper. Avoid a font that is unusual or hard to read.

Title page   Include the full title of your paper, your name, the course title, the instructor's name, and the date. See page 248 for a sample title page.

Pagination   Using arabic numerals, number the pages in the upper right corner. Do not number the title page but count it in the manuscript numbering; that is, the first page of the text will be numbered 2. Depending on your instructor's preference, you may also use a short title or your last name before the page numbers to help identify pages.

Margins and line spacing   Leave margins of at least one inch at the top, bottom, and sides of the page. Double-space the body of the paper, including long quotations that have been set off from the text. (For line spacing in notes and the bibliography, see p. 247.) Left-align the text.

Long quotations   You can choose to set off a long quotation of five to ten typed lines by indenting the entire quotation one-half inch from the left margin. (You should always set off quotations of ten or more lines.) Double-space the quotation; do not use quotation marks. (See pp. 250 and 252 for a long quotation in the text of a paper.)

Capitalization and italics   In titles of works, capitalize all words except articles (*a, an, the*), prepositions (*at, from, between,* and so on), coordinating conjunctions (*and, but, or, nor, for, so, yet*), and *to* and *as*—unless one of these words is first or last in the title or subtitle. Follow these guidelines in your paper even if the title is styled differently in the source.

Lowercase the first word following a colon even if the word begins a complete sentence. When the colon introduces a series of sentences or questions, capitalize all sentences in the series, including the first.

Italicize the titles of books and other long works. Use quotation marks around the titles of periodical articles, poems, short stories, and other short works.

Visuals   *Chicago* classifies visuals as tables and illustrations (illustrations, or figures, include drawings, photographs, maps, and charts). Keep visuals as simple as possible. Label each table with an arabic numeral (Table 1, Table 2, and so on) and provide a clear title that identifies the table's subject. The label and the title should appear on separate lines above the table, flush left. Below the table, give its source in a note like this one:

Source: Edna Bonacich and Richard P. Appelbaum, *Behind the Label* (Berkeley: University of California Press, 2000), 145.

For each figure, place a label and a caption below the figure, flush left. The label and caption need not appear on separate lines. The word "Figure" may be abbreviated to "Fig."

In the text of your paper, discuss the most significant features of each visual. Place visuals as close as possible to the sentences that relate to them unless your instructor prefers visuals in an appendix.

URLs (Web addresses)   When a URL must break across lines, do not insert a hyphen or break at a hyphen if the URL contains one. Instead, break the URL after a colon or a double slash or before any other mark of punctuation. If your word processing program automatically turns Web addresses into links (by underlining them and changing the color), turn off this feature.

Headings   *Chicago* does not provide guidelines for the use of headings in student papers. If you would like to insert headings in a long essay or research paper, check first with your instructor. See the sample pages from a *Chicago*-style paper on pages 248–56 for typical placement and formatting of headings.

Preparing the endnotes

Begin the endnotes on a new page at the end of the paper. Center the title Notes about one inch from the top of the page, and number the pages consecutively with the rest of the manuscript. See page 254 for an example.

Indenting and numbering   Indent the first line of each note one-half inch from the left margin; do not indent additional lines in the note. Begin the note with the arabic numeral that corresponds to the number in the text. Put a period after the number.

Line spacing   Single-space each note and double-space between notes (unless your instructor prefers double-spacing throughout).

Preparing the bibliography

Typically, the notes in *Chicago*-style papers are followed by a bibliography, an alphabetically arranged list of all the works cited or consulted. Center the title Bibliography about one inch from the top of the page. Number bibliography pages consecutively with the rest of the paper. See page 256 for a sample bibliography.

Alphabetizing the list   Alphabetize the bibliography by the last names of the authors (or editors); when a work has no author or editor, alphabetize it by the first word of the title other than *A*, *An*, or *The*.

If your list includes two or more works by the same author, use six hyphens instead of the author's name in all entries after the first. Arrange the entries alphabetically by title.

Indenting and line spacing   Begin each entry at the left margin, and indent any additional lines one-half inch. Single-space each entry and double-space between entries (unless your instructor prefers double-spacing throughout).

Sample research paper: *Chicago* style

Following is a sample research paper by Ned Bishop, a student in a history class. Bishop was asked to document his paper using *Chicago*-style endnotes and bibliography. In preparing his manuscript, Bishop also followed *Chicago* guidelines.

Title of paper.

The Massacre at Fort Pillow:

Holding Nathan Bedford Forrest Accountable

Writer's name.

Ned Bishop

Title of course,
instructor's name,
and date.

History 214

Professor Citro

March 22, 2001

Marginal annotations indicate *Chicago*-style formatting.

Bishop 2

Although Northern newspapers of the time no doubt exaggerated some of the Confederate atrocities at Fort Pillow, most modern sources agree that a massacre of Union troops took place there on April 12, 1864. It seems clear that Union soldiers, particularly black soldiers, were killed after they had stopped fighting or had surrendered or were being held prisoner. Less clear is the role played by Major General Nathan Bedford Forrest in leading his troops. Although we will never know whether Forrest directly ordered the massacre, evidence suggests that he was responsible for it.

What happened at Fort Pillow?

Fort Pillow, Tennessee, which sat on a bluff overlooking the Mississippi River, had been held by the Union for two years. It was garrisoned by 580 men, 292 of them from United States Colored Heavy and Light Artillery regiments, 285 from the white Thirteenth Tennessee Cavalry. Nathan Bedford Forrest commanded about 1,500 troops.[1]

Statistics are cited with an endnote.

The Confederates attacked Fort Pillow on April 12, 1864, and had virtually surrounded the fort by the time Forrest arrived on the battlefield. At 3:30 p.m., Forrest demanded the surrender of the Union forces, sending in a message of the sort he had used before: "The conduct of the officers and men garrisoning Fort Pillow has been such as to entitle them to being treated as prisoners of war. . . . Should my demand be refused, I cannot be responsible for the fate of your command."[2] Union Major William Bradford, who had replaced Major Booth, killed earlier by sharpshooters, asked for an hour to consider the demand. Forrest, worried that vessels in the river were bringing in more troops, "shortened the time to twenty minutes."[3] Bradford refused to surrender, and Forrest quickly ordered the attack.

Quotation is cited with an endnote.

The Confederates charged to the fort, scaled the parapet, and fired on the forces within. Victory came quickly, with the Union forces running toward the river or surrendering. Shelby Foote describes the scene like this:

Long quotation is set off from text by indenting. Quotation marks are omitted.

> Some kept going, right on into the river, where a number
> drowned and the swimmers became targets for marksmen on
> the bluff. Others, dropping their guns in terror, ran back toward
> the Confederates with their hands up, and of these some were
> spared as prisoners, while others were shot down in the act of
> surrender.[4]

In his own official report, Forrest makes no mention of the massacre. He does make much of the fact that the Union flag was not lowered by the Union forces, saying that if his own men had not taken down the flag, "few, if any, would have survived unhurt another

Quotation is introduced with a signal phrase.

volley."[5] However, as Jack Hurst points out and Forrest must have known, in this twenty-minute battle, "Federals running for their lives had little time to concern themselves with a flag."[6]

The federal congressional report on Fort Pillow, which charged the Confederates with appalling atrocities, was strongly criticized by Southerners. Respected writer Shelby Foote, while agreeing that the report was "largely" fabrication, points out that the "casualty figures . . . indicated strongly that unnecessary killing had occurred."[7] In an important article, John Cimprich and Robert C. Mainfort Jr. argue that the most trustworthy evidence is that written within about ten days of the battle, before word of the congressional hearings circulated and Southerners realized the extent of Northern outrage. The article reprints a group of letters and newspaper sources written before April 22 and thus "untainted by the political overtones the controversy later assumed."[8] Cimprich and Mainfort conclude that these sources "support the case for the occurrence of a massacre" but that Forrest's role "remains clouded" because of inconsistencies in testimony.[9]

Did Forrest order the massacre?

We will never really know whether Forrest directly ordered the massacre, but it seems unlikely. True, Confederate soldier Achilles Clark, who had no reason to lie, wrote to his sisters that "I with several others tried to stop the butchery . . . but Gen. Forrest ordered them [Negro and white Union troops] shot down like dogs[,] and the carnage continued."[10] But it is not clear whether Clark heard Forrest giving the orders or was just reporting hearsay. Many Confederates had been shouting "No quarter! No quarter!" and, as Shelby Foote points out, these shouts were "thought by some to be at Forrest's command."[11] A Union soldier, Jacob Thompson, claimed to have seen Forrest order the killing, but when asked to describe the six-foot-two general, he called him "a little bit of a man."[12]

Perhaps the most convincing evidence that Forrest did not order the massacre is that he tried to stop it once it had begun. Historian Albert Castel quotes several eyewitnesses on both the Union and Confederate sides as saying that Forrest ordered his men to stop firing.[13] In a letter to his wife three days after the battle, Confederate soldier Samuel Caldwell wrote that "if General Forrest had not run between our men & the Yanks with his pistol and sabre drawn not a man would have been spared."[14]

In a respected biography of Nathan Bedford Forrest, Hurst suggests that the temperamental Forrest "may have ragingly ordered a massacre and even intended to carry it out—until he rode inside the fort and viewed the horrifying result" and ordered it stopped.[15] While this is an intriguing interpretation of events, even Hurst would probably admit that it is merely speculation.

Can Forrest be held responsible for the massacre?

Even assuming that Forrest did not order the massacre, he can still be held accountable for it. That is because he created an atmosphere ripe for the possibility of atrocities and did nothing to ensure that it wouldn't happen. Throughout his career Forrest repeatedly threatened "no quarter," particularly with respect to black soldiers, so Confederate troops had good reason to think that in massacring the enemy they were carrying out his orders. As Hurst writes, "About all he had to do to produce a massacre was issue no order against one."[16] Dudley Taylor Cornish agrees:

> It has been asserted again and again that Forrest did not order a massacre. He did not need to. He had sought to terrify the Fort Pillow garrison by a threat of no quarter, as he had done at Union City and at Paducah in the days just before he turned on Pillow. If his men did enter the fort shouting "Give them no quarter; kill them; kill them; it is General Forrest's orders," he should not have been surprised.[17]

The slaughter at Fort Pillow was no doubt driven in large part by racial hatred. Numbers alone suggest this: of 295 white troops, 168 were taken prisoner, but of 262 black troops, only 58 were taken into custody, with the rest either dead or too badly wounded to walk.[18] A Southern reporter traveling with Forrest makes clear that the discrimination was deliberate: "Our troops maddened by the excitement, shot down the ret[r]eating Yankees, and not until they had attained t[h]e water's edge and turned to beg for mercy, did any prisoners fall in [t]o our hands—Thus the whites received quarter, but the negroes were shown no mercy."[19] Union surgeon Dr. Charles Fitch, who was taken prisoner by Forrest, testified that after he was in custody he "saw" Confederate soldiers "kill every negro that made his appearance dressed in Federal uniform."[20]

Fort Pillow is not the only instance of a massacre or threatened massacre of black soldiers by troops under Forrest's command.

Bishop 6

Biographer Brian Steel Wills points out that at Brice's Cross Roads
in June 1864, "black soldiers suffered inordinately" as Forrest
looked the other way and Confederate soldiers deliberately sought
out those they termed "the damned negroes."[21] Just a day after
Fort Pillow, on April 13, 1864, one of Forrest's generals, Abraham
Buford, after consulting with Forrest, demanded that the federal
garrison in Columbus, Kentucky, surrender. The demand stated that
if an attack became necessary, "no quarter will be shown to the
negro troops whatever; the white troops will be treated as prisoners
of war."[22]

Nathan Bedford Forrest, a crude man who had made his fortune
as a slave trader, was noted for both his violence and his hatred of
blacks. In the words of historian James M. McPherson, "Forrest
possessed a killer instinct toward . . . blacks in any capacity other
than slave."[23] Forrest's battle successes were largely due to his brazen
tactics—tactics that Hurst says would not have occurred to the
"aristocratic, well-educated Confederate military hierarchy." [24] Some
Southerners, in fact, found Forrest's leadership style distasteful. As one
Mississippi aristocrat put it, "Forrest may be, and no doubt is, the best
cavalry officer in the West, but I object to a tyrrannical [*sic*],
hot-headed vulgarian's commanding me."[25]

Because he was so crudely racist, Forrest surely understood the
rage that his troops felt toward the very idea of blacks as soldiers.
Further, he must have known that his standard threats of "No quarter"
would fuel the Confederate soldiers' rage. Although Forrest may have
tried to prevent the massacre once it was under way, he can still be
held accountable for it. That is because he created the conditions
that led to the massacre (especially of black troops) and with full
knowledge of those conditions took no steps to prevent what was a
nearly inevitable bloodbath.

Ellipsis mark
indicates that
words have been
omitted.

Notes begin on a
new page.

Notes

First line of each
note is indented
½".

    1. John Cimprich and Robert C. Mainfort Jr., eds., "Fort
Pillow Revisited: New Evidence about an Old Controversy," *Civil War
History* 28, no. 4 (1982): 293-94.

Note number is
not raised and
is followed by a
period.

    2. Quoted in Brian Steel Wills, *A Battle from the Start:
The Life of Nathan Bedford Forrest* (New York: HarperCollins, 1992),
182.

    3. Ibid., 183.

    4. Shelby Foote, *The Civil War, a Narrative: Red River to
Appomattox* (New York: Vintage, 1986), 110.

Authors' names
are not inverted.

    5. Nathan Bedford Forrest, "Report of Maj. Gen. Nathan
B. Forrest, C. S. Army, Commanding Cavalry, of the Capture
of Fort Pillow," Shotgun's Home of the American Civil War,
http://www.civilwarhome.com/forrest.htm.

    6. Jack Hurst, *Nathan Bedford Forrest: A Biography*
(New York: Knopf, 1993), 174.

Last name and
title refer to an
earlier note by the
same author.

    7. Foote, *Civil War*, 111.

    8. Cimprich and Mainfort, "Fort Pillow," 295.

    9. Ibid., 305.

    10. Ibid., 299.

    11. Foote, *Civil War*, 110.

    12. Quoted in Wills, *Battle from the Start*, 187.

Notes are single-
spaced, with
double-spacing
between notes.
(Some instructors
may prefer
double-spacing
throughout.)

    13. Albert Castel, "The Fort Pillow Massacre: A Fresh
Examination of the Evidence," *Civil War History* 4, no. 1 (1958):
44-45.

    14. Cimprich and Mainfort, "Fort Pillow," 300.

    15. Hurst, *Nathan Bedford Forrest*, 177.

    16. Ibid.

17. Dudley Taylor Cornish, *The Sable Arm: Black Troops in the Union Army, 1861-1865* (Lawrence, KS: University Press of Kansas, 1987), 175.

18. Foote, *Civil War*, 111.

19. Cimprich and Mainfort, "Fort Pillow," 304.

20. Quoted in Wills, *Battle from the Start*, 189.

21. Ibid., 215.

22. Quoted in Hurst, *Nathan Bedford Forrest*, 177.

23. Quoted in James M. McPherson, *Battle Cry of Freedom: The Civil War Era* (New York: Oxford University Press, 1988), 402.

24. Hurst, *Nathan Bedford Forrest*, 74.

25. Quoted in Foote, *Civil War*, 106.

Bibliography

Castel, Albert. "The Fort Pillow Massacre: A Fresh Examination of the
        Evidence." *Civil War History* 4, no. 1 (1958): 37-50.

Cimprich, John, and Robert C. Mainfort Jr., eds. "Fort Pillow Revisited:
        New Evidence about an Old Controversy." *Civil War History* 28,
        no. 4 (1982): 293-306.

Cornish, Dudley Taylor. *The Sable Arm: Black Troops in the Union Army,
        1861-1865*. Lawrence: University Press of Kansas, 1987.

Foote, Shelby. *The Civil War, a Narrative: Red River to Appomattox*.
        New York: Vintage, 1986.

Forrest, Nathan Bedford. "Report of Maj. Gen. Nathan B. Forrest,
        C. S. Army, Commanding Cavalry, of the Capture of Fort Pillow."
        Shotgun's Home of the American Civil War. http://www
        .civilwarhome.com/forrest.htm.

Hurst, Jack. *Nathan Bedford Forrest: A Biography*. New York: Knopf,
        1993.

McPherson, James M. *Battle Cry of Freedom: The Civil War Era*. New York:
        Oxford University Press, 1988.

Wills, Brian Steel. *A Battle from the Start: The Life of Nathan Bedford
        Forrest*. New York: HarperCollins, 1992.

Bibliography
begins on a new
page.

Entries are
alphabetized
by authors' last
names.

First line of entry
is at left margin;
additional lines are
indented ½".

Entries are single-
spaced, with
double-spacing
between entries.
(Some instructors
may prefer
double-spacing
throughout.)

CSE Style: Biology and Other Sciences

CSE documentation systems

Though scientific publications document sources in similar ways, the details of presenting source information vary from journal to journal. Often publications provide prospective authors with style sheets that outline formats for presenting sources. Before submitting an article to a scientific publication, you should request its style sheet. If one is not available, examine a copy of the publication to see how sources are documented. When writing for a science course, check with your instructor about how to cite and list your sources.

Most biologists, zoologists, earth scientists, geneticists, and other scientists use one of three systems of documentation specified by the Council of Science Editors in *Scientific Style and Format: The CSE Manual for Authors, Editors, and Publishers* (7th ed., 2006).

In the CSE *name-year* system, the author of the source is named in the text and the date is given in parentheses. The APA documentation section of this book (see pp. 182–218) describes an author-date system that is similar to the CSE name-year system.

In the CSE *citation-sequence* system, each source cited in the paper is given a number the first time it appears in the text. Anytime the source is referred to again, the text is marked with the same number. At the end of the paper, a list of references provides full publication information for each numbered source. Entries in the reference list are numbered in the order in which they are mentioned in the paper.

In the CSE *citation-name* system, the list of references is first put in alphabetical order and then the entries are numbered in that order. Those numbers are used in the text to cite the sources from the list. This section describes formatting of in-text citations and the reference list in all three systems and gives specific models for entries in a citation-sequence reference list.

CSE in-text citations

In the text of a paper using the citation-sequence or citation-name system, the source is referenced by a superscript number.

IN-TEXT CITATION

Scientists are beginning to question the validity of linking genes to a number of human traits and disorders [1].

At the end of the paper, on a page titled References or Cited References, the source is fully identified according to CSE style.

ENTRY IN THE REFERENCE LIST

1. Horgan J. Eugenics revisited. Sci Am. 1993;268(6):122-130.

If the author or publication date of a particular work is important to your discussion, add this information to the sentence.

Smith [11], studying three species of tree frogs in South Carolina, was the first to observe. . . .

This species was not listed in early floras of New York; however, in 1985 it was reported in a botanical survey of Chenango County [13] and has since been verified [14].

In the name-year system, the author's name and the date are given in parentheses in the text of the paper. Alternatively, the author's name can be given in a signal phrase and the date in parentheses.

This species was not listed in early floras of New York; however, it was reported in a botanical survey of Chenango County (Osiecki and Smith 1985).

Smith (2003), studying three species of tree frogs in South Carolina, was the first to observe. . . .

Sometimes you will refer to a specific part of a source (such as a figure or a table) or will quote the exact words of a source. CSE does not provide guidelines for citing a specific part of a source, but your instructor will probably expect you to include an exact reference. The following style is consistent with CSE's other guidelines.

> My data thus differ markedly from Markam's study on the same species in New York [5](Figs. 2,7).

> Researchers observed an immune response in "19 of 20 people who ate a potato vaccine aimed at the Norwalk virus," according to Langridge [3](p. 68).

CSE reference list

Basic format   Center the title References (or Cited References) and then list the works you have cited in the paper; do not include other works you may have read. Double-space throughout.

Organization of the list   In the citation-sequence system, number the entries in the order in which they appear in the text. In the citation-name system, first alphabetize all the entries by authors' last names (or by organization name or by title for a work with no author). Then number the entries in the order in which they appear in the list. In both systems, use the number in the reference list every time you refer to the corresponding source in the paper. Make the entire entry flush with the left margin.

In the name-year system, the entries in the reference list are not numbered. They are alphabetized by authors' last names (or by organization name or by title for a work with no author). The year is placed after the last author's name, followed by a period. To convert the models shown here to the name-year system, omit the number and move the date of publication after the last author's name. CSE provides no guidelines for formatting a reference list in the name-year system in a student paper, but you can use a hanging indent for readability: Type the first line of each entry flush left, and indent any additional lines one-half inch.

Authors' names   List authors' names last name first. Use initials for first and middle names, with no periods after the initials and no space between them. Do not use a comma between the last name and the initials. Use all authors' names if a work has up to ten authors; for a work with eleven or more authors, list the first ten names followed by a comma and "et al." (for "and others").

Titles of books and articles   Capitalize only the first word in the title of a book or article (and all proper nouns). Do not underline or italicize the titles of books; do not place titles of articles in quotation marks.

Titles of journals   Abbreviate titles of journals that consist of more than one word. Omit the words *the* and *of*; do not use apostrophes. Capitalize all the words or abbreviated words in the title; do not underline or italicize the title: Science, Sci Am, N Engl J Med, Womens Health.

Page ranges   Do not abbreviate page ranges for articles in journals or periodicals and for chapters in edited volumes. When an article appears on discontinuous pages, list all pages or page ranges, separated by commas: 145-149, 162-174. For chapters in edited volumes, use the abbreviation "p." before the numbers (p. 63-90).

Books

1. Basic format for a book   After the author(s) and title, give the place of publication, the name of the publisher, and the date of publication.

1. Melchias G. Biodiversity and conservation. Enfield (NH): Science; 2001.

2. Two or more authors   List the authors in the order in which they appear on the title page. For a work with two to ten

Directory to CSE reference list

authors, list all the authors. For eleven or more authors, list the first ten followed by "et al." (for "and others").

2. Ennos R, Sheffield E. Plant life. Boston: Blackwell Scientific; 2000.

3. Edition other than the first   Include the number of the edition after the title.

3. Mai J, Paxinos G, Assheuer J. Atlas of the human brain. 2nd ed. Burlington (MA): Elsevier; 2004.

4. Article or chapter in an edited volume   Begin with the name of the author and the title of the article or chapter. Then write "In:" and name the editor or editors, followed by a comma and the word "editor" or "editors." Place the title of the book and publication information next. End with the page numbers on which the article or chapter appears.

4. Underwood AJ, Chapman MG. Intertidal ecosystems. In: Levin SA, editor. Encyclopedia of biodiversity. Vol. 3. San Diego: Academic Press; 2000. p. 485-499.

Articles

5. Article in a magazine   Provide the year, month, and day (for weekly publications), followed by the page numbers of the article.

5. Stevens MH. Heavenly harbingers. Smithsonian. 2001 Nov:20, 22.

6. Article in a journal   After the author(s) and the title of the article, give the journal title, the year, the volume number, the issue number if there is one (in parentheses), and the page numbers on which the article appears.

6. Gulbins E, Lang F. Pathogens, host-cell invasion and disease. Am Sci. 2001;89(5):406-413.

7. Article in a newspaper   After the name of the newspaper, give the edition name in parentheses, the date of publication, the section letter (or number), the page number, and the column number. If the newspaper does not have section designations, use a colon between the date and the page number.

7. O'Neil J. A closer look at medical marijuana. New York Times (National Ed.). 2001 Jul 17;Sect. D:6 (col. 4).

8. Article with multiple authors   For a work with up to ten authors, list the names of all authors. For a work with eleven or more authors, list the first ten names followed by a comma and "et al." (for "and others").

8. Longini IM Jr, Halloran ME, Nizam A, Yang Y. Containing pandemic influenza with antiviral agents. Am J Epidemiol. 2004;159(7):623-633.

9. Article with a corporate author   When a work has a corporate author, begin with the authoring organization, followed by the article title, journal title, and all other publication information.

9. International Committee of Medical Journal Editors. Clinical trial registration: a statement from the International Committee of Medical Journal Editors. JAMA. 2004;292(11):1363-1364.

In the name-year system, a familiar abbreviation for an organization is given in brackets at the beginning of the entry: [NCI] National Cancer Institute. 2004. The abbreviation is used in the in-text citation: (NCI 2004).

Electronic sources

CSE guidelines for Web sites and subscription services require publication information as for books: city, publisher, and publication date. This information can usually be found on the home page of a Web site and in a copyright link in a subscription service. Ask a reference librarian if you have trouble locating the information. In addition, include an update date if one is available and your date of access. Do not use a period at the end of a URL unless the URL ends in a slash. Break a URL only after a slash.

10. Home page of a Web site   Begin with the author, whether an individual or an organization. Include the title of the home page (if it is different from the author's name), followed in brackets by the word "Internet." Provide the place of publication, the publisher (or the site's sponsor), and the date of publication. Include the copyright date if no date of publication is given or if the publication date and the copyright date are different: 2010, c2009. Include in brackets the date the page was last modified or updated and the date you accessed the site: [modified 2009 Mar 14; cited 2010 Feb 3]. Use the phrase "Available from:" followed by the URL.

10. American Society of Gene and Cell Therapy [Internet]. Milwaukee (WI): The Society; c2000-2010 [modified 2010 Jan 8; cited 2010 Jan 16]. Available from: http://www.asgt.org/.

11. Short work from a Web site If the short work does not have an author or if the author is the same as the author of the site, begin as for a home page. After the publication information, give the title of the short work, the date of publication or most recent update, and the date of access. Indicate in brackets the number of pages, screens, paragraphs, lines, or bytes: about 5 p., about 3 screens, 12 paragraphs, 26 lines, 125K bytes. End with "Available from:" and the URL.

11. Cleveland Clinic. The Cleveland Clinic Health Information Center [Internet]. Cleveland (OH): The Clinic; c2006. Smoking cessation; 2009 [cited 2010 Feb 8]; [about 3 screens]. Available from: http://www.clevelandclinic.org/services/smoking_cessation/hic_quitting_smoking.aspx

If the short work has an author different from the author of the site, begin with the author and title of the short work, followed by the word "In:" and the home page information as in item 10. End with the URL for the short work.

12. Online book To cite an online book, follow the instructions for a home page, but include the description "Internet" in brackets following the title.

12. Wilson DE, Reeder DM, editors. Mammal species of the world [Internet]. Washington (DC): Smithsonian Institution Press; 3rd ed. Baltimore (MD): Johns Hopkins University Press; c2005 [cited 2007 Oct 14]; [about 200 screens]. Available from: http://vertebrates.si.edu/mammals/msw/.

If you are referring to a specific chapter or section in an online book, begin the citation with the author and the title of the specific part. Follow with the word "In:" and the author, editor, title, and publication information for the entire book. End with access information about the specific part.

12. Olson S. The path to a PhD. In: Jarmul D, editor. Beyond bio 101: the transformation of undergraduate biology education [Internet]. Chevy Chase (MD): Howard Hughes Medical Institute; c2001 [cited 2009 Nov 19]; [about 2 screens]. Available from: http://www.hhmi.org/beyondbio101/phdpath.htm

13. Article in an online periodical   Begin with the name of the author and the title of the article. Include the name of the journal, followed by the word "Internet" in brackets. Give the date of publication or the copyright date. Include in brackets the date the article was updated or modified, if any, and the date you accessed it, followed by a semicolon. Then provide the volume, issue, and page numbers. If the article is unpaginated, include in brackets the number or an estimated number of pages, screens, paragraphs, lines, or bytes. Write "Available from:" and the URL.

13. Isaacs FJ, Blake WJ, Collins JJ. Signal processing in single cells. Science [Internet]. 2005 Mar 25 [cited 2009 Jun 17];307(5717): 1886-1888. Available from: http://www.sciencemag.org/cgi/content/full/307/5717/1886

14. Work from a subscription service   CSE does not provide guidelines for an article accessed through a subscription service, such as *InfoTrac* or *EBSCOhost*. The guidelines presented here are based on CSE's models for an article in an online periodical and for a complete database.

Begin with information about the online article, as in item 13. Follow with the name of the database, the place of publication, the publisher, and the date of publication or the copyright date. End with the phrase "Available from:" followed by the URL for the database. Include an article or document number, if the database assigns one, after the URL.

14. Cantor RM, Kono N, Duvall JA, Alvarez-Retuerto A, Stone JL, Alarcon M, Nelson SF, Geschwind DH. Replication of autism linkage: fine-mapping peak at 17q21. Am J Hum Genet [Internet]. 2005 [cited 2009 Jun 17];76(6):1050-1056. Expanded Academic ASAP. Farmington Hills (MI): Thomson Gale; c2005. Available from: http://web4.infotrac.galegroup.com/. Document No.: A133015879.

15. E-mail   CSE recommends not including personal communications such as e-mail in the reference list. A parenthetical note in the text usually suffices: (2010 e-mail to me; unreferenced).

16. Online posting Online postings include messages to e-mail discussion lists (often called Listservs), Web forums, newsgroups, or bulletin boards. CSE does not provide guidelines for including postings in the reference list, but the following formatting is consistent with other CSE advice. Begin with the author initiating the message and the subject line of the message. Next use the word "In:" followed by the name of the host system and in brackets the phrase "discussion list on the Internet." Give the place where the discussion list is issued and the individual or organization that hosts the discussion list. Provide the date and time the message was posted, the date you accessed it, and the length of the message in screens, paragraphs, lines, or bytes. End with the phrase "Available from:" followed by the e-mail address by which the list can be accessed or the URL at which the list is archived.

16. Buxbaum E. Bradford protein assay in membrane crystals. In: BIOSCI/ Bionet: protein-analysis [discussion list on the Internet]. Bloomington: Indiana University; 2005 Jan 26, 10:45 am [cited 2005 Jun 22]; [about 16 lines]. Available from: http://www.bio.net/bionet/mm/proteins/ 2005-January/000010.html

Other sources (print and online)

The advice in this section refers to the print versions of the following sources, but in each case an example is also given for an online version.

17. Government report Begin with the name of the agency and, in parentheses, the country of origin if it is not part of the agency name. Next include the title of the report, a description of the report (if any), the place of publication, the publisher, and the date of publication. Give any relevant identifying information, such as a document number, and then the phrase "Available from:" followed by the name, city, and state of the organization that makes the report available or the URL for an online source.

17. National Institute on Drug Abuse (US). Inhalant abuse. Research Report
Series. Bethesda (MD): National Institutes of Health (US); 2005 Mar. NIH
Pub. No.: 00-3818. Available from: National Clearinghouse on Alcohol and
Drug Information, Rockville, MD 20852.

17. National Institute on Drug Abuse (US). Inhalant abuse [Internet].
Research Report Series. Bethesda (MD): National Institutes of Health (US);
2005 Mar [cited 2005 Jun 23]; [about 13 screens]. NIH Pub. No.: 00-3818.
Available from: http://www.drugabuse.gov/ResearchReports/Inhalants/
Inhalants.html

In the name-year system, begin with the abbreviation of
the organization, if any, in brackets. (You will use the abbreviation in your in-text citations.) Use the complete name of
the organization when you alphabetize the reference list.

[NIDA] National Institute on Drug Abuse (US). 2005 Mar. Inhalant abuse. . . .

18. Report from a private organization   Begin with the name of
the sponsoring organization. Next include the title of the report, a description of the report, the place of publication, the
publisher, the year and month of publication, and the product number (if any).

18. American Cancer Society. Cancer facts and figures for African Americans
2005-2006. Report. Atlanta (GA): The Society; 2005.

18. American Cancer Society. Cancer facts and figures for African Americans
2005-2006 [report on the Internet]. Atlanta (GA): The Society; 2005
[cited 2005 Jun 23]; [535K bytes]. Available from: http://www.cancer.org/
downloads/STT/CAFF2005AACorrPWSecured.pdf

19. Unpublished dissertation or thesis   After the author and title
of the work, indicate the type of work in brackets. List the city
and state of the institution granting the degree, followed by
the name of the institution and the date of the degree. Include
an availability statement if the work is archived somewhere

other than the sponsoring university's library (for example: Available from: University Microfilms, Ann Arbor, MI).

19. Warner DA. Phenotypes and survival of hatchling lizards [master's thesis]. Blacksburg: Virginia Polytechnic Institute and State University; 2001 Jan 16.

19. Warner DA. Phenotypes and survival of hatchling lizards [master's thesis on the Internet]. Blacksburg: Virginia Polytechnic Institute and State University; 2001 Jan 16 [cited 2005 Jun 22]; [125 p.]. Available from: http://scholar.lib.vt.edu/theses/available/etd-01232001-123230/.

20. Conference presentation Begin with the author and title of the presentation. After the word "In:" give any editors and the name of the conference if it is not included in the title of the publication. Give the dates and location of the conference, followed by publication information and the inclusive page numbers for the presentation. Give an availability statement if appropriate.

20. Pendleton L. The cost of beach water monitoring errors in southern California. In: Proceedings of the 2004 National Beaches Conference; 2004 Oct 13-15; San Diego, CA. Washington (DC): Environmental Protection Agency (US); 2005 Mar. p. 104-110.

20. Pendleton L. The cost of beach water monitoring errors in southern California [conference presentation on the Internet]. In: Proceedings of the 2004 National Beaches Conference [Internet]; 2004 Oct 13-15; San Diego, CA. Washington (DC): Environmental Protection Agency (US); 2005 Mar [cited 2005 Jun 30]. p. 104-110. Available from: http://www.epa.gov/waterscience/beaches/meetings/2004/.

21. Map First name the cartographer, if any, followed by the area represented, the title of the map, and, in brackets, the type of map. Provide the place of publication, publisher, and date of publication. If it is relevant, include a brief physical description of the map: the number of sheets, size, color or black and white, and scale.

21. Northeastern United States. West Nile virus: wild bird cases [demographic map]. Washington (DC): Department of the Interior (US); 2001 Jun 1. 1 sheet: color.

21. Northeastern United States. West Nile virus: wild bird cases [demographic map on the Internet]. Washington (DC): Department of the Interior (US); 2001 Jun 1 [cited 2005 Jun 22]; [1 screen]; color. Available from: http://nationalatlas.gov/printable/wnv.html

22. Audio or video recording   Begin with the title of the work, followed by the medium in brackets. Next include, if available, the author, editor, and producer. Provide the place of publication, the publisher, and the date of publication. Give a brief physical description of the work and, in parentheses, identifying information, if any. End the citation with "Available from:" followed by the name, city, and state of the organization that distributes the work or the URL for an online source.

22. NOVA: cancer warrior [videocassette]. Quade D, editor; WGBH Boston, producer. Boston: WGBH Educational Foundation; 2001 Feb 27. 1 videocassette: 60 min., sound, color. Available from: WGBH Boston Video, Boston, MA.

22. NOVA: cancer warrior [video on the Internet]. Quade D, editor; WGBH Boston, producer. Boston: WGBH Educational Foundation; 2001 Feb 27 [cited 2005 June 22]; 60 min., sound, color. Available from: http://www.pbs.org/wgbh/nova/cancer/program.html

CSE manuscript format

Although the style manual of the Council of Science Editors does not include manuscript guidelines for student papers, most instructors will want you to format your manuscript in ways consistent with common scientific practice. The following guidelines for student writers have been adapted from CSE advice directed to professional authors. When in doubt, check with your instructor. For sample pages of a college biology paper, see pages 272–76.

Materials   Use good-quality 8½″ × 11″ white paper. Secure the pages with a paper clip.

Title   Begin a college paper with an unnumbered title page. Center all information on the page: the title of your paper, your name, the name of the course, and the date. See page 272 for an example.

Pagination   The title page is counted as page 1, although a number does not appear. Number the first page of the paper as page 2. Type the number in the top right corner of the page. Many instructors will want you to use a shortened form of the title before the page number.

Margins, spacing, and indentation   Leave margins of at least one inch on all sides of the page, and double-space throughout the paper. Indent the first line of each paragraph one-half inch. When a quotation is set off from the text, indent it one-half inch from the left margin.

Abstract   Many science instructors require an abstract, a single paragraph that summarizes your paper. If your paper reports on research you conducted, use the abstract to describe your research methods, findings, and conclusions. Do not include bibliographic references in the abstract.

Headings   CSE encourages the use of headings to help readers follow the organization of a paper. Common headings for papers reporting research are Introduction, Methods (or Methods and Materials), Results, and Discussion. If you use both headings and subheadings for a long paper, make sure to distinguish clearly between them with your choice of typography.

Visuals   A visual should be placed as close as possible to the text that discusses it. In general, try to place visuals at the top of a page.

Appendixes   Appendixes may be used for relevant information that is too long to include in the body of the paper. Label each appendix and give it a title (for example, Appendix 1: Methodologies Used by Previous Researchers).

Acknowledgments   An acknowledgments section is common in scientific writing because research is often conducted with help from others. For example, you might give credit to colleagues who reviewed your work, to organizations that funded your work, and to writers who allowed you to cite their unpublished work.

List of references   For advice on constructing a CSE reference list, see pages 259–60.

Sample pages from a research paper: CSE style

The following sample pages are from a review of the literature written by student Briana Martin for a biology class. Martin follows the style of the Council of Science Editors (CSE) in the text of her paper and uses the CSE citation-sequence system for citing her sources.

Hypothermia, the Diving Reflex,
and Survival

Briana Martin

Biology 281
Professor McMillan
April 17, 2002

Hypothermia and Diving Reflex 2

ABSTRACT

This paper reviews the contributions of hypothermia and the mammalian diving reflex (MDR) to human survival of cold-water immersion incidents. It also examines the relationship between the victim's age and MDR and considers the protective role played by hypothermia. Hypothermia is the result of a reduced metabolic rate and lowered oxygen consumption by body tissues. Although hypothermia may produce fatal cardiac arrhythmias such as ventricular fibrillation, it is also associated with bradycardia and peripheral vasoconstriction, both of which enhance oxygen supply to the heart and brain. The MDR also causes bradycardia and reduced peripheral blood flow as well as laryngospasm, which protects victims against rapid inhalation of water. Studies of drowning and near drowning of children and adults suggest that victim survival depends on the presence of both hypothermia and the MDR, as neither alone can provide adequate cerebral protection during long periods of hypoxia. Future research is suggested to improve patient care.

INTRODUCTION

Drowning and near-drowning incidents are leading causes of mortality and morbidity in both children [1] and adults [2]. Over the past 30 years, there has been considerable interest in cold-water immersion incidents, particularly the reasons for the survival of some victims under seemingly fatal conditions. Research suggests that both hypothermia and a "mammalian diving reflex" (MDR) may account for survival in many near-drowning episodes [3]. However, the extent to which these two processes interact is not fully understood. Controversy also exists regarding the effect of the victim's age on the physiological responses to cold-water immersion. In this paper, I provide an overview of recent research on the protective value of hypothermia and the MDR in cold-water immersions. I also examine hypotheses concerning the effects of age on these processes and conclude with suggestions about future lines of research that may lead to improved patient care.

Hypoxia during drowning and near-drowning incidents

The major physiological problem facing drowning victims is hypoxia, or lack of adequate oxygen perfusion to body cells [1,4]. Hypoxia results in damage to many organs, including the heart, lungs, kidneys, liver, and intestines [4]. Generally, the length of time the body has been deprived of oxygen is closely related to patient prognosis. Only 6-7 s of hypoxia may cause unconsciousness; if hypoxia lasts longer than 5 min at relatively warm temperatures, death or irreversible brain damage may result [5]. However, some victims of cold-water immersion have survived after periods of oxygen deprivation lasting up to 2 h [4]. . . .

[*The student goes on to highlight the major controversies and to add interpretation and analysis.*]

CONCLUSIONS

Recent research on cold-water immersion incidents has provided a better understanding of the physiological processes occurring during drowning and near-drowning accidents. Current findings suggest that the cooperative effect of the MDR and hypothermia plays a critical role in patient survival during a cold-water immersion incident [3]. However, the relationship between the two processes is still unclear. Because it is impossible to provide an exact reproduction of a particular drowning incident within the laboratory, research is hampered by the lack of complete details. Consequently, it is difficult to draw comparisons among published case studies.

More complete and accurate documentation of cold-water immersion incidents—including time of submersion; time of recovery; and a profile of the victim including age, sex, and physical condition—will facilitate easier comparison of individual situations and lead to a more complete knowledge of the processes affecting long-term survival rates for drowning victims. Once we have a clearer understanding of the relationship between hypothermia and the MDR—and of the effect of such factors as the age of the victim—physicians and rescue personnel can take steps to improve patient care at the scene and in the hospital.

ACKNOWLEDGMENTS

I would like to thank V. McMillan and D. Huerta for their support and suggestions throughout the research and writing of this paper. I am also grateful to my classmates in Biology 281 for their thoughtful comments during writing workshops. Finally, I thank Colgate University's interlibrary loan staff for help securing the sources I needed for this review.

CITED REFERENCES

1. Kallas HJ, O'Rourke PP. Drowning and immersion injuries in children. Curr Opin Pediatr. 1993;5(3):295-302.

2. Keatinge WR. Accidental immersion hypothermia and drowning. Practitioner 1997;219(1310):183-187.

3. Gooden BA. Why some people do not drown—hypothermia versus the diving response. Med J Aust. 1992;157(9):629-632.

4. Biggart MJ, Bohn DJ. Effect of hypothermia and cardiac arrest on outcome of near-drowning accidents in children. J Pediatr. 1999;117(2 Pt 1):179-183.

5. Gooden BA. Drowning and the diving reflex in man. Med J Aust. 1972;2(11):583-587.

6. Bierens JJ, van der Velde EA. Submersion in the Netherlands: prognostic indicators and the results of resuscitation. Ann Emerg Med. 1999;19(12):1390-1395.

7. Ramey CA, Ramey DN, Hayward JS. Dive response of children in relation to cold-water near drowning. J Appl Physiol. 1987;62(2):665-688.

List of Style Manuals

Research and Documentation in the Electronic Age describes four commonly used systems of documentation: MLA, used in English and the humanities (see pp. 119–81); APA, used in psychology and the social sciences (see pp. 182–229); *Chicago*, used in history and some humanities (see pp. 230–56); and CSE, used in biology and other sciences (see pp. 257–76). Following is a list of style manuals used in a variety of disciplines.

BIOLOGY (See pp. 257–76.)

Council of Science Editors. *Scientific Style and Format: The CSE Manual for Authors, Editors, and Publishers.* 7th ed. Reston: Council of Science Eds., 2006. Print.

BUSINESS

American Management Association. *The AMA Style Guide for Business Writing.* New York: AMACOM, 1996. Print.

CHEMISTRY

Coghill, Anne M., and Lorrin R. Garson, eds. *The ACS Style Guide: Effective Communication of Scientific Information.* 3rd ed. Washington: Amer. Chemical Soc., 2006. Print.

ENGINEERING

Institute of Electrical and Electronics Engineers. *IEEE Editorial Style Manual.* IEEE, n.d. Web. 9 Sept. 2009.

ENGLISH AND OTHER HUMANITIES (See pp. 119–81.)

MLA Handbook for Writers of Research Papers. 7th ed. New York: Mod. Lang. Assn., 2009. Print.

GEOLOGY

Bates, Robert L., Rex Buchanan, and Marla Adkins-Heljeson, eds. *Geowriting: A Guide to Writing, Editing, and Printing in Earth Science.* 5th ed. rev. Alexandria: Amer. Geological Inst., 2004. Print.

GOVERNMENT DOCUMENTS

Garner, Diane L. *The Complete Guide to Citing Government Information Resources: A Manual for Social Science and Business Research.* 3rd ed. Bethesda: Congressional Information Service, 2002. Print.

United States Government Printing Office. *Style Manual.* 30th ed. GPO, 2008. Web. 9 Sept. 2009.

HISTORY (See pp. 230–56.)

The Chicago Manual of Style. 15th ed. Chicago: U of Chicago P, 2003. Print.

JOURNALISM

Goldstein, Norm, ed. *Associated Press Stylebook and Briefing on Media Law.* Rev. ed. New York: Associated Press, 2008. Print.

LAW

Harvard Law Review et al. *The Bluebook: A Uniform System of Citation.* 18th ed. Cambridge: Harvard Law Rev. Assn., 2005. Print.

LINGUISTICS

Linguistic Society of America. *Language Style Sheet.* LSA, n.d. Web. 9 Sept. 2009.

MATHEMATICS

American Mathematical Society. *AMS Author Handbook.* AMS, 2008. Web. 9 Sept. 2009.

MEDICINE

American Medical Association. *AMA Manual of Style: A Guide for Authors and Editors.* 10th ed. New York: Oxford UP, 2007. Print.

MUSIC

Holoman, D. Kern, ed. *Writing about Music: A Style Sheet from the Editors of* 19th-Century Music. Berkeley: U of California P, 1988. Print.

PHYSICS

American Institute of Physics. *Style Manual: Instructions to Authors and Volume Editors for the Preparation of AIP Book Manuscripts.* 5th ed. New York: AIP, 1995. Print.

POLITICAL SCIENCE

American Political Science Association. *APSA Style Manual for Political Science.* Rev. ed. Washington: APSA, 2006. Print.

PSYCHOLOGY AND OTHER SOCIAL SCIENCES (See pp. 182–229.)

American Psychological Association. *Publication Manual of the American Psychological Association.* 6th ed. Washington: APA, 2010. Print.

SCIENCE AND TECHNICAL WRITING

American National Standards Institute. *American National Standard for the Preparation of Scientific Papers for Written or Oral Presentation.* ANSI, 2005. Web. 9 Sept. 2009.

Microsoft Corporation. *Microsoft Manual of Style for Technical Publications.* 3rd ed. Redmond: Microsoft, 2004. Print.

Rubens, Philip, ed. *Science and Technical Writing: A Manual of Style.* 2nd ed. New York: Routledge, 2001. Print.

SOCIAL WORK

National Association of Social Workers Press. *NASW Press Author Guidelines.* NASW P, 2009. Web. 9 Sept. 2009.

Part V. Glossary of Research Terms

abstract A summary of a work's contents. An abstract usually appears at the beginning of a scholarly or technical article. Databases and indexes often contain abstracts that can help you decide whether an article is relevant for your purposes.

annotated bibliography A list of sources that gives the publication information and a short description—or annotation—for each source. Each annotation is generally three to seven sentences long. In some bibliographies, the annotation merely describes the content and scope of the source; in others, the annotation also evaluates the source's reliability, currency, and relevance to a researcher's purpose.

anthology A collection of writings compiled into a book. The selections in anthologies are usually connected by a common topic, time period, or group of authors.

archives A collection of documents and artifacts, usually unpublished, that constitute the organized historical record of an organization or of an individual's life. Many academic libraries house their institution's archives and may have other archival materials as well. *See also* **special collections**.

authentication An online verification process that allows users to access library resources such as databases from off campus. Authentication generally requires logging in with a campus ID.

bibliography (1) A list of sources, usually appearing at the end of a research paper, an article, a book, or a chapter in a book. The list documents sources used in the work and points out sources that might be useful for further research. Entries provide publication information so that interested readers can track down and examine sources for themselves. (2) A list of recommended readings on a given topic, usually sorted into subcategories.

blog A blog (short for *Weblog*) is a site that contains dated text or multimedia entries usually written and maintained by one person, with comments contributed by readers. Though some blogs are personal diaries and others are devoted to partisan politics, many journalists and academics maintain blogs that cover topics of interest to researchers. Blogs frequently provide links to other sources.

Boolean operators The words *and*, *or*, and *not* used in search queries to relate the contents of two or more sets of data in different ways. When search terms are combined with *and*, the search results contain only those items that include all the terms. When *or* is used, the results include items that contain any one of the terms. *Not* is used to exclude items containing a term.

call number The letter and number combination that indicates where a book is kept on a library's shelves. Call numbers are assigned using a system that locates books on the same subject next to one another for easy browsing. Most academic libraries use the Library of Congress (LC) system; public libraries typically use the Dewey decimal system.

catalog A set of records for the location information and other details about materials owned by a library. Most catalogs are online, though a library may have all or part of its catalog on printed cards. Online catalogs usually can be searched by author, title, subject heading, or keyword; search results provide a basic description of the item (book, journal title, video, or other) and a call number. *See also* **call number**; **subject heading**.

citation A reference to a book, an article, a Web page, or another source that provides enough information about the source to allow a reader to retrieve it. Citations in a paper must be given in a standard format (such as MLA, APA, *Chicago*, or CSE), depending on the discipline in which the paper is written.

citation management software A computer program that stores bibliographic references and notes in a personal database and that can automatically format bibliographies, reference lists, or lists of works cited based on a particular documentation style (MLA, APA, *Chicago*, CSE, for example). Such programs may generate inaccurate or incomplete citations, so writers should proofread all results.

citation trail The network of citations formed when a reference work refers to sources that in turn refer to other sources. The process used by researchers to track down additional sources on a topic is sometimes referred to as following the path of a "citation trail" or "citation network."

cite (1) As a verb, to provide a reference to a source. (2) As a noun, a shortened form of *citation*. (*Note:* This term is frequently confused with *site*, as in *Web site*.)

corporate author An organization, an agency, an institution, or a corporation identified as the author of a work.

database A collection of information organized for retrieval. In libraries, databases usually contain references to sources retrievable by a variety of means. Databases may contain bibliographic citations, descriptive abstracts, full-text documents, or a combination.

descriptors Terms assigned by compilers of a database to describe the subject content of a document. Descriptors are chosen so that all of the work on a particular topic can be found with a single word or phrase, even though there may be many different ways of expressing the same idea. For example, the *PsycINFO* database uses *academic achievement* as a descriptor to help researchers locate texts on the subject of scholastic achievement or grade-point average. *See also* **database**; **subject heading**; **tags**.

digital object identifier (DOI) A persistent code assigned to online or digital material. The DOI can be entered into a Web site called a DOI resolver or used in a database to retrieve an item.

discipline An academic field of study such as history, psychology, or biology. Often books and articles published by members of a discipline and intended for other scholars are called *the literature of the discipline*—referring not to literary expression but to research publications in the field.

field (1) An area of study within an academic discipline. (2) A particular area in a database in which the same type of information is regularly recorded. One field in an article database may contain the titles of articles, for example, while another field may contain the names of journals the articles are in. Some search engines allow a user to limit a search to one or more specific fields.

full text A complete document contained in a database or on a Web site. (*Note:* Illustrations and diagrams may be omitted from a full-text document.) Some databases search full-text documents; others search only the citation or abstract. In some cases researchers can set their own preferences.

hits (1) The results called up by a search of a database, a Web site, or the Internet. (2) The number of times a Web site has been visited. Web site owners track hits as a measure of the popularity of a site.

holdings The exact items a library owns. The term typically refers to the specific issues of a magazine or journal in a library. This information is often listed in a library's catalog as a *holdings statement*.

index (1) In a book, an alphabetical listing of topics and the pages on which information about them can be found. The index is located at the back of the book. (2) A publication that lists articles or other publications by topic. (3) An alphabetical listing of elements that can be found in a database.

journal A type of periodical usually sold by subscription and containing articles written for specialized or scholarly audiences. *See also* **scholarly journal**.

keyword A word used to search a library database, a Web site, or the Internet. Keyword searches locate results by matching the search word to an item in the resource being searched. Keyword searches often retrieve broad results through many database fields. However, researchers who perform a keyword search using terms that are different from those used by the database may not retrieve all of the information in the database related to their topic. For example, a search using the keyword *third world* will find items containing that term but may not include related items using the term *developing countries*. *See also* **descriptors**; **subject heading**; **tags**.

library catalog *See* **catalog**.

licensed database *See* **subscription database**.

literature review An article or paper describing published research on a particular topic. The purpose of a literature review (sometimes called a *review article*) is to select the most important publications on the topic, sort them into categories, and comment on them to provide a quick overview of leading scholarship in that area. Published articles often include a literature review section to place their research in the context of other work in the field.

magazine A type of periodical containing articles that are usually written for general and popular audiences. Magazines are sold on newsstands or by subscription and earn a part of their revenue through advertising.

microform A process that reproduces texts in greatly reduced size on plastic film called *microfilm*. Flat sheets of microfilm are called *microfiche*. Both forms must be read on special machines that magnify the text.

online catalog *See* **catalog**.

OPAC (online public access catalog) *See* **catalog**.

peer review Part of the publication process for scholarly publications in which a group of experts examines a document to determine whether it is worthy of publication. Journals and other publications use a peer review process—usually arranged so that reviewers do not know who the author of the document is—to assess articles for quality and relevance. *See also* **refereed publication**.

periodical A publication issued at regular intervals. Periodicals may be magazines, journals, newspapers, or newsletters. *See also* **serial**.

periodical index A list of all the articles that have been published in a magazine, journal, newspaper, or newsletter or in a set of periodicals. Many periodical indexes have been converted to online databases, though many online versions are limited to recent decades. For access to all years of a periodical's publication, you may need to consult a print index. The *MLA Bibliography*, for example, covers publications since 1963 in the online version, but the print version goes back to 1921.

plagiarism The unattributed use of a source of information that is not considered common knowledge. In general, the following acts are considered plagiarism: (1) failing to cite quotations or borrowed ideas, (2) failing to enclose borrowed language in quotation marks, (3) failing to put summaries or paraphrases in your own words, and (4) submitting someone else's work as your own.

popular Often used to refer to sources written for a general audience; not scholarly. *See also* **scholarly**.

primary source An original source, such as a speech, a diary, a novel, a legislative bill, a laboratory study, a field research report, or an eyewitness account. While not necessarily more reliable than a secondary source, a primary source has the advantage of being closely related to the information it conveys and as such is often considered essential for research, particularly in history. In the sciences, reports of new research written by the scientists who conducted it are considered primary sources.

professional journal A journal containing scholarly articles addressed to a particular professional audience such as doctors, lawyers, teachers, engineers, or accountants. Professional journals differ from trade publications, which usually do not include in-depth research articles. *See also* **scholarly journal**; **trade publications**.

record An entry in a database or a library catalog. Records contain the details about the books, articles, or other sources that users will find in a database.

refereed publication A publication for which every submission is screened through a peer review process. Refereed publications are considered authoritative because experts have reviewed the material in advance of publication to determine its quality. *See also* **peer review**.

reference (1) A source used in research and mentioned by a researcher in a paper or an article. (2) In libraries, a part of the library's collection that includes encyclopedias, handbooks, directories, and other publications that provide useful overviews, common practices, and facts. (*Note*: *Reference* may also indicate a desk or counter where librarians provide assistance to researchers.)

review article *See* **literature review**.

RSS Short for *rich site summary*, a system for collecting and viewing recent updates to Web sources such as blogs or news sites. These updates are often collected through personal accounts set up on sites such as *Bloglines* or *Google Reader*.

scholarly Often used to describe books, periodicals, or articles that are written for a specialized audience of academics or researchers. These sources are generally formal in style and include references to other published sources. *See also* **popular**.

scholarly journal A journal that is primarily addressed to scholars, often focusing on a particular discipline. Scholarly journals are often refereed publications and for some purposes may be considered more authoritative than magazines. Articles in scholarly journals usually are substantial in length, use specialized language, contain footnotes or endnotes, and are written by academic researchers rather than by journalists. *See also* **refereed publication**; **magazine**.

search engine (1) A program that allows users to search for material on the Internet or on a Web site. (2) The search function of a database.

secondary source A source that comments on, analyzes, or otherwise relies on primary sources. An article in a newspaper that reports on a scientific discovery or a book that analyzes a writer's work is a secondary source. *See also* **primary source**.

serial A term used in libraries to encompass all publications that appear in a series: magazines, journals, newspapers, and books that are published regularly (such as annual reviews). *See also* **periodical**.

special collections A section of a library devoted to unusual or valuable materials that cannot be checked out, including rare books, artwork, photographs, posters, and pamphlets. Researchers are generally required to use these rare materials in a reading room with special assistance. Many rare materials are being scanned for easier access through digital archives or repositories. *See also* **archives**.

subject heading A word or phrase assigned to an item in a database to describe the item's content. This content information can help a researcher evaluate whether a book or an article is worth further examination. Subject headings also suggest alternative terms or phrases to use in a search. Most academic library catalogs use the *Library of Congress Subject Headings* to describe the subjects of books in the catalog. Other databases create their own list, or thesaurus, of accepted descriptive terms. In some databases, subject headings are called *descriptors*. *See also* **descriptors**; **tags**; **thesaurus**.

subscription database A database that can be accessed only by paying a fee. Most of the online materials that libraries provide free to their patrons are paid for by the library through a subscription. Often the material provided in a subscription database is more selective and quality-controlled than sources that are freely available on the Web. Because these databases are often provided through a license agreement, they are sometimes referred to as *licensed databases*.

tags User-supplied words or phrases describing the subject of a document, image, or video. Tags are frequently used in social media forums such as *Flickr*. Unlike subject headings or descriptors used in databases, the wording of tags is often determined by individual users. *See also* **descriptors**; **subject headings**; **thesaurus**.

thesaurus (1) A collection of words and synonyms. (2) In a database, a list of the subject headings or descriptors that are used in a particular catalog or database to describe the subject matter of each item. A thesaurus is useful to researchers because it identifies which term among available synonyms has been used by the database compilers to describe a topic. Some databases provide a searchable thesaurus that helps researchers choose the most effective search terms before they start searching.

trade publications Periodical publications, such as magazines or newsletters, covering specialized news and information for members of a particular profession or industry. Unlike scholarly journals, trade publications do not include in-depth research articles.

truncation In search engine or database queries, a shortened version of a search term. In some search engines and databases, the truncated term plus a wildcard symbol (such as an asterisk or a question mark) can be used to search all possible variations of the word. *See also* **wildcard**.

URL (uniform resource locator) An Internet address. Most URLs consist of a protocol type (such as *http*), a domain name and extension (such as *hackerhandbooks.com*), and a series of letters and / or numbers to identify an exact resource or page within the domain. Many electronic databases have long URLs that are generated in the course of a search and vary each time a search is conducted. In some cases, a database record may contain a "persistent URL" that can be used to locate the item again.

wiki A collaborative Web site with content that is written by many contributors and that may change frequently. *Wikipedia*, a collaborative online encyclopedia, is one of the most frequently consulted wikis.

wildcard A symbol used to substitute any letter or combination of letters in a search word or phrase. A wildcard may replace a single letter (as in *wom*n*, to search for *women* or *woman* in one search) or any number of letters (as in *psycholog** to search for *psychology*, *psychologist*, and *psychological*). Typical wildcard symbols are asterisks, question marks, and exclamation points. *See also* **truncation**.

(continued from page iv)

Constance M. Ruzich. Page 428, "For the Love of Joe: The Language of Starbucks." From *The Journal of Popular Culture*, Volume 41, No. 3, 2008. © 2008 Constance M. Ruzich. Journal compilation © 2008, Blackwell Publishing, Inc. Reprinted with permission of the publisher.

David Whitman. "An Appeal to Authority: The New Paternalism in Urban Schools" front page from *Education Next*, vol. 8 (4): 53-58 screen shot. Fall 2008/*Education Next*. Copyright © 2008. Reprinted by permission of the Education Next Program on Education Policy & Governance, Harvard Kennedy School.

Brenda Wineapple. Title page from *White Heat: The Friendship of Emily Dickinson and Thomas Wentworth Higginson* by Brenda Wineapple. Copyright © 2008 by Brenda Wineapple. Used by permission of Alfred A. Knopf, a division of Random House, Inc.

Authors' names   Reverse the order of the first author's name. Use first and last names and middle initials. For an organization or a government agency as author, give the group's name. For a work with no author, begin with the title.

Titles   Capitalize all major words. Italicize titles of books, periodicals, and Web sites. Use quotation marks for titles of articles or short works from Web sites, followed by the title of the periodical or the Web site.

Publication information

Book   Give the publisher's city and name and the date.

> Holton, Woody. *Unruly Americans and the Origins of the Constitution*. New York: Hill and Wang, 2008.

> Purdy, Jedediah. *The Meaning of Property: Freedom, Community, and the Legal Imagination*. New Haven: Yale University Press, 2010.

Article in a print periodical   For a journal, give the volume and issue numbers, the date, and page numbers. For a monthly or weekly publication, give the month, day (if there is one), and year followed by the page numbers.

> Derbyshire, John. "Summertime Blues." *National Review*, August 10, 2009, 47.

> Freeman, Allen. "The Uses of Re-Enchantment." *American Scholar* 78, no. 3 (2009): 10-11.

Article in an online periodical   Give the date of publication and the URL.

> Rossmeier, Vincent. "One Small Step: A Look Back." *Salon*, July 20, 2009. http://www.salon.com/news/feature/2009/07/20/moon_landing/index.html.

Article from a database   Give publication information for the periodical, followed by the URL for the database at the end.

> Kozloff, Sarah. "Wyler's Wars." *Film History* 20, no. 4 (2008): 456-73. http://find.galegroup.com/.

Page numbers   Provide the range of pages (210-43).

Authors' names Reverse the order of all authors' names. Use initials for first and middle names, with no periods or spaces. For an organization or a government agency as author, give the group's name followed by the country (abbreviated) unless the country is part of the name. For a work with no author, begin with the title.

Titles Capitalize the first word and proper nouns for books, articles in periodicals, and Web sites. Do not italicize or place titles in quotation marks. Abbreviate journal titles of more than one word.

Publication and retrieval information

Book Give the publisher's location, its name, and the publication date.

> Weinberg S. Lake views: this world and the universe. Cambridge (MA): Harvard University Press; 2010.

Article in a print periodical Follow the periodical title with the year of publication. For a journal, add volume and issue numbers. For a magazine, add the month and the day (if there is one).

> Saey TH. Better flu-fighting models. Sci News. 2010;177(1):11.

Article in an online periodical Follow the periodical title with "Internet" in brackets. Provide the publication date; the retrieval date; volume, issue, and page numbers; and the URL. No period follows the URL unless the URL ends in a slash.

> Heimann M. How stable is the methane cycle? Science [Internet]. 2010 Mar 5 [cited 2010 Apr 10];327(5970):1211-1212. Available from: http://www.sciencemag.org/cgi/content/short/327/5970/1211

Article from a subscription service Give publication information as for an article in an online periodical. Provide publication information for the database publisher, including the copyright date. End with the URL of the database and the document number, if any.

> Heyes A, Kapur S. Enforcement missions: targets vs budgets. J Environ Econ Manag [Internet]. 2009 [cited 2010 Jan 8];58(2):129-140. Expanded Academic ASAP. Farmington Hills (MI): Gale Cengage Learning; c2009. Available from: http://find.galegroup.com.ezproxy.bpl.org/. Document No.: A217951659.

Page numbers For consecutive pages, give the range (210-243). For nonconsecutive pages, list all pages (7, 8-12). For online sources with no page numbers, estimate the number of pages, screens, paragraphs, lines, or bytes in brackets ([about 10 p.]).

Authors' names Reverse the order of all authors' names. Use initials for first and middle names. For an organization or a government agency as author, use the group's name. For a work with no author, begin with the title.

Titles Capitalize the first word and proper nouns for books, articles, and on-line works. Capitalize major words for journal titles. Italicize titles of books, periodicals, and documents from Web sites. Do not use quotation marks for titles of short works.

Publication and retrieval information

Book Follow the author's name with the year of publication. Follow the title with the publisher's city, state, and name. Give the state (abbreviated) or the country for all cities; also give the province for Canadian cities.

> Pellegrini, A. (2009). *The role of play in human development*. New York, NY:
> Oxford University Press.

Article in a periodical Follow the author's name with the year; add the month for monthly publications and month and day for weekly publications. Include the volume number in italics; give the issue number in parentheses (not italicized) for journals paginated by issue. For an online article, include the DOI (digital object identifier). If the article does not have one, give the URL for the periodical's home page. Use a retrieval date only if the content is likely to change.

> Bower, B. (2009, June 20). Think like a scientist. *Science News, 175*(13), 20-23.
>
> Guerrero, V. (2009). Peru embraces biotech. *Nature Biotechnology, 27*, 685.
> doi:10.1038/nbt0809-685b
>
> Liu, H. (2009). Recycling economy and sustainable development. *Journal of Sustainable Development, 2*(1), 209-212. Retrieved from http:// ccsenet.org/journal/index.php/jsd/

Article from a database Give the print information followed by the DOI (digital object identifier), if the article has one. If it does not, give the URL for the home page of the journal. Do not include the database name.

> Nakamura, E. (2009). Deconstructing the success of real business cycles.
> *Economic Inquiry, 47*, 739-753. Retrieved from http://www.wiley.com/bw /journal.asp?ref=0095-2583
>
> Perspectives on neuroscience and behavior. (2008). *The Neuroscientist, 14*, 405-406. doi:10.1177/10738584080140050201

Page numbers For consecutive pages, give the complete range (310-330). For nonconsecutive pages, list all pages (7-8, 12-15).